Prolegomena to a Philosophy of Religion

Prolegomena to a Philosophy of Religion

J. L. SCHELLENBERG

Cornell University Press

ITHACA AND LONDON

First published 2005 by Cornell University Press

Printed in the United States of America

Library of Congress Cataloging-in-Publication Data

Schellenberg, J. L.
    Prolegomena to a philosophy of religion / J. L. Schellenberg.
        p. cm.
    Includes bibliographical references and index.
    ISBN-13: 978-0-8014-4358-9 (cloth : alk. paper)
    ISBN-10: 0-8014-4358-X (cloth : alk. paper)
    1. Religion—Philosophy.   I. Title.
    BL51.S426 2005
    210—dc22   2005013977

Cornell University Press strives to use environmentally responsible suppliers and materials to the fullest extent possible in the publishing of its books. Such materials include vegetable-based, low-VOC inks and acid-free papers that are recycled, totally chlorine-free, or partly composed of nonwood fibers. For further information, visit our website at www.cornellpress.cornell.edu.

Cloth printing   10 9 8 7 6 5 4 3 2 1

for regina
the love of my life

Contents

Preface

A few years ago, in a fit of optimism, I sought to develop in a single book certain new thoughts I had conceived on the reconciliation of reason and religion. But the manuscript I completed will remain unpublished, as it turned out to be impossible to do well between two covers all that I had in mind to do. In the wake of this discovery I devised a different plan, the first part of which has now been put into effect. To provide a proper basis for what lay ahead, so it immediately seemed to me, this first part of the plan should involve considering more fully than I had previously done some foundational issues concerning the nature of religion, belief, skepticism, faith (and so on) which kept cropping up in my work. But recognizing that there is in philosophy no thorough and systematic treatment of these issues—or of these issues together with certain others apparently belonging to the same general category, concerning the identity and aims and principles of assessment of philosophy of religion—I soon arrived at the richer idea of writing something that might both serve as my opening volley and open up this overlooked subfield of foundations or prolegomena.[1]

---

[1] Despite much talk of religious belief and religious faith, for example, relatively little reflection has been devoted to determining exactly what faith is and what makes a state of belief religious, or to identifying the standards by which assessments of religious belief and religious faith are to be made. Still more rare are attempts to deal with various fundamentals at once, in a sensitive and systematic way. (Some recent works, it is true, seem to be moving in this direction. I think particularly of Richard Swinburne's *Faith and Reason* [Oxford: Clarendon Press, 1981] and William Alston's "Belief, Acceptance, and Religious Faith," in *Faith, Freedom, and Rationality*, ed. Jeff Jordan and Daniel Howard-Snyder [Lanham, MD: Rowman & Littlefield, 1996]. But it is illuminating to observe that both these works have been neglected. Moreover, it must be said that even in them there is

The book you hold in your hands is the result. Its title, *Prolegomena to a Philosophy of Religion,* must accordingly be understood as having a double sense: it not only identifies the more immediate role of my results, to serve as material underlying and informing a particular philosophy of religion (namely, my own, to be developed in subsequent volumes), but also encapsulates the subject that this book may, at another level, be seen as addressing: the subject of the understandings of basic issues that *ought* to underlie a (i.e., any) philosophy of religion—a subject I hope my work will prompt others also to address.

Put otherwise, there are two layers of discussion in the book; both are concerned with prolegomena, though in different ways, and both are to be discerned throughout. In one layer I am developing concepts and principles that I will be utilizing in subsequent volumes, outlining the starting points of my philosophy of religion. Here my *chapters*—more exactly, the positions and arguments developed therein—are the prolegomena. In the other layer my positions and arguments serve as proposals for how philosophers in general might look upon (some) important matters in the subfield I have mentioned (though I expanded my list of topics when I hit on the idea of functioning as a standard-bearer for prolegomenous inquiry, I have still not touched on nearly everything that might be discussed in this area)—proposals put forward as part of what I hope will be a continuing discussion, joined by many, of how properly to deal with this neglected category of fundamental start-up issues. In this case the *correct* views on all these matters, whatever they may be, are the prolegomena, and although I can be seen as suggesting some of what I presently think may be involved in the correct views, my aim in this layer is not so much to facilitate a final consensus on anything as to start a discussion rolling, and to take it some distance in a promising direction. The questions of which issues count as prolegomenous and how they are best dealt with will remain long after I pick up, in subsequent volumes, where the first layer leaves off and finish the task I have set for myself. And that, as I see it, is all to the good.

I hope it will be evident from the foregoing that everything I have to say in this book, at both levels, is up for discussion in philosophy of religion (the field); there is no attempt here to lay down as inviolable or to

---

sometimes a one-sidedness that derives from a particular [Christian] orientation.) In the absence of sensitive and systematic discussion of this sort, there is—among other things— a danger that writers will draw their understandings of basic concepts and their basic principles somewhat unreflectively from one source with which they are familiar while ignoring others, or else from a variety of sources that do not speak with one voice and thus generate subtle inconsistencies that go undetected.

legislate certain ways of looking at things or ways of proceeding for philosophers of religion, only proposals for how to deal with a range of basic issues—proposals that I hope will ignite much fruitful discussion and which, in any case, I shall take as a basis for my own ongoing work in the field. Nor (as already suggested) do I suppose that the issues I discuss or my manner of discussing them exhaust what properly belongs to the area of prolegomena. The presence of two layers, two things going on at once, means that what I do in seeking to contribute to the subfield concerned with "prolegomena to a philosophy of religion" must at the same time have some bearing on my own ongoing work. Prolegomenous issues that are only indirectly or very distantly related to the latter will not often be putting in an appearance here. Other writers may make a different selection from among prolegomenous issues or find a different pathway through them. My selection and my pathway are determined by what is needed to frame the discussion of other volumes in the series of books on which I am embarked. For example, it will serve my later purposes for me to get clear about the phenomenology of belief—what it is *like* to be a believer—and so in the chapter on the nature of belief I focus on phenomenology and give short shrift to some recent theories in philosophy of mind. That chapter might therefore seem incomplete, but it gets at what I need for future arguments and at the same time clarifies certain matters that anyone in philosophy of religion concerned with prolegomena might find it important to address, thus advancing the latter cause as well.

Having said that, I must also emphasize that I am very serious about what I am doing at both levels of the book. I think that philosophical discussions of religion (past and present) often suffer from unfortunate tendencies ultimately derived from *inattention* to prolegomena (a tendency toward parochialism is especially common), and I argue vigorously for various claims supporting this view and for certain understandings of basic issues— for example, the nature of religion—that I think may serve to put philosophy of religion on a better footing. Perhaps these arguments can be successfully challenged. I am of course open to that. But my task, as I see it, is to make them clear and advance them as far as I can, in the interest of undogmatic wakefulness. I do not shrink from this task. Furthermore, it seems to me that some of the understandings for which I argue are especially critical to a correct view of the prolegomena and to the future usefulness of work done by philosophers of religion. Here especially it will be evident that what I am supporting is not always properly called a return to basics; such efforts as I am recommending may often take one to terrain not previously visited or properly explored. For when we give sustained attention to prolegomenous issues in philosophy of religion, we may find that some of the central ideas of the field have been inadequately formulated and that fresh thoughts are called for on various fronts. Only if we are open to *this* will we be able to move forward in a manner that does justice to the lofty ideal that should animate any area and any style of philosophy: an investigation of the deepest of intellectual problems and possibilities that is critical yet creative, analytically precise yet imaginative, tough-minded yet willing to follow wherever the truth might lead, and actively seeking an ever richer and more adequate overall understanding.[2]

It is in response to this ideal, and, I hope, in a manner consonant with its demands, that certain issues fundamental to any philosophy of religion are systematically addressed in this volume. My aim is to get clearer about how philosophy should understand the nature and interrelationships of religion, belief, religious belief, religious disbelief, religious skepticism, and religious faith (Chapters 1–6);[3] the nature of philosophy's proper aims in respect of such phenomena (Chapter 7); and the principles governing the evaluative activity to which, as we shall see, an understanding of these aims most urgently invites us (Chapter 8). To that end, I have thought through the issues and presented and defended the views that seem to me, on reflection, most adequate. (I have sought to develop all this material rigorously and systematically, laying aside some popular assumptions—including some I used to accept—and thinking everything through from the ground up.) I hope that a deeper understanding of the fundamentals, and a wider interest in taking such an understanding further, will be the result. And, of course, I also hope that a proper foundation will have been laid for understanding and being convinced by the arguments I shall go on to develop in future work.[4]

---

[2] An objection that may be found tempting in this connection is that philosophers of religion cannot expect to reach agreement on all the prolegomenous issues before beginning other inquiries. But I am not advising everyone to defer all other investigations until the prolegomena have been dealt with. Inquiries into various such matters should, I would rather say, be going on continually alongside all the more common forms of investigation into the staples of the field; and the latter should be seen in light of and undertaken with a sensitivity to (and an openness to being modified by) the results of the former.

[3] The first aspect of the task mentioned here I shall treat as equivalent to the task of getting clearer about how philosophers should *define* the *concepts* of "religion," "belief," etc. (Notice that—as to some extent suggested above—we cannot assume that ordinary or accepted linguistic practices will always provide a quick or completely adequate answer to this question.)

[4] Someone might—despite what I have said—see in what I am doing the danger of seeking to make philosophy of religion (the field) conform to preconceived ideas about what I wish to do in *my* philosophy of religion (the particular set of positions and arguments I am developing). I am aware of this danger and can only reply that it is also possible to reverse the point—to see in what I am doing an attempt to make my own project conform to what can responsibly be applied to the field as a whole. Perhaps my work in this book exists in a tension between these two possibilities. But if so, it is a creative tension.

I have many people to thank for their help with my ongoing project. I think especially of John Ackerman, William Alston, David Burton, Stephen Maitzen, Paul Moser, William Rowe, Terence Penelhum, Richard Swinburne, and William Wainwright, and also the students of upper-level courses on philosophy of religion at Mount Saint Vincent University and members of audiences in Halifax, Truro, Calgary, Boston, and Miami (you know who you are). Paul Draper and Daniel Howard-Snyder I single out for special mention because of the extent and detail of their comments, which have led to many improvements. For this generosity far beyond the call of duty I am immensely grateful. The Social Sciences and Humanities Research Council of Canada and Mount Saint Vincent University provided much-needed financial support and occasional release from teaching duties; I am very thankful to them. Last (but also first) come the members of my immediate family, whose effects on my life are deep and no doubt invisibly present on every page. My sons, Matthew and Justin, have in the time of this writing grown into fine young men, and their speedy development reminds me daily that time waits for no one. My artist wife and muse, Regina Coupar, is she on account of whom I will hold on to time for as long as I can. To her this book of new beginnings is dedicated, with deepest love and gratitude.

J. L. S.

Chester Basin, Nova Scotia

Prolegomena to a Philosophy of Religion

On Religion

A rather large concept, which contributes its color to every part of the map whose configurations we are seeking to discern, is the concept of religion. Because of its pervasiveness in philosophy of religion, a book on prolegomena to inquiry in that field might be expected to have something to say about this concept. Indeed, a careful analysis would seem warranted. Yet the need for this can be contested, and its justification can be misunderstood. I therefore begin this discussion by considering more closely why it ought to be undertaken.

1. Why Discuss This Issue?

One reason that might be put forward for analyzing "religion" involves the goal of better understanding the meaning of "philosophy of religion." Someone might be led to ask what religion is, hoping thereby to acquire a deeper understanding of what this field of study is all about. But it is a mistake to think that a discussion of how to define "religion" which seeks to settle this notoriously disputed matter will help one more fully understand what philosophy of religion is about. Such thinking assumes that there is agreement among those who competently use the term "philosophy of religion" as to what religion is, and also that analysis will inevitably lead one to a clarified version of their understanding. But there is no agreement. This is, as I have noted, a disputed matter, featuring endless wrangles among students of religion of various stripes over the correct understanding of that obdurate term. Indeed, we might better say that philosophy of religion has been concerned with what philosophers have *taken* as religion and so advise those seeking a fuller understanding of what that field is about to consider what *has* been so taken. Since this is not the same for every philosopher who sees herself or himself as commenting on religious matters, it seems appropriate to say that the word "religion" in "philosophy of religion" really expresses quite a generous, collective idea—the idea of the conjunction of all the items that philosophers have ever used the word "religion" to name!

This thought might seem to support the view that there is no point in philosophers' seeking to arrive at a more precise understanding of "religion"; the diversity of usage we see here, which might seem to cry out for philosophical tidying up, instead renders the search for a single definition superfluous. *Any* of the questions philosophers have taken to concern religion, so it may be said, make appropriate topics of discussion for philosophers of religion; thus, to determine whether one's inquiry remains within the boundaries of their field or falls outside, one need only consult past practice.

Yet that conclusion, it seems to me, does not quite get it right, for we have not only the past to think about but also the future. We look to the practices and preoccupations of the past to formulate our understanding of "philosophy of religion," but in the present, and from within the field thus named, we may arrive at a new or revised understanding of what it *should* be about, and this understanding may involve, among other things, a proffered and accepted definition of "religion" appropriate to the purposes by which, according to a new consensus, it *ought* to be animated.[1] I suggest that adequate attention to the matters I have called prolegomena may in time produce just such a state of affairs. Philosophers who want (inter alia) to address religious belief or religious faith need a criterion by which to determine, of any state that might seem to instantiate one of these phenomena, whether it is religious or not. Otherwise put, philosophers who offer or criticize evaluations purportedly applicable to all members of the general classes of religious belief and religious faith require a criterion by which to determine the extension of these classes. Only thus, it seems, can definite results from the field as a whole, criticized and checked and confirmed by a wide body of inquirers, be forthcoming. Now if such points were to be taken seriously, and the consensus mentioned above should come to be, we could of course continue to understand the term "religion" as it appears in "philosophy of religion" collectively (indeed, we might have a new understanding of the former term to add to the collection), but we

---

[1] It might be argued that more than one definition could be utilized at the same time by different groups: parceling out the possibilities, we might have different understandings followed through by different research programs. This possibility is considered more fully later on, but for now I assume the preferability of a single definition that all accept.

would also recognize that in its current phase the field had adopted a narrower, technical definition to suit its purposes.

I suggest that these considerations provide an adequate reason for pursuing a fuller understanding of "religion," even though the first consideration mentioned above does not. (What this implies is that the question of how "religion" should be understood by philosophers of religion as they go about their work and the question of how "religion" functions in the phrase "philosophy of religion" are to be distinguished as different questions.) Philosophers of religion need to do something about the unclarity and inconsistency in usage of such fundamental terms of their field, not necessarily by seeking to solve the problem once and for all in a manner suitable for just any form of inquiry into religious matters (though it would be good to know what the problems are that prevent such a solution and whether they must remain intractable) but by discussing and determining the range of the phenomena into which *they* wish to inquire, and the nature of items within that range, and also by behaving accordingly in a consistent manner. What is taken as religion in the field may thus in time come to reflect a wider agreement, and as a result, coherent and mutually illuminating discussion in the field may be greatly facilitated. Otherwise, where, for example, discussions of religious belief and faith are concerned, we will be passing each other like ships in the night and perhaps leaving our readers in the dark as well. In sum, a reference point for discussion in the field is desirable, and this a closer look at "religion" might provide.

Let us therefore consider this term more carefully. I will impose no special constraint on the exercise of intellectual curiosity at first—we begin with some of the most general issues about the nature of religion, which anyone thinking about religion, in whatever field, might encounter—but it may be expected that, as we progress, the question of how the various insights we glean should affect the understanding(s) of "religion" utilized in philosophy will come ever more to dominate.

2. *Religion and the Religions*

The first thing to notice is that there is really more than one concept lurking here: the word "religion" is ambiguous. This point is implicit in the work of William James[2] and developed at length by the well-known scholar of religion Wilfred Cantwell Smith.[3] Smith distinguishes two basic

---

[2] See William James, *The Varieties of Religious Experience* (1902; New York: Penguin, 1982), pp. 28–31. James speaks of two "branches" of "the religious field" but then also of there being more than one "sort" of religion.

[3] In Wilfred Cantwell Smith, *The Meaning and End of Religion* (New York: New American

senses—call them *personal* and *institutional*, or, if you like, *internal* and *external*—of "religion." (The former labels are appropriated from James; the latter are mine.) Employing the once familiar but now little used personal sense, we may explain such things as new references to spiritual matters in someone's conversation and accompanying changes in behavior by remarking that they have "got" religion, or observe that a certain community's religion is generous and sincere while another's is judgmental and exclusionary. Here we are talking primarily about the personal dispositions of individuals. We are talking about religiousness or religiosity— what many today might call "spirituality" and what Smith calls "piety." Notice that in this context the article and the plural form are at best awkward and often inappropriate.

Using the word "religion" in the more common institutional sense, on the other hand, we can say that Islam is a world religion, or ask individuals filling out application forms to name their religion (we don't really expect them to tell us what they think about God or whether they went to synagogue last week, do we?), or speak in the plural of the world religions. Here we are talking about a thing to which one might adhere or belong, something in an important sense external to individual persons—what Smith calls a "cumulative tradition," a huge phenomenon straddling the centuries. (Or we may be speaking, more narrowly, of one part of such a tradition, the kind of thing on which many of us tend to become fixated when thinking about religious matters: namely, a belief or symbol system of the sort exemplified by one of the Christian creeds.)

Both James and Smith think that the former, personal, notion of religion is the more basic of the two. Why? Because institutional religion appears to be the result—as Smith puts it, the "deposit"—of religion in the personal sense. Perhaps there are other and yet deeper factors at work here, such as psychological tendencies or neurological patterns or the activity of a Divine being or earlier institutions, but there certainly seems to be a relation of causal dependence between particular instances of institutional religion and personal religion: without the Buddha's experiencing "enlightenment" under the bodhi tree and embodying its principles in his behavior, without many others' similar patterns of action and interaction, there would be no such religion as Buddhism. Without the experiences that enlivened the disciples of Jesus after his death and without the actions they took in developing and propagating their understanding of what had transpired among them, there would be no such thing as Christianity. And such connections, a follower of Smith and James will say, have implications

---

Library, 1964), esp. pp. 47–48, 141, 174–175.

for the decisions we ought to make in academic study. Surely, for example, we should begin by seeking to understand the relevant *personal* facts when our aim is to understand the religions of Buddhism and Christianity.

Now all of this seems both sensible and important. Of course we need to recognize that items in the category of "traditions" and items in the category of "personal religiousness" can be causally linked in a variety of ways. Thus it may also be possible to learn much about what is in the latter category from what we know about the former. (The religiousness of members of one generation, for example, will be causally dependent in many ways on aspects of traditions dominant in previous generations.) Nevertheless, it remains plausible to hold that religion of the personal kind is in an important sense more fundamental than its institutional counterpart. Significant changes in religious tradition can usually be traced to what some*one* has been *thinking* or *feeling* or *doing*—here we need to be reminded of the importance of "founder figures" in explanations of such changes. Traditions, whatever their ultimate source may be, are deeply influenced by people and will tend to go where people choose to take them, and the meaning of "religious tradition" will always be constrained by what we are willing to identify as personal religiosity, in its individual and communal manifestations. It follows that *even if their concern ought ultimately to be with traditions,* it is natural and appropriate for philosophers of religion thinking about the parameters of their discipline to begin by considering what is included in the personal sense of the term "religion."

Another closely related reason for philosophers of religion to begin with this personal sense is the following. Although just about any general proposition or creed will be of potential interest to philosophers, in order for a proposition or creed to be rightly identified as deserving the attention specifically of a philosopher of religion, it will need to be the sort of thing that can properly be the object of *religious* attitudes such as religious belief or faith. And, of course, one cannot distinguish such attitudes from others without first knowing something of what religion in the personal sense is about. A slightly different way of addressing this issue would point out that even at an elementary level, philosophy of religion is bound up with discussion of the meaning and justification of religious claims, as well as the nature and rational appropriateness of religious attitudes; that "claims" evidently may be and are made by people; and that attitudes are in the relevant way "personal." Add to these points the fact that full and proper attention to the nature and possible realizations and outputs of religion in the personal sense has in any case been neglected by philosophers in their single-minded concern with assessing certain particular and common religious attitudes and creeds (or elements thereof), and you can see the appropriateness of recommending urgent and first attention to this issue and of concentrating on the personal sense of "religion" in a book on prolegomena to a philosophy of religion. In any case, these considerations are influencing my decisions here. Hence, unless otherwise indicated, it is the personal sense that I have in mind when I use that term in future discussion.

But what sort of notion have we latched on to here? Speaking of "religiosity" or "spirituality" or "piety" may get us into the right neighborhood when thinking about how to understand "religion" but clearly leaves a lot to be desired. Having distinguished one meaning the word may have from others, we therefore still need to consider whether a satisfactory definition of the meaning that concerns us can be provided. The distinction urged by James and Smith may of course be expected to help us: in considering the multitude of definitions to be found in the literature, we can now leave aside those referring specifically and exclusively to traditions or belief systems.[4] But even then, a great profusion of offerings remains.[5] And it has proved rather difficult to find anywhere in this array a definition that cannot be undermined by counterexamples. A possible response to this state of affairs is to say that no one definition of the usual sort will do, and that those who think otherwise have fundamentally misconstrued the nature of language and of concepts. Now this position, if correct, might be expected to have important implications for philosophy of religion. I therefore propose to begin consideration of whether a definition for religion in the personal sense can be found by examining it more carefully, focusing the discussion on its most popular contemporary representative—the so-called family resemblance approach.

---

[4] Because of an apparent failure to recognize the distinction we have made, however, the personal and the nonpersonal are sometimes conflated in discussions of "religion." Take, for example, the definition, very influential in the social sciences (and so in religious studies), offered by Clifford Geertz in his "Religion as a Cultural System," in *Anthropological Approaches to the Study of Religion,* ASA Monographs, vol. 3, ed. Michael Bainton (London: Tavistock, 1966). Geertz writes: "Religion is (1) a system of symbols which acts to (2) establish powerful, pervasive, and long-lasting moods and motivations in men by (3) formulating conceptions of a general order of existence and (4) clothing these conceptions with such an aura of factuality that (5) the moods and motivations seem uniquely realistic" (p. 4). Clearly, Geertz means to be speaking of institutional religion, but it appears that he wishes to slip much belonging to personal religion in on the side. Without going into details, we can observe that, as well as insights, there are at least two other limitations in this definition. First, it suggests that the "system" is primary and that personal religiosity is secondary and derivative (whereas there is at least reciprocity of influence). Second, the definition seems too broad: on Geertz's understanding, an entirely pessimistic and destructive system or orientation could count as religious, and this seems a rather too generous use of the term, perhaps even for those not specially concerned to meet the needs of philosophy of religion.

[5] William Alston, touching the tip of the iceberg, lists nine alternative definitions in his "Religion," in *The Encyclopedia of Philosophy,* ed. Paul Edwards (New York: Macmillan, 1967), 7:140.

3. *The Family Resemblance Approach*

The family resemblance idea, derived from Wittgenstein's later philosophy, is that we need not find some way to make all the pieces from the ordinary usage of a word like "religion" fit into a single necessary-and-sufficient-conditions definition of the term. Instead, we ought to accept that the different pieces reflect different applications of it which are "bound together in a family by a network of overlapping similarities and not by any strict identity."[6] According to Peter B. Clarke and Peter Byrne, who defend this approach, if the family resemblance idea applies to it, we should find the following facts when considering our uses of the word "religion":

> (a) There will be a characteristic set of features to be seen in the examples of religion. . . . (b) Over and above the fact that they are religions, there will be no single feature or set of features to be found in each and every example of religion. (c) There will be no limits to be set in advance to the kind of combinations of characteristic features [that] newly discovered or developing religions might be found to exemplify, nor will there be absolute limits to the additional features [that] such new examples could add to the set. (d) The various examples of religion will then be related by a network of relationships rather than shared possession of necessary and sufficient conditions for membership of the class. (e) The meaning of the word "religion" will nonetheless be projectible: that is, having rehearsed the characteristic features of religion in an inclusive family resemblance definition or having become acquainted with some central examples of religion, one will be able to say of newly found examples whether they are religions or not.[7]

I will respond to this in a moment, but before I do, I want to get clearer about points (a) and (b). In giving their own gloss to point (a), Clarke and Byrne speak of certain characteristic dimensions of religion: "theoretical, practical, experiential and social." These are distinguished from nonreligious versions of the same dimensions by "characteristic kinds of objects (gods or transcendent things), goals (salvation or liberation) and

---

[6] Peter B. Clarke and Peter Byrne, *Religion Defined and Explained* (London: Macmillan, 1993), p. 7.

[7] Ibid., pp. 11–12. Clearly, the focus of Clarke and Byrne is on what I have called institutional religion (or else they conflate the two senses of the term "religion" that we have distinguished), but almost everything they say can be taken as applying to personal religion as well. That, at any rate, is how their proposal will be taken here.

functions (the provision of meaning and unity to group or individual life)."[8] There are apparently two (related) sets of things here: the dimensions of religion; and their objects, goals, and functions. And although there is some unclarity, it appears that Clarke and Byrne are best taken as saying that whereas the concepts "dimension," "object," "goal," and "function" apply to all cases of religion, the manner in which these constants are *exemplified* will vary: we can speak only of typical or characteristic dimensions and typical or characteristic objects, goals, and functions. The judgment as to whether something is a case of religion will depend on whether we judge it to exemplify a sufficient selection of the characteristic dimensions, as well as a sufficient selection of the characteristic objects, goals, and functions. And so this example of religion may possess one combination of the characteristic dimensions and objects, goals, and functions; that example, another. But—and here we come to point (b)— no one combination is necessary and sufficient for something to count as a case of religion, and indeed, no one feature (that is, no one dimension or object or goal or function) will be found in every case of religion.

Now let me respond. First, although the last claim here mentioned— that no one feature (dimension or object or goal or function) will be found in every case of religion—is to be expected in a family resemblance approach (since otherwise we are back to being able to talk about at least necessary conditions), Clarke and Byrne are not consistent in their affirmation of it. Second, that claim is in any case false—or, at the very least, the intuitive plausibility of a consideration that supports its falsity and has yet to be defeated appears to outweigh any intuitive plausibility attaching to the family resemblance approach as applied to "religion"—and so both it and the approach of which it is a part seem unworthy of our acceptance.

To see my first point, notice that although the characteristic dimensions of religion are, according to Clarke and Byrne, four in number and so can appear in varying combinations, these authors seem to mention and to have in mind but one characteristic object, one characteristic goal, and one characteristic function (or, at any rate, the number is in each case reducible to one), from which it follows, if—as they assume—religion always has an object, goal, and function, that there are *three* features that *each* instance of religion must possess. The objects mentioned, as we have seen, are "gods or transcendent things," but since gods are taken to *be* transcendent things, the simpler expression "transcendent things" would do just as well.[9] The goals mentioned are salvation or liberation,

---

[8] Ibid., p. 13.

[9] P. 13 refers to "god-like beings or more generally sacred, non-empirical realities." Clearly,

but both of these instantiate the general idea that is elsewhere taken as specifying a goal of religion: the idea of achieving "states of being in which such basic facts as death, suffering, conflict can be overcome."[10] And the functions mentioned are the "provision of meaning and unity to group or individual life." Although providing meaning might seem to be different from providing unity, it is clear that religion does both if it does either, and so again we do not really have ideas that can be separately realized. Therefore, Clarke and Byrne, it appears, are committed to the view that in *all* instances of religion one will find the idea of transcendent things, the pursuit of states of being in which such basic facts as death, suffering, conflict can be overcome, and the provision of meaning and unity to group or individual life. But this view is contrary to what is explicitly stated by and essential to their family resemblance approach. Thus we have an inconsistency.

There is a passage in which it seems that Clarke and Byrne recognize the possibility of such a complaint and seek to deal with it:

> We can accept that the specific distinguishing features of religion (object, goal and function) are exemplified in different degrees, and manifested in quite different ways in different religions. If we say that all religions have as their object "the sacred" this does not point to a determinate property which all religions share. "Sacred" is an umbrella term which hides differences rather than reveals obvious unity. A general contrast between sacred and profane is implied in it but how this contrast is drawn will differ from case to case, as different religions will be seen to have particular ways of distinguishing the special type of object or state which is their focus.[11]

But this will not do. We are now being told, in effect, that yet another layer of properties represents the features no one of which is shared in common between examples of religion—namely, those identical to the *ways* in which the features mentioned by Clarke and Byrne (e.g., the provision of unity) are realized—which is compatible with the latter features being in some form always present. But this is a shift, since earlier it was the latter features themselves that were said to be not uniformly present in religion. And, of course, just the fact that those features can be spoken of as such at

---

the realm of the "sacred" is here taken to include the gods, and since in the next sentence the word "transcendent" is taken as a synonym, we may infer that, on the view here discussed, gods are transcendent things.

[10] Ibid., p. 9.

[11] Ibid., p. 13.

all—can be picked out and distinguished from other things of the same sorts, other objects, goals, and functions—shows that they possess the "determinateness" denied them in this passage.

An analogy may help to drive this point home. Suppose I define "car" as "any object having four wheels and an internal-combustion engine." Someone employing the Clarke/Byrne move could respond by saying that this is inadequate since "having four wheels" and "having an internal-combustion engine" are umbrella terms that hide differences rather than revealing obvious unity; because different cars will realize these properties in quite different ways, any definition of "car" must refer to these *specific* distinguishing features. But although this would, if correct, clear the way for a family resemblance approach to the definition even of the term "car" (since such specific features could not be expected to be shared by all cars), it is clearly not correct. A definition must (by definition!) remain general. And so long as the features to which it refers are illuminating and distinguishable from others, it may live up to its name. These conditions are satisfied by "having four wheels" and "having an internal-combustion engine" in the case of car, and apparently also by the features introduced by Clarke and Byrne in the case of "religion."

Thus the strategy they suggest for dealing with the inconsistency in question is unsuccessful. The inconsistency remains. But a deeper problem lies behind the inconsistency (and here I come to my second point): the claim that no one feature will be found in every case of religion is in any event intuitively false. To show this, I introduce the idea of a *disqualifying feature*—a feature that necessarily disqualifies its possessor from being religious, showing that someone is *not* religious. I would suggest that it is intuitively easier to identify such disqualifying features than to identify necessary conditions of religion straight off. But, of course, if such disqualifying features exist, then we can generate the relevant necessary conditions, since then the *absence* of any such feature will be necessary for someone to count as religious—as instantiating religion in the personal sense. And though this sounds purely negative, there are ways of supporting a move to a positive property constitutive of religion in some cases, while in others a negative property is all we need, or else the disqualifying feature we start off with must be stated in negative terms so that the upshot—the absence of that negative property—is a positive property.

Let us now consider how this might be worked out. It seems, most obviously, that someone whose dominant and persistent view was that nothing in life has meaning or value could not be religious. The concept of religion may not wear its meaning on its face, but surely we can see that someone like this could not instantiate it. But if so, then it is necessary, for someone to be religious, that it *not* be the case that her dominant and persistent view is of this sort. Now this is, of course, not the same as it being the case that her dominant and persistent view is that something significantly meaningful or valuable is attainable—to suppose otherwise is to confuse a contradictory with a contrary. But we can, perhaps, negotiate a move from the purely negative contradictory to the positive contrary representing a useful and illuminating property if we recognize that the best *explanation* for the truth of the disqualifying intuition in question—the intuition that meaning and value nihilism is incompatible with religion—is that religion entails an emphasis on meaning or value.

In other cases, no such move as the latter is required, because all we need is a negative property, or else because we begin with one. For example, it also seems that someone whose thoughts were restricted completely to the mundane realm could not be religious—and let us understand by "the mundane realm" those aspects of human life and its environment to which just any mature human always has quick and natural cognitive and experiential access, what might (in two senses) be called the *common* elements of human life, which all who eat, drink, sleep, play, think, relate, and so on, will explicitly know and regularly encounter.[12] It follows that to be religious, one must have thoughts of something *not* thus restricted, which is to say, thoughts of a *trans*mundane reality. (This property, though essentially negative, is not unilluminating.) And it further seems that someone who was not in any way seeking to *bring about* something or actively engaged in pursuing goals, who had no focus in life of any kind (even the focus provided by seeking to have no focus!), could not be religious. Here the absence of the negatively expressed disqualifying feature is the *presence of goal-oriented behavior,* which adds useful content. The approach that focuses on disqualifying features thus appears to show, contrary to the claim of the family resemblance approach, that there *are* features we may expect to find in all cases of religion.

Notice another attractive aspect of the "disqualifying features" strategy: it places a clear onus on representatives of the family resemblance approach to come up with possible examples of religion that *include* the (allegedly) disqualifying features in question. The family resemblance approach rests on the intuition that religion is too variously realized to be correctly characterized in terms of necessary conditions, and so a challenge is issued to show that some condition thought of as necessary

---

[12] No doubt there is more to eating, drinking, working, etc., than we recognize as belonging to them—perhaps even something "spiritual." So when identifying the mundane realm, which any religious reality exceeds, we cannot simply refer to such entities, events, and relations and all they include. Hence my reference to *aspects,* and to what is *common.*

really is present in all cases of religion. How could this be done? Should we not expect that there will be some example of religion, whether present now or revealed in the future, to which the condition does not apply? But all of this is answered if competent users of the language of religion have an initial sense that some things are just incompatible with religion. Now there is a new challenge: show us evident examples of religion that involve no goal-oriented behavior, or that are completely nihilistic, or that remain entirely within the mundane realm. Unless examples of each kind are made available, we have no reason to deny the initial sense, which entails that there are conditions necessary for religion, and so we have no reason to accept—indeed, we have reason to oppose—the central claim of the family resemblance approach as applied to "religion."

That being said, it must also be said that what we have at this stage is still somewhat sketchy and programmatic. Some "disqualifying intuitions" may be stronger than others, and so independent forms of support may be needed in some cases. And, of course, not just necessity but also joint sufficiency needs to be more fully demonstrated for members of the set of conditions earlier offered, or—and this is more likely, given the relative vagueness of what we have got so far—for some expanded set, in order to arrive at a complete definition. Is this possible? Can our opposition to the family resemblance approach and its ilk be turned into a full-blooded and convincing alternative? Can the opposite to the position represented by the family resemblance approach be adequately defended after all? I want now to explore this question by developing as strongly as possible a certain definitional idea which—borrowing from some of the results above but also moving beyond them—seems at least initially to bring an affirmative answer within reach.

4. A Definition of "Religion"?

Four features, it may be said, appear to be especially closely tied to the nature of religiosity—to be defining features, if any are. These are (1) frequent thoughts of a transmundane reality; (2) an emphasis on a significant good, for oneself and others, that may be realized through a proper relation to this reality; (3) the cultivation of such a relation; and (4) a disposition or tendency, when attending to matters in which they are implicated, to—as I shall put it—*totalize* or *ultimize* in some way the central elements of features (1) to (3). Some of these notions we have already encountered in at least an inchoate form. Here I have more to say about each of them.

(1) *Frequent thoughts of a transmundane reality.* Religious persons can appear to be, among other things, those whose thoughts are often turned to something "beyond" or "more" (consider, for example, the thought life lying behind Hindu statements about Brahman, or Taoist utterances concerning the mysterious Tao, or aboriginal talk of the grandmothers and the grandfathers and of the Creator, or the ancient Greek stories of the gods).[13] I put this vaguely at first because the precise force of the relevant use of "beyond" is elusive, and what such a reality is more *than* is difficult to specify; these facts need to be acknowledged up front. Perhaps, however, we will not go far wrong if we speak, as we did earlier, of a "transmundane reality," understanding by that phrase a reality that exceeds the mundane realm, and by "the mundane realm" those aspects of human life and its environment to which just any mature human always has quick and natural cognitive and experiential access—the common elements of human life mentioned before.[14]

And here we immediately find ourselves needing to make some further clarifications: Do we mean that the transmundane reality is *thought of* as exceeding the mundane: that is, that religious people one and all explicitly utilize, in connection with some object of thought, if not the terms "mundane," "transmundane," and so on, at least the concepts they denote? Or are we leaving open the possibility that it might not be conceptualized as such, and asserting simply that what is thought of has properties entailing that it *does* go beyond the realm of the mundane? The former, internal or subjective, interpretation appears too restrictive, since someone might confusedly think of something transmundane as mundane, or fail to make any distinction between what is mundane and what is not, without lacking thoughts of the sort that I am suggesting are central to religion. (For example, someone might operate on the assumption that spirit penetrates everything, making no distinction corresponding to the distinction between a "spirit world" and the "mundane world," and

---

[13] It might seem that we should say "beliefs" instead of "thoughts," but the latter, vaguer notion is more appropriate at this stage. Religious thoughts, as we shall see, are not always instantiated as beliefs; in any case, the idea I am trying to get at here is just that *mental attention* is given to the transmundane.

[14] Daniel Howard-Snyder has suggested to me the objection that there is a possible world in which *God* is a part of the mundane realm as I have defined it, since accessible to the experience of all, and that my definition has the implausible result that in that world no one is religious, even though one and all commune with God, since in thinking of God no one would be thinking of a transmundane reality! This objection can be answered by noting that even if there were aspects of God, responsible for our well-being, to which we continually had access, these would, given human finitude, never be completely penetrable, and there would always be further aspects of the Divine to which we *lacked* access—which is to say that God would remain transmundane.

yet we would want to ascribe to her such thoughts as are here at issue, precisely because what she thinks of when she thinks of spirit is something that has properties distinguishing it from the common aspects of human experience as we are understanding them.) Thus, I suggest we go with the latter, external or objective, interpretation. This will, among other things, help us deal with some common counterexamples to philosophical definitions of "religion," which point out that religious people sometimes lack the concepts ascribed to them by the definitions (such concepts as that of a "transmundane reality").

The relevant notion of "going beyond" can apparently be cashed out either metaphysically or axiologically or in both ways. That is, it can be linked simply to there being *more to reality* than is included in the mundane realm, or to that more embodying or facilitating *greater value* than can be realized in the mundane realm, or to both these things. At first sight there is no uniformity in this respect among the items focused on in various forms of religion, but as shown under (2) below, there is reason to go with the latter, more inclusive, interpretation. So let us say that if religious claims are true, then there are more entities or states or relations to be listed in the correct inventory of what there is than would be mentioned by a full description of the "common" features belonging to the mundane realm (this is the metaphysical aspect), and also their value or importance exceeds that of anything in the mundane realm (this is the axiological aspect).

Notice—this is important—that although the thoughts of a religious person *may* often concern something that would be nonphysical or would transcend the universe, were it to exist (think of the Creator-God of any Western form of religion), something could be transmundane in the (no doubt technical) sense I have given that notion *without* metaphysically transcending the realm of the physical or natural. So we must beware of confusing "transmundane" with "transcendent." The Greek and Scandinavian gods come to mind here, as does the Mormon conception of God the Father (who is said to have a body of flesh and bone), and also—to introduce something rather different—certain aspects of nature's order that are not noticed or appreciated by all human beings but sometimes inspire responses in people—as, for example, in Einstein[15]—that lead them to think of themselves as belonging to the category of the religious. (Each of these, it may be noted, has played a role in *other* counterexamples to definitions of the past, definitions that put too much into the notion of a transmundane reality.) Notice,

---

[15] See "The World as I See It," in Albert Einstein, *Ideas and Opinions* (New York: Wings Books, 1954), p. 11.

further, that a form of religion such as Zen, which on most construals emphasizes *engaging* the mundane with an attitude of acceptance or detachment, and is often said to introduce one to nothing exotic or exciting or unusual or supernatural, still involves thinking of something transmundane, on my understanding of that term. For here the *attitude* (and what it facilitates) is transmundane.

(2) *An emphasis on a significant good, for oneself and others, that may be realized through a proper relation to this reality.* Whether it really is so or not, religion is at any rate seen as a positive thing by those in whom it is realized. It appears to bring with it a promise of deliverance from evil or of harmony and peace in one's everyday existence or, more strongly, of spiritual transformation. It contributes to the religious person's sense of meaning in life. This, by the way, provides support for including feature (1) above, as I have interpreted it. For it is precisely in connection with perceived or possible inadequacies encountered in the mundane realm that the importance of deliverance or peace or transformation or meaning most commonly arises (suffering and moral and spiritual disorder grow out of a *lack* of food and drink, etc., and out of *conflict* with others, and out of the *noncompliance* with our wishes and needs of the everyday reality). So if religion involves a concern with rising above such inadequacies, it may quite naturally involve thoughts of something (at least objectively) other than and greater than the mundane. The manner in which religion is thought to be a power for good may vary from one form to another, but it seems impossible to conceive of religion where *nothing* good is promised. To be a religious good, moreover, something must be thought to be more than trifling (it is similarly inconceivable that religion should *emphasize* something viewed by the religious as trifling): hence, "significant." And though not all forms of religion are truly universal in orientation (take tribal religion, in most of its manifestations), it does seem that to focus on a good tailored to a single person—namely, oneself—would be to step outside the realm of the religious: hence a possibility for oneself *and others*. Though there is a distinction between personal and institutional religion, the former has a strong tendency to turn into the latter which it arguably would not have if focusing on a good tailored to oneself alone could be religious. And there are, in any event, fairly plausible counterexamples to the claim that such a focus is religious. Think, for instance, of someone whose elevated thoughts and newly formed disposition to live a better life are due to a new romance which he invests with an ultimate status. Should we think that this person might, on that account, literally be religious? This would, it seems, be an offense against ordinary usage of the term, and apparently it would be so because this person's "religiosity" is not something he is likely to see himself sharing with anyone. It is

arguably only if he perceives his personal changes as associated not just with his beloved, with whom (so long as they retain their present character) he will seek an exclusive relationship, but attached instead to something more generally accessible and perceived as such—say, some vital force suffusing the universe, to which others can in principle also relate—that we would begin to think of what we see here in terms of religion.

(3) *The cultivation of such a relation.* The religious way is a religious *way*: the religious person, as some of my previous points already suggest, sees himself as headed somewhere, though perhaps a "somewhere" that is to some extent or in some measure visited every step along the way. And to travel along such a way one must, in some manner and to some extent, seek to be more intimately connected to the delivering or transforming reality. It is within this context that we can understand what is going on when the religious person meditates or sacrifices or sings or befriends the helpless: his life is bound up with a quest for the good referred to under (2), sometimes for self-interested reasons (in the crudest forms this appears, for example, as a concern to "go to heaven instead of hell") but also, in more ethically mature forms of religion, for its own sake and for the sake of others.

(4) *A disposition or tendency, when attending to matters in which they are implicated, to totalize or ultimize in some way the central elements of features (1)–(3).*[16] What I have in mind here can be stated more fully as follows: a tendency, when attending to the relevant matters, to treat the object of the thoughts referred to by (1), the good referred to by (2), and the activity referred to by (3) as in some way unlimited or *ultimate*. To treat these things thus can certainly involve thinking of them as ultimate, but it need not, especially in the case of (1), where we have seen the need to allow for the absence of concepts of the mundane and the transmundane (perhaps one could not think of something as ultimate without also thinking of it as transmundane). A more sensitive and accurate characterization might speak disjunctively of a tendency to experience ultimizing (i.e., limit-removing) thoughts, or to engage in limit-removing behavior, or else to feel limit-removing emotions (of course the disjunction should be viewed

---

[16] In this book I treat "disposition" and "tendency" synonymously and think of the basic notion involved here as follows: *S* has a disposition or tendency to exemplify a certain mental or physical behavior *B* in circumstances *C* if and only if the constitution of *S* is such that, were *S* to find herself in *C*, *S* would normally (i.e., unless things fail to proceed as they usually do and the production of *B* is in some way blocked) exemplify *B*. It is of course compatible with this understanding that a disposition may exist without ever being activated: whether it is activated depends on how commonly we may expect the relevant circumstances to be realized. But in the present case—the case of ultimization in religion—and in the large majority of cases we will encounter, it is obvious that the relevant circumstances are fairly commonly realized for most of the individuals involved.

as inclusive), in respect of the central elements of features (1) to (3). One's behavior in relation to x is limit-removing or ultimizing if it is such as makes sense only if x is ultimate (perhaps rituals involved in worship would be an example), and emotions are ultimizing if they are appropriate only given that x is ultimate (a certain kind of awe would be an example here). In ultimizing, the religious person relates to the items in question, represented by (1) to (3), *as though they were* ultimate. And of course they may not be, even given the properties the religious person is independently inclined to ascribe to them. This possibility affects especially the object of the thoughts referred to by (1), which may have properties *excluding* its ultimacy if, for example, it is conceptualized as only one among various creative powers or processes. (Notice that thus interpreted, the tendency in question will be immune to counterexamples affecting other definitions referring to ultimacy, which require that the object of religious concern be such as *really would be* ultimate, were it to exist.)

Take the previous three features in turn. The suggestion here is that talk of a "beyond" or "more," when it is religious, tends toward the removal of all limitations from its object. It gestures at something that cannot be limited to the mundane or even the physical world but is transcendent, whose status in reality is (moving beyond simple transcendence, which in the sense indicated could be realized by a ghost!) indeed the deepest, the most fundamental; and whose value is the greatest and the fullest possible.[17] In other words, religious persons tend to treat the object of their concern as though it were ultimate (whether they explicitly think of it as such or not). One similarly finds a tendency not only to emphasize the possibility, for oneself and others, of realizing significant good in relation to this reality but of realizing in relation to this reality the highest or deepest good possible for humankind, often with ramifications that are said to embrace the whole world or, if not that, with ramifications that generate a radical asymmetry between what is realizable by the religious and the lot of those outside the fold (ultimately great disvalue or perhaps an absence of personal status). One notices, further, not only the cultivation of such a relation but a tendency to seek to make the cultivation of the deepest possible relation to the religious reality absolutely central to one's whole life. And bound up with all these things one also commonly finds ultimizing emotions—such as feelings of

[17] Analytical philosophers may immediately be inclined to make this notion of an ultimate reality more precise, but as it appears in the actual practice of religion, the notion is far from precise and probably should be seen as representing a disjunction of possibilities. At this point I do not wish to speculate as to how large a disjunction this might be, and how its disjuncts should be construed, but simply to identify the general notion behind it.

absolute allegiance. If one considers where an emphasis on the ultimate, the infinite, the unlimited is most naturally to be found—which aspect of human life provides the most natural home for such talk—the answer "religion" must surely be inevitable.[18] The notions of an ultimate reality (notice the commonness of god-language), an ultimate human good (think of salvation or liberation), and an ultimate commitment (consider how references to devotion are woven into religious talk) appear to be at the heart of almost anything that goes by that name.

But not *just* anything—or so the careful student of religion will now suggest. That is, the last of our four features, despite the subtleties involved in its formulation, seems not as closely tied to the nature of religion as the first three. Some of our own examples—for instance, ancient Greek religion—appear to make this obvious. So we cannot say that features (1) to (4) represent jointly sufficient as well as individually *necessary* conditions of religion, as the tidiest sort of philosophical definition of "religion" would require. And, sadly, when (4) is dropped from consideration, we are left with a definition that is obviously too broad: even if the remaining three conditions are necessary, as our earlier "disqualifying feature approach" suggested, satisfying each of (1) to (3) is still not *sufficient* to make something a genuine instance of religion, as counterexamples—take a passionate gym teacher, for one—will show. What we have arrived at, so the student of religion will continue, is therefore just another good example of the frustrating nature of the search for a definition of "religion." And this frustration is not relieved by tinkering with the four features. If we expand the idea of a transmundane reality, introducing into it the notion of something inaccessible to the senses or completely supernatural or transcendent, we immediately leave plausible examples of religion behind. And similar results follow if we speak simply of the highest good or of complete devotion, or—inserting this alteration into feature (4)—if we say that religious people ultimize with respect to only *one or more* of features (1) to (3).

But perhaps these animadversions are beside the point. It is, after all, only a tendency that I refer to in respect of feature (4). And this is the sort of thing that can exist without being always—or even in all relevant circumstances—activated or evident and that can reasonably be inferred to exist even where we are not acquainted with every aspect of a person's life (thus we will infer that someone is an example of an angry person—has a disposition to display the behavior(s) we use this label to cover—when we

---

[18] One wants to say that since ultimization is a distinctive and striking feature of human life, there must be *some* important category to which it belongs and in which it is indeed dominant, and what would this be if not religion?

often see him angry in representative situations, even if there are many corners of his life we have not examined). It also bears repeating that, given our generous conception of what is involved in treating something as ultimate, the fact (if it is a fact) that the object of this or that religious concern is furnished with properties entailing that it is *not* ultimate need not deter us. Now with these points in mind, we can see, I think, that even the Greeks and the Norse and Mormons and Einstein and practitioners of Zen, in those cases where we are inclined to call them religious, may be said to exhibit a tendency to treat the objects of their religious concern, and the concern itself, as ultimate.

For some of this there is direct evidence. Here is the sober scientist, Einstein: "The most beautiful experience we can have is the mysterious . . . knowledge of the existence of something we cannot penetrate, . . . perceptions of the profoundest reason and the most radiant beauty, which only in their most primitive forms are accessible to our minds."[19] And here is a modern-day teacher of Zen: "Now the truth of the matter is that we're not separate. We are all expressions or emanations of a central point—call it multidimensional energy. We can't picture this; the central point or energy has no size, no space, no time. I'm speaking metaphorically about what can't really be spoken of in ordinary terms."[20] And we all know that religious Greeks and the Norse worshiped their gods and understood the world in terms of them and organized their lives around them, and that Mormons worship their God, and also that worship is a form of ultimization. Indeed, this is precisely what gives point to the criticism of god-worship leveled at his fellow Greeks by the pre-Socratic philosopher Xenophanes, who pointed out flaws in the gods, suggesting that they were therefore unfit to be worshiped. The god he himself believes in, he says, is by contrast "one god, greatest among gods and men, in no way similar to mortals either in body or mind," a god who "sees all over, thinks all over, and hears all over."[21] There is a clear resemblance between this idea and the conception of a completely unlimited God at the heart of Judaism, Christianity, and Islam, a conception which, as we all know, has deeply influenced Western culture over many centuries. Now I am not suggesting that examples like these show that all practitioners of anything worthy of the label "religion" always and inevitably ultimize in the manner in question, only that these examples (which could easily be multiplied) provide support for the view that even

---

[19] Einstein, "The World as I See It," p. 11.

[20] Charlotte Joko Beck, *Nothing Special: Living Zen* (New York: HarperCollins, 1993), p. 76.

[21] Quoted in Norman Melchert, *The Great Conversation*, vol. 1: *Pre-Socratics through Descartes*, 4th ed. (New York: McGraw-Hill, 2002), p. 16; see also p. 15.

in instances of religion where surface indications may suggest otherwise, a *tendency* toward ultimization exists.

To these points certain others can be added. We can note that religion is a matter of degree—one can be more or less religious—and that any obvious move *toward* ultimization, however much it might reflect conceptual misunderstanding, would normally be taken by the religious as marking an increase in religiosity. The Hindu devotee who treats the actually limited object of her concern as if it were ultimate gives us more reason to regard her as religious rather than less. We can also observe how those who are most obviously religious are themselves inclined to regard those who do not ultimize as only nominally religious, as having no degree of real religiosity at all. (Think of the evangelical Christian's response to church members who sleep in on Sundays or in other ways make the Christian way less than completely central to their lives.) There is, further, the fact that taking feature (4) as necessary for religion permits us to explain certain otherwise puzzling phenomena. We can then explain, for example, why the passionate gym teacher is yet not religious: whatever her enthusiasm, it would be too much to say that, *qua* gym teacher, she has any tendency to treat the realities with which she is putting her students in touch, or the reality with which she herself is put in touch while teaching them, as metaphysically and axiologically ultimate.[22] Then we can also—to take an example often utilized in this sort of discussion—explain why we are at the same time attracted to and repelled by the idea that the ardent Communist is religious: we are attracted to this idea because, in addition to expressing features (1) to (3), he *is ardent* (that is, his form of life displays a tendency toward ultimization of the central items connected with features (2) and (3)); we are repelled because he does not treat anything as transcendent of the physical universe in the manner that ultimization with respect to feature (1) would require.[23]

---

[22] Perhaps it will be thought that there is another problem here—that if, strangely enough, the gym teacher *did* come to treat health or fitness (or whatever) as though it were metaphysically and axiologically ultimate, my argument would require that we think of her as religious, when this is clearly not the case. (And—so says Daniel Howard-Snyder, to whom I owe this objection—we can think of plenty of similar examples involving atypical attitudes that generate a similar problem.) But I think the speed with which we are inclined to conclude that persons in such examples are not literally religious owes something to the fact that, although they have now become rather odd, we are still back thinking about *ordinary* gym teachers (or whatever) who display no religious tendencies—we have not carefully enough considered *what it would be* for them to display truly ultimizing behavior or emotion. I submit that if we really saw ultimizing behavior or emotion in such cases—the health of students treated as of a piece with the health of the universe, itself treated as inconceivably important?—the category of religion, quite literally construed, would seem to us to be the only one adequate to the situation.

[23] Remember here that the concept of being transmundane and the concept of being

It may still seem to some, however, that anyone who accepted my argument as developed so far would have to be overly sanguine about the possibility of defining "religion." Is it not obvious that what each of us has experienced in connection with the use of the word will influence our understanding of its meaning? I have clearly encountered ultimate attitudes and naturally assume that others are thinking of the same thing when they use the word, when in fact they may be thinking something very different. Someone growing up in an atheistic family, for example, may define religion as superstition; someone who is evangelical may think of it as empty formalism or inefficacious ritual. Academics may have a more detailed understanding, but even they—notoriously—differ among themselves as to what religion is. (And these differences may of course reflect the aforementioned differences in ordinary usage, to which academics often appeal in justifying their definitions.) Even if I *can* include under my definition much of what others would call religion, there is no guarantee that my definition is mapping their uses of the word (that I am identifying what we all agree on). They may be thinking very differently about what I take over from them, combining it with other phenomena I would *not* include as religious. Or else they may view as central certain aspects that my definition relegates to a peripheral status. In general, sensitivity to the complexities and subtleties of language will rightly lead us to look askance upon any definition of the sort I have proffered, insofar as it purports to accommodate actual usage.

I would reply as follows. The relevant variability in usage of the term "religion" will be diminished if, as in our case, one distinguishes its personal and institutional senses. In any event, attention to language will reveal that it is not quite so private a phenomenon as the objector's first remarks suggest it to be; our individual contexts of language use are, all of them, strongly shaped by cultural patterns and other realities of human life much larger and more general than they. Thus there will be much more in common between our linguistic activities than is here allowed. (Applying this point to our present concern we might note, for example, that if the objection is correct, we should hardly expect to find ourselves understanding and resonating with even the details of much that is written on the nature of religion by, say, William James, many years ago—but we do.) Another point worth noting is that what appears to be disagreement over the referent of a term may often instead be a

---

transcendent are not coextensive: for something to be transmundane, as my earlier discussion shows, it need not transcend the physical universe. The ardent Communist is focused on a utopian ideal, which takes him beyond the mundane but does not prompt him to treat anything as transcendent.

difference in the *interpretation* or *evaluation* of it. This applies, arguably, to the atheist who thinks of religion as superstition and the evangelical who thinks of it as empty formalism. In addition to possible factual errors—by which, presumably, definitions need not be influenced—what one sees here are different (but equally negative) *assessments* of what "religion" names. The atheist and evangelical in question may not (and typically do not) have any trouble agreeing over what it is that is being evaluated. We also find people picking out, when they speak of religion, what is of particular concern to them at the moment, which may suggest a different usage, whereas it is really only a one-sided emphasis explained by their purposes. (Here too the example of the atheist and the evangelical is useful: the former, concerned with intellectual issues, emphasizes what we might call the *cognitive* side of religion, what the religious (in the atheist's view, erroneously) hold to be true about the world; the latter, concerned with practical and spiritual matters, focuses on the *conative* side, what the religious are (in the evangelical's view, fruitlessly) endeavoring to accomplish in the world. But we should not expect either to claim that the side she has latched on to is all there is to religion.) Thus when people "view certain aspects as central," it is not immediately obvious, as the objector assumes, that the aspects thus viewed are thought to be central to the *nature* of religion.

So have we arrived at an adequate definition, suitable for general consumption? I think that the definition I have been discussing, when examined closely, can be seen to have quite a lot going for it—especially when we notice that we can make use of the notion of ultimacy without implying that religious persons themselves deploy it (this, it may be recalled, is how we were able to include such apparent counterexamples as Norse and Greek religiosity, which would otherwise strike a powerful blow at condition (4)).[24] It seems reasonably likely, however, that some will disagree. What I want to point out at this stage is that even if they are right, and the approach we have just been discussing is no more successful at the most general level than the family resemblance approach to which it is opposed, we may still make use of material from our discussion of these

---

[24] This feature of the definition also helps to deal with cases where we have apparently religious persons in intellectual discussion *denying* that the God they worship, say, is in every significant respect unlimited. What they assert may be belied by their behavior and their emotion, which are appropriate only to a truly ultimate being. If such is not the case—if they are in no way inclined to ultimate—then on the present view we are mistaken in calling them religious (which, it should be noted, is quite compatible with their performing actions similar to those that religious persons perform, or belonging to a group called religious, or thinking of themselves as religious, or being thought of as such by others, and so on).

two approaches to provide all that is needed to deal with the problem of defining "religion" *for philosophy.* Where the concern is with prolegomena to a *philosophy* of religion, there is, I suggest, a way of avoiding any dispute between those who say there is and those who say there isn't a good general definition of "religion" on offer—a way that is made possible by the special character of philosophy.[25]

5. *Defining "Religion" for Philosophy*

Even if no one definition best accommodates everything that has been or might be counted as belonging to the world of religion, it may still be possible to craft an appropriate and adequate *technical* definition of "religion": a definition accommodating everything in a *significant tract* of religious phenomena which philosophy has special reason to find interesting, and satisfying various desiderata in connection with the needs and obligations of philosophy of religion. Let me put my cards on the table right away. In my view, such a definition would make ultimization central. It would say, to be specific, that "*S* is religious (or exhibits religion)" should be viewed as synonymous with the conjunction of the following propositions:

(1) *S* takes there to be a reality that is ultimate, in relation to which an ultimate good can be attained.
(2) *S*'s ultimate commitment is to the cultivation of dispositions appropriate to this state of affairs.[26]

Before I make a number of elucidatory remarks about the details of this definition, let me comment briefly on why it might be found appealing by philosophers of religion, so as not to leave the reader hanging (after the elucidations I will have more to say about why I

---

[25] I do not assume that the family resemblance approach is the only approach that might be seen as representing the negative side of the dispute referred to here ("There *isn't* a good general definition"), or that the approach I have just defended is the only approach that might be seen as representing the affirmative side ("There *is* a good general definition"). My aim has been and is to represent both sides and then to show a way of transcending them both—which, if it succeeds, takes us past other representatives of these conflicting positions as well.

[26] There is of course another use of the word "religion" that can be derived from this one, which refers to *all the instances of such religion or religiousness taken together.* Sometimes it will be convenient or necessary to speak of religion in this general way (compare the way we sometimes use the word "science" for science-in-general or "art" for art-in-general). It should be clear from the context when I am doing so and when not.

consider this definition to be the one most appropriate to investigation in philosophy).

Notice first that this definition, while somewhat narrower than the one discussed in the previous section (for it makes necessary an explicit deployment of the concepts of ultimacy), does satisfy the conditions the latter considers necessary and would also be viewed by the latter's advocates as specifying a sufficient condition of religiosity. (Indeed, similar judgments would have to be rendered by advocates of most candidates for the status of "good, general definition of 'religion.'") Notice also that even when judged in the light of the family resemblance approach, it counts as satisfying a sufficient condition of religiosity: a defender of this approach would concede that it does indeed identify something (the "significant tract" mentioned above) belonging to the sprawling world of religion. These points show that my definition is at any rate not wildly unrelated to what contenders on either side of the dispute over the nature of religion have considered to be important.

A much more compelling point in its defense, though, is that a concern with matters it makes central is *clearly* at the heart of *philosophy*. It may indeed with some justification be said that the tendency for a philosopher like me to notice ultimization when considering the nature of religion owes as much to the special character of philosophy as to the character of religion, neutrally considered. But though it might at first appear otherwise, that is not really the basis for an objection to my results. It is, after all, the aim of finding an understanding of religion relevant to philosophical investigation that drives this inquiry. And in this connection the fact that metaphysics is concerned to discover the deepest truths about the nature of reality, and ethics the deepest truths about goodness and value, must be deemed relevant, for given this fact, anything that ultimizes generates claims that offer answers, whether illuminating or misleading, to the questions of metaphysics and ethics. Since metaphysics and ethics lie at the heart of philosophy, it is perhaps not surprising that ultimizing religion should be of special interest to philosophy.

Here we might also note, more specifically, that an emphasis on transcendence of the physical universe, which (as I argue below) the explicit deployment of concepts of ultimacy entails, must make any form of life in which it is found a subject of interest for philosophers, because of its obvious connection to the questions of metaphysics which ask whether reality is most fundamentally physical or rather in some important sense or respect nonphysical. I suggest that it is because it both emphasizes transcendence *and* ultimizes that traditional *theistic* religion—focused on the idea of a personal and perfect creator of the universe—has been of such interest to philosophy.

But of course not only theistic religion does this. Theistic religion is an instance of a type, of which there are many other instances in today's world, to which philosophy (at least philosophy in the West) is only now starting to give proper attention. The traditional idea of God shared by most Jews, Christians, and Muslims is a conception of someone transcendent and ultimate, relationship with whom constitutes our highest good, and absolute devotion to whom is clearly considered appropriate. But both monistic and dualistic Hindus say something very like this about Brahman and emphasize the overriding importance of commitment to the religious path in one of its many possible forms as a way of finally securing release from samsara, or the wheel of rebirth. And for Buddhists the idea of the Buddha-nature or of Nirvana, the emphasis on enlightenment, and the wholehearted pursuit of the Noble Eightfold Path function in a similar fashion. A central type of which these main contemporary forms of religion and also many others, both known and waiting to be discovered, are instances seems clearly to be *ultimizing* religion. Thus it is natural and appropriate for philosophers of religion—who are seeking to be true to their historical preoccupations and to the most well-known of today's religious options while at the same time moving imaginatively and creatively beyond them—to choose an ultimistic definition of "religion" to structure and guide and facilitate their efforts.

Finally, in this opening set of comments, I suggest we consider that ultimizing religion also offers more to the religious *practitioner* than does any other form of religion there may be. (Could there be anything better than an ultimate good?) This is important. For now it is not only when paying attention to the aims of theoretical philosophical inquiry but also when concerning themselves with the natural interests of persons reflecting on the rationality of religious practice—an obvious audience for them—that philosophers of religion will find a reason to focus on ultimizing religion. (There is more on this duality of concern in Chapter 7.)

Now to the elucidatory remarks.

(i) We may begin here by noticing that I have collapsed the first two elements of "ultimized" religion mentioned earlier into one: the ideas of an ultimate reality and an ultimate good both appear in proposition (1). This allows us to keep everything that is, in a broad sense, cognitive in one part of the definition, and everything conative in the other. This division is not only tidy but will be useful later, when we are identifying what I shall call the central or basic religious proposition.

(ii) A second point is that in understanding (1) we have no need of the distinction, utilized earlier, between the object of a thought having a certain status and the religious person subjectively appreciating it as such: the central thoughts of a religious person, as we shall understand them

from now on, concern something that really would be ultimate if it were
to exist, and we will assume that she also thinks of it as having this status.
Now this is not to say that every religious person will be assumed to use
regularly such terms as "ultimate reality," "ultimate good," "metaphysical"
and "axiological." Quite obviously, not many do. The religious are rather
inclined to refer to the object of their concern as (for example) "our
heavenly Father" or "the Lord Jesus" or "Allah" or "Brahman," and to
think of their religious goal as "the Kingdom of God" or "a personal relationship with Jesus" or "paradise" or "realizing identity with Brahman."
But that is not a mark against my definition (which must, after all, remain
general). For one can take a reality to be ultimate, both metaphysically
and axiologically, and a good to be ultimate without ever actually employing this terminology: if, for example, it emerges in discussion with a religious person that she believes in God, and understands God to be the
nonphysical creator of the physical universe, the most perfect reality possible, the beatific vision of whom constitutes our highest fulfilment, it is
perfectly appropriate to say of her that she takes God to be a reality that is
ultimate in both senses and that she supposes an ultimate good to be
attainable in relation to God, even if these words and this configuration
of words are not part of her vocabulary, since she clearly possesses the *concepts* denoted by these terms and considers them to be realized.

   (iii) The point just made reminds us of some details concerning "ultimate reality": specifically, that the relevant notion is associated with both
the idea of metaphysical ultimacy and the idea of axiological ultimacy.
Among further features of this notion, one is hidden precisely in the joint
affirmation just noted: namely, that such a reality would have to be a transcendent reality. As suggested earlier, something is properly called a transcendent reality if it is more than or other than—if it in some way goes
beyond—the physical universe studied by science. (It need not oppose
physical nature; it might indeed include it in some sense, if that is conceivable.) The content of all these expressions can be identified a bit
more precisely by saying that a reality of the sort in question will not be
ontologically or causally reducible to the universe.[27] Something nonphysical—for example, a mental state, on some interpretations—might still be
completely caused by physical states. If so, then, appearances to the contrary notwithstanding, it does not "go beyond" the universe in the relevant sense. Here, of course, we bump into the notorious problem of the
nebulousness of "physical universe" (a problem to which both of the

-----

[27] Here I am drawing on some thoughts of Paul Draper; see his "God, Science, and
Naturalism," in *The Oxford Handbook of Philosophy of Religion*, ed. William Wainwright
(Oxford: Oxford University Press, 2004).

terms involved, "physical" and "universe," contribute) and the corresponding question of what, really, a transcendent reality transcends if it transcends the physical universe. I suggest that we may deal with this question as follows. Consider the set of interpretations of the meaning of "physical universe" that have been offered or suggested by scientists or philosophers (including any that view the universe as a *multi*verse, embodying perhaps an infinite number of what on other interpretations would count as universes). Consider, next, the disjunction of different versions of the claim that there exists a physical universe that can be generated from this set. A reality is a transcendent reality, let us say, if and only if it is *more than or other than (not ontologically or causally reducible to) anything whose existence would make this disjunction true.*

Now, clearly, something could be metaphysically ultimate, representing the deepest fact about the nature of reality, without being transcendent in this sense; a materialist who thinks that nothing is transcendent may still hold that something—perhaps particles in fields of force—is metaphysically ultimate. But it does seem that nothing could be metaphysically and axiologically ultimate, representing both the deepest fact about the nature of reality and unsurpassable excellence, without being a transcendent reality. Why? Well, some rather well-known limitations and deficiencies are displayed by the physical universe and everything in it or causally reducible to it; what we see here, more generally, are realities than which greater ones can fairly easily be conceived (e.g., we can think of realities not subject to physical deterioration, or capable of operating independently of physical laws). So if the physical universe and what it spawns is all there is, nothing is *unsurpassably* excellent. Thus, if something is both metaphysically and axiologically ultimate, it must be transcendent.

This conclusion ties in nicely, as we may briefly note, with the way the idea of a transmundane reality is filled out in major contemporary forms of religion (I do not assume that these are the only forms of life that could with any plausibility be called religious, but facts about major contemporary religious options do provide one strand of support for my claim about the proper focus of philosophy of religion, and so they may be expected to emerge from time to time). Here one clearly finds references to ultimacy in both senses and also to transcendence. The "more" of these forms of religion is always something ontologically and causally independent of the physical universe, whether that be—in John Hick's words—"the Jahweh of the Torah, or the Vishnu of the Bhagavad Gita, or the Heavenly Father of the New Testament, or the Brahman of the Upanishads, or the Dharmakaya of Mahayana Buddhism."[28] Clearly, even

---

[28] John Hick, *An Interpretation of Religion* (London: Macmillan, 1989), p. 6.

nontheistic forms of religion (such as that of Theravada Buddhists) buy into this. As Hick suggests, the "direction" of transcendence can be "inward" as well as "outward," and although this language is metaphorical, it is not hard to see Christian religion, for example, as emphasizing both directions, and Theravada Buddhists—with their notion of Nirvana as a "permanent, immortal, supramundane state"[29]—as accepting at least the former.

Might we in a similar fashion seek to incorporate the idea of an ultimate good for humanity that can be attained in relation to the ultimate reality within the notion of such a reality? That is, does the idea of an ultimate reality entail that there is such a good, as it entails that something is transcendent? Must an ultimate reality, as we might say, be *salvific*? If so, we could, at least for some purposes, speak only of there being an ultimate reality while not failing to include either of these other notions. But I think we would be going too far were we to attempt to do so. Ultimacy in the relevant (combined) sense does not clearly entail the attribute here labeled by the term "salvific," for it is hard to rule out the idea that a reality unsurpassably great might be so far out of our league as to be eternally unavailable to us. (Of course, religion denies that this is *in fact* so.) For this reason, it seems appropriate to distinguish the notions of an ultimate reality and an ultimate good attainable in relation to it, as I have done in proposition (1) of my definition.

(iv) An assumption of what I have just said should be clarified, in relation to the word "relation" in proposition (1). To maintain the religious character of this proposition, we must assume that the relation to which it refers, which is said to mediate the attainment of an ultimate good, is an *explicit* relation: as all our previous discussion and also proposition (2) clearly suggest, a relation that we never think about or cultivate—one that is, as we might say, never more than *anonymous*—would not count as the sort of relation through which, according to proposition (1), our ultimate good can be attained. Such an explicit relation would be out of our reach

---

[29] Narada Mahathera, quoted in Hick, *Interpretation of Religion*, p. 287. Consider also the famous passage asserting the existence of a transcendent reality that appears twice in the Theravada scriptures (the Pali Canon). Here is how it is translated by Steven Collins, *Nirvana and Other Buddhist Felicities* (Cambridge: Cambridge University Press, 1998, p. 167): "There exists, monks, that [no substantive is used] in which there is no birth, where nothing has come into existence, where nothing has been made, where there is nothing conditioned. If that in which there is no birth . . . [etc.] did not exist, no escape here from what is [or: for one who is] born, become, made, conditioned would be known. But since there is that in which there is no birth, where nothing has come into existence, where nothing has been made, where there is nothing conditioned, an escape here for what is [or: for one who is] born, become, made, conditioned is known." (The material in square brackets is from Collins.)

if the ultimate were to be eternally incomprehensible and unavailable to us. Here we might also bring out the fact that it is not just any old explicit relation that proposition (1) refers to but rather a *proper* relation—the relation, whichever it is (and of course there can be much disagreement between forms of religion on this), that is appropriate to the attainment of the ultimate good.

(v) What the conjunction of the previous points makes clear is that whether what any traditional form of religion says in filling it out is coherent or correct or not, the concept of ultimacy I am working with (and also the related idea of an ultimate good) is not to be taken as the concept of something forever beyond our grasp, something of which no positive properties we know about can ever appropriately be predicated. Such a notion is already belied by the ideas of metaphysical fundamentality and unsurpassable greatness—both of them positive properties of which we have some understanding. And though it may be that no human being or human community will ever make much progress in understanding metaphysical fundamentality and unsurpassable greatness more fully, I am certainly not ruling that out. It follows that despite superficial resemblances, my notion of an ultimate reality is very different from John Hick's well-known notion of the "Real" (which he sometimes calls the "Ultimate").[30] According to Hick, none of our positive, nonformal concepts *can* apply to the Real as it is in itself. But this Kantian constraint is decidedly not to be attached to the notion of an ultimate reality found in my proposition (1).

(vi) Now a word about the word "takes" in that same proposition (1). Why not just say "believes"? Because, as we will see in later chapters, some serious questions about the relation between belief and faith, and between both of these and religion, would be begged if we did so. Despite this fact (and indeed in light of it), if one wanted to elucidate "takes there to be" further, one might not inappropriately say "believes or has faith that there is."

(vii) A brief remark is also required concerning what *S* represents in the definition. It may appear that *S* should be taken to represent any human subject, as is usually the case in such definitions, and that I am therefore construing religion individualistically. This appearance can be remedied by stipulating, as I now do, that *S* shall represent any subject *or set* of subjects. Some such stipulation is clearly needed because of the importance of community in religion: religion in the personal sense I am defining is instantiated not just individually but collectively as well. Here is another way of putting this point: in talking about personal states, we should not be misled into supposing that "personal" implies "individual."

---

[30] See Hick, *Interpretation of Religion,* esp. chap. 14.

Though religion is carried out by individuals, it may be shared by many individuals. We speak legitimately of the religion of a social group where certain patterns are present within the life of that group, and in certain contexts it might even be impossible to describe religion adequately *without* reference to a group.

(viii) Now some remarks concerning proposition (2) of the definition. This proposition may be thought to misstate the commitment of a religious person by saying that it is a commitment to the cultivation of certain dispositions rather than to the ultimate reality itself. Is not a Muslim, for example, committed to *Allah,* rather than to doing this or that? But it seems that a false choice is insisted upon here. What does it mean to be committed to Allah if not doing the things involved in cultivating a disposition of submission to Allah—a disposition appropriate to Allah's being real and ultimate, as well as the One in relation to whom one's own deepest good can be found? In any case, what *I* mean by "ultimate commitment" is connected to action—something like "deepest focus of action and dedication in the realm of action" might do. So for me to spell out such a commitment necessarily involves reference to what the committed individual has bound himself to in the way of action. (It might also be observed here that if the critic means something *else* by "ultimate commitment," it will most likely turn out to be a disposition or set of dispositions—perhaps loyalty?—*appropriate to the state of affairs referred to by proposition (1),* and so the ultimate action commitment I refer to will necessarily involve cultivating it.)[31]

The idea of religion as including an ultimate commitment may bear a little further probing. It is an idea not uncommonly represented in definitions of "religion." Paul Tillich's well-known definition of "religion" in terms of "ultimate concern," for example, can be seen as making something like the same point.[32] But what exactly does the ultimacy of such a commitment entail? I suggest that we think of a commitment that is basic or fundamental in one's life—in the sense of determining or at least most strongly influencing the course of that life—and perceived as fundamental and also as most deeply important by the one whose commitment it is. (So aspects objective and subjective, as well as axiological and in a broad sense metaphysical, are to be discerned here too.) This view is supported

---

[31] And even if this disposition or set of dispositions involves certain action dispositions, the action focus to which I am referring in speaking of "ultimate commitment" must be deeper than any they might represent, since it embraces and unifies both those dispositions and those together with many others that might be mentioned, which a religious person has reason to seek to cultivate.

[32] See, for example, Paul Tillich, *Systematic Theology* (Chicago: University of Chicago Press, 1963), 3:157–161.

by our tendency to link paradigmatic forms of religion with a devotion that is all-embracing and by the incompatibility of such devotion with the presence of something else as deeply or yet more deeply influential.[33] Though one in whom such an ultimate commitment is operating may lapse, now and then, from behavior appropriate to it, acting in ways that suggest a commitment not as deeply important to her or as formative as it might once have seemed to be (displaying, for example, a ho-hum approach to participation in her religious community, or suspending participation altogether for a time), she will, upon reflection, consider this a lapse and less than her commitment deserves, and her commitment will continue to have the deep and wide effects in question. If she does not think this way, or if what we are inclined to call her ultimate commitment ceases to (or never begins to) play that fundamental causal role, it is not an ultimate commitment—even if, for example, she appears in church or synagogue regularly.

Should we think of the notion of such commitment as a *graded* notion? Can one person or community show more or less of such commitment than another, or more or less of it at one time than at another? It might seem that our designation "ultimate" rules this out. But a moment's reflection reveals otherwise: both in a relative and in an absolute sense an ultimate commitment may be said to be a matter of degree. (We must not be misled by the fact that an ultimate reality would be unsurpassably great into thinking that a commitment, if ultimate in the relevant sense, is unsurpassably influential or strong.) For it may include more or less of one's life even when it includes the most (while representing one's deepest concern, there may be pockets of emotion it has not reached, or motives that remain resistant to its influence, and these may be dealt with over time). Also, the extent of its force may vary within and between lives (even when it includes the same proportion of one's life at different times, it may still be more intense at some times than at others, and someone else's religious intensity may be yet greater). All of this is of course just what we should expect, given the emphasis among the paradigmatically religious on matters of *growth* and *development* in the pursuit of a religious way.

(ix) An interesting related matter, suggested by what I have just now written, concerns whether not only commitment to the cultivation of certain forms of personal involvement but also *their expression* ought to be deemed part of religion. Specifically, my definition seems compatible with a religious person's only being disposed to *act* in certain ways—the idea of

---

[33] Notice the connection to devotion even in such nonliteral uses of the term as "He attends baseball games religiously."

cultivation seems to require no more than this—and thus with such an individual's entirely lacking *emotions* of the sort that are surely characteristic of religion. And this seems to render the definition inadequate.

But we have already seen that more or less of one's life may be governed by one's religion. Although ideally (or so a religious person would say) all one's dispositions should reflect the religious concern, in most persons some of these will not (or not fully) be brought under the sway of religion. What *is* essential is that one's deepest commitment be to doing what one can to bring often stubborn aspects of human nature into line with the religious vision, whatever it may be; and such a commitment clearly involves a disposition to act in certain ways, ways that will intensify this very disposition as well as promote others—which will no doubt include a panoply of emotions, different in different cases of religion. Because of these facts it is hard to justify references to specific emotional dispositions in a definition of religion: where would one draw the line? It may be replied that it is also hard to imagine a completely feelingless religious actor, or someone with a religious propositional attitude—say, the belief that God exists and is perfectly good—who is not in any way affected by this attitude in other areas of her life. States like these are typically psychologically intertwined in important ways. Yes indeed, but that is how things *are,* and we are trying to develop a definition whose central claims must cover all relevant *possibilities.*[34] When one thinks about which aspects of personal involvement to make defining features, surely action leaps to mind. Without being inclined to *do* something, the course of one's life can hardly be deeply affected by religion, and as we have seen, religion deeply affects the course of one's life. And it is in acting religiously—through prayer or meditation or study or singing or rebuilding devastated houses in the name of God—that someone shows most clearly that her religion matters to her.

Religion, in short, could hardly involve an "ultimate concern" without a disposition to act; if it did not include such a disposition, then any competing concern capable of prompting action in pursuit of alternative goals would be more ultimate. And if the right sort of action disposition—together with the propositional attitude already discussed, represented by proposition (1))—is present, surely we have religion, regardless of what else may be absent. Imagine someone who, because of some strange psychological event, is left with only a disposition to perform religious actions but who sincerely orients himself toward a reality construed as ultimate, and so on, and makes the aforementioned disposition

---

[34] And what one considers possible must be influenced not just by the past but by various unexperienced (and also possible future) scenarios.

(which, we may imagine, for him involves, among other things, a tendency to seek appropriate emotions) central to his life. Would we really want to say that such a person is not religious? Thus, while recognizing that quite commonly and indeed typically religiousness involves more than just such dispositions to act in certain ways, I am inclined to include only the latter in the definition of religion.[35]

So much for elucidatory remarks. I return now to the all-important question of why my definition of "religion" should be accepted by philosophers of religion. I want to approach the matter afresh, though incorporating here and there the points concerning it that were briefly set out at the beginning of this section. My response has several parts, which may be distinguished as follows.

(i) First, there is the fact that my definition does indeed provide a point of orientation for work in philosophy of religion, a central idea through which the various activities of the field may be better understood and also facilitated, and in terms of which its central concepts (concepts of religious belief and religious faith, etc.) may be defined.

(ii) There is, second, the significant fact that it does so without ignoring any of the paradigms of religion in the world today; indeed, as we have seen, "ultimization" is a central feature of them all.

(iii) Third, we may note that with such a definition we have a clear criterion by reference to which *new* forms of religion may easily be identified—a much more clear, precise, and helpful criterion, by the way, than a family resemblance approach could ever supply (one can imagine much disagreement, given only a family resemblance criterion, with regard to whether some new phenomenon put forward as religious really is religious or not).[36]

---

[35] Here we must be careful not to be misled by a natural tendency to suppose that everything we are inclined to regard as involved in the religiousness of particular individuals must be included in the general *concept* "religion." It is no more true to suppose that because emotional dispositions would commonly be said to be part of the religiousness of many particular individuals, reference to them must be included in the general definition of "religion" than it is to suppose that because living alone is commonly part of bachelorhood for particular bachelors, it must be referred to in the correct definition of "bachelor." (I am of course counting on the reader's recognition that the only terms required in the definition of "bachelor" are those in the phrase "unmarried adult human male"!)

[36] A family resemblance approach—whatever its merits where a more general understanding of "religion," applicable both within and outside philosophy, is concerned—cannot produce a definition that will serve as an adequate technical definition to guide the activities of philosophers of religion. Here we have one more example of how different understandings of "religion" may be required for different purposes. For a contrary view, to which my arguments here provide an answer, see Charles Taliaferro, *Contemporary Philosophy of Religion* (Oxford: Blackwell, 1998), pp. 21–24.

(iv) What has already been said shows that my definition satisfies what we might call an obvious *minimum requirement* that any definition utilized by philosophers of religion must satisfy if it is to be adequate: namely, the conjunction of the requirements that can be derived from points (i) to (iii). But, of course, other definitions might satisfy it too. A fourth point or set of points, which begins to show why this definition is to be preferred to others, includes the central point made above: that a concern with matters most general and fundamental is at the heart of *philosophy*. With this may be paired the point about the natural interest in ultimacy of persons reflecting on the viability of religious practice. Ultimizing religion might be expected to be of special interest to philosophy and also to those who come to philosophy for guidance in religious matters. Of course, nonultimizing forms of religion, if such there be, may also (for various reasons) be of interest to philosophers and religious practitioners.[37] But our fourth point provides a convincing rationale for making religion that ultimizes the *focus* of investigation in philosophy of religion and adopting a technical definition of "religion" to match. Because of the special character of philosophy we might think of religion that ultimizes as constituting a first tier of religious phenomena, of deepest interest for philosophers of religion and the first object of their consideration; and we might think of nonultimistic forms of religion, if such there be, as a second tier, reserved for later exploration (perhaps on the conditions that further investigation into the concept of religion confirms their status as religious and that investigation into the first tier reveals nothing of enduring religious and philosophical value).

A possible objection to this way of proceeding may now be considered. So far, we have been working with the assumption that philosophy of religion should have a single definition of "religion" to guide all its efforts. But perhaps instead of seeking a single definition, philosophy of religion should entertain *several* definitions, corresponding to different "significant tracts" of religious phenomena, broader or narrower, or with different distinctive features *all* of which are of interest to philosophy (though perhaps not of equal interest). One could imagine picking out of the

---

[37] In this connection it may be noted that no matter what technical restrictions to the use of "religion" philosophy of religion observes, there will remain reasons for philosophers to consider, from time to time, the more general questions about the concept of religion addressed in earlier parts of this chapter. Just for example, there may turn out to be other ways of achieving, at least in part, some of the goals religious people are often inclined to think require transcendence and ultimacy, and these might conceivably generate forms of practice that a future philosophy of religion considers part of its mandate to explore if (after proper investigation) it judges the ideas of transcendence and ultimacy to be irremediably problematic.

buzzing, blooming confusion of the religious domain purely supernaturalistic forms of life, or forms of life that seek unified meaningfulness without supernaturalism, in addition to ultimistic forms of life. Why should there not be different philosophical research programs corresponding to different arguably religious forms of life, which structure their understanding of the major concepts—religious belief, religious faith, and so on—according to the form of life of greatest interest to them, and which seek out solutions to the problems of philosophy of religion in those terms? These research programs would then take care of the various possibilities among them and *together* carry out the work of the field. In this way, all the various concerns and also judgments about the nature of religion could be accommodated at once, and the pluralistic nature of human life and interest would receive more conspicuous respect.

This idea might seem to have at least as much merit, as a proposal for philosophers of religion mulling over prolegomenous issues to consider, as my original proposal above. But I do not think it can survive scrutiny.[38] Let me point out why. First, if it really is a concern with accommodating diverse judgments about the nature of religion that is (among other things) animating this proposal, then it is pertinent to observe that despite the controversy over that subject, not all definitions of "religion" are created equal. In the previous section I provided some reasons for supposing that ultimizing trends are central to religion, but no one would even entertain the idea that religion is *purely* supernaturalistic (and thus that ultimizing religion is not really religion at all), or that *only* forms of life seeking meaningfulness without supernaturalism are religious. What we see in these suggested additional definitions is an *artificiality* that is the inevitable result of refining them to the point where they do not overlap with others. For example, the category of supernaturalistic religion, as it would normally be construed, includes everything belonging to ultimistic religion (an ultimate reality, as we have seen, must be transcendent). And so, to avoid massive redundancy of effort and arrive at a true alternative, the pluralistic approach has to imagine someone focusing on a category of religion that is *merely* supernaturalistic

---

[38] Let me acknowledge that it may seem unrealistic, at least as things stand at present, to give *any* proposal of this nature much chance of being implemented or of seriously influencing how things go in the field, no matter how well it is defended. Perhaps it would be to underestimate the complexity of the factors involved and to be overly naive about human interaction to think any differently. But it would also be unrealistic to suppose that positive structural changes will come about *without* careful attention to such things, and I do not in any case see myself as doing anything more than starting the discussion—a discussion that precisely because of the complexity of factors involved may lead to a variety of benefits both for the philosophical community and for individuals, flowing in quite unpredictable ways from a sharpening of the reflective orientation involved.

(focused on transmundane realities that are also supernatural or transcendent but not ultimate). And this, as I say, leads to artificiality and to definitions of "religion" that, unlike the definition focusing on ultimizing trends, cannot claim to represent a serious or live option in the discussion of what religion is.

Another problem for the proposal stems from its claim to accommodate more flexibly the diversity of philosophical interests. Here the important point to note is that a focus on ultimizing trends has—as I have sought to show—the merit of connecting with a variety of concerns that not just some but *all* philosophers will share. The argument in its defense therefore applies to *any* would-be philosopher of religion, and it must remain a serious question why any philosopher of religion would prefer an understanding of religion that embraces fewer of her concerns to one that covers more. So perhaps the set of philosophers whose interests are better accommodated by the alternative proposal is empty. At the very least, it seems that there could hardly be a philosopher concerned with religion who upon reflection wished to focus all her investigations on, say, forms of life that seek unified meaningfulness without supernaturalism who hadn't first *ruled out* more metaphysically and ethically ambitious forms of religion as embodying untenable claims. And this in its own way shows the priority that must be placed on investigating such forms of religion in philosophy, and the preferability of the original proposal! I therefore conclude that the objection questioning that proposal does not succeed.

(v) A fifth and final point in defense of the idea that the ultimistic definition of "religion" set out above should be accepted by philosophers of religion is that this definition provides a useful and quite natural expansion of what is at present the focus of much inquiry in philosophy of religion—namely, the claim of traditional theism and various more specific claims entailing it—and also, thereby, a proper context or home for continuing inquiry into theistic matters. As already suggested, selecting the foregoing definition to guide their activities will permit philosophers of religion to keep clearly in view that their concern ought to be not only with theism but with the central type of which it is an *instance*. Traditional theism ultimizes, but so do many other actual and possible religious claims. Philosophers of religion, with their concern for no-holds-barred exploration of the deepest issues of religious truth and rationality, must surely be interested in them all. This concern appears most adequately reflected by the definition of religion I have put forward, which, among other things, acts as a powerful tool of investigation, concentrating our attention on the heart of philosophical concern and pointing us in the direction that future investigations ought to take. It also puts investigation into matters theistic in its proper context, clearly sanctioning such investigation while at the same time balancing it with other aspects of the broader concern of which it should be seen as a part.

6. *From Theism to Ultimism*

I suggest, therefore, that we have arrived at a definition of "religion" that philosophy of religion has good reason to accept. Before moving on to other, related, prolegomena, we may bring into clearer focus an immediate result of this inquiry that is of obvious philosophical interest: namely, a new understanding of what we might call the *central or basic religious proposition*. If religion is construed in the suggested manner, then that proposition will be the one embedded in the first part of our definition: that there is an ultimate reality in relation to which an ultimate good can be attained. This is to be viewed as the central or basic religious proposition because all more specific religious claims of the sort actually adhered to in the various forms of religion that philosophy examines must, according to our definition, entail this proposition—and it entails none of them but only the disjunction of all such claims. Traditional theism is not the most basic religious proposition, for it is not the case that all other religious claims entail it; rather it too entails this more general proposition (which entails not theism but only the disjunction of theism and similar claims). Or, at least, traditional theism entails the larger proposition if—as our inquiry suggests is required in order for it to qualify as a religious claim—we construe it as averring not only that there is a certain being, an omnipotent, omniscient, and omnibenevolent creator of the universe, but also that our deepest good involves properly relating ourselves to this being. Let us now give a name to the aforementioned more general proposition that theism, thus construed, entails. I call it *ultimism*. This has echoes of *theism* but reminds us that theism itself qualifies as a religious claim only because it entails this larger claim, which is therefore a more appropriate point of reference for investigation in philosophy of religion.

What we have been discussing so far might be called *generic* ultimism, the idea that there is an ultimate reality of some sort in relation to which an ultimate good of some sort can be attained. But of course, as already observed, religious claims tend to come clad in more particular garb: in the real religious world we have, for example, both the claim that there is a personal God and the claim that there is a nonpersonal Absolute (the Brahman of nondualistic Hindu religion). All such specific religious claims—claims that entail generic ultimism but also fill it out in some way—are forms of what I call *elaborated* ultimism.

In the chapters that follow, the idea given expression by generic ultimism will naturally loom large, for it is the idea in terms of which other general concepts of philosophy of religion will now need to be defined. So we have already achieved an important result. But each of the matters yet to be discussed not only turns on issues already considered, which affect them all, but also brings with it many special problems of its own. Thus, although an important base color of our map has been filled in, many further occasions for conceptual artistry await us.

On Belief

Having clarified "religion" as far as we have, we are closer to being in a position to tackle the ideas of religious belief and a generalized religious disbelief. Philosophers of religion are obviously very interested in the former attitude; one could go on for pages listing the titles referring to it. There is less mention of the latter, but clearly it is something in which philosophers are interested and should be interested, for it represents an important answer to the question of what response to religious claims is rationally most appropriate—an answer about as opposed, intellectually, to religious belief as anything could be.[1] There are other answers too, and we will be exploring the main ones in due course. But before doing so I want to color in the borders of the discussion by considering the outermost responses to religious claims. To do *that* properly, however, we must first spend some time on the very important element these opposites have in common: namely, belief.[2]

---

[1] Strictly speaking, one or two of the attitudes I explore (in particular, belief-in—or affective belief, as I call it) are not entailed by any such response. My reasons for exploring them will become apparent as we proceed.

[2] I am indebted in what follows to the work on belief of L. Jonathan Cohen; see his *An Essay on Belief and Acceptance* (Oxford: Clarendon Press, 1992). Though I have come to disagree with some elements of it, Cohen's positive account—"belief that p is a disposition, when one is attending to issues raised, or items referred to, by the proposition that p, normally to feel it true that p and false that not-p" (p. 4)—provides a starting point and continuing stimulation for my own thinking. And I am still persuaded, as will be evident, that the simplicity of his account (the reference to *but one* disposition) is worth preserving.

1. *Propositional Belief as a Form of Thought*

The main sort of belief at issue here, as a glance at philosophical discussions will attest, is so-called *propositional* belief, the psychological
state of believing *that* so-and-so. (Near the end of the chapter I also
have something to say about the somewhat different notion of believing *in*.) But what is propositional belief? The answer to this question is
not immediately evident, even though we all have innumerable beliefs
of this sort, and despite the fact that we all seem to have immediate
access to such beliefs through introspection. Indeed, there are many
subtleties here, as well as possibilities for confusion. So we shall need to
tread carefully.

I begin with a small but not insignificant clarification, which will help
to ensure that we are all singing from the same page of the hymnbook,
or at least from the same hymnbook. We are, I have said, concerned with
belief as a psychological state—with believing. But this is not the only
meaning attached to the English word "belief." The word is ambiguous:
we use "belief" to refer both to the psychological state of believing and to
what one is claiming when one gives expression to it (which philosophers call the propositional content of that state). We may, for example,
speak both of someone's belief that there are UFOs (the psychological
state) as being hastily or carefully formed, rational or irrational, and so
on, and of the belief that there are UFOs (the claim or propositional
content now) as credible or incredible, as true or false, and as entailing
or not entailing other propositions. From now on I use "belief" primarily
in the former sense.

It is interesting to note that the ambiguity here is quite parallel to that
observed by Wilfred Cantwell Smith and noted in Chapter 1. "Belief," like
"religion," has both an internal and an external sense. It is not surprising,
therefore, that some of the confusion surrounding the meaning(s) of
"religion" is expressed in terms of "belief." A recent college textbook on
philosophy of religion, for example, after spelling out what is to all
appearances an understanding of religion in the internal sense (in which
beliefs are mentioned alongside emotions), suggests that its concern is
with the belief element of religion: namely, the *propositions believed* by religious persons.

This is of course only a small matter, easily dealt with by noticing the
ambiguity in question and avoiding equivocation. Other matters concerning the proper understanding of belief as psychological state will,
however, require considerably more attention. For example, what *sort* of
state or condition is it? A first broad answer, for which it is not hard to
find support and on which there is widespread agreement, is that belief is

a *disposition* of some kind. If that were not the case—if belief were restricted to conscious episodes—then for some time now (that period of time in which I have not thought of what these propositions report) I have not believed that I exist or that the earth is round, and this is absurd.[3] But what sort of disposition? A disposition to do or think or feel what, and under what conditions? In formulating my answers to these questions, I focus on certain matters related to *how it feels from the inside* to be a believer. Such a phenomenological approach can yield some important insights about belief and also about the justification of religious and irreligious belief.

To lay the groundwork for my answers, answers which emphasize thought, it is necessary to draw attention to some important aspects of our mental life and the language we use to speak of it. There is, to begin, our ability as humans mentally to put (or else involuntarily to view) things or possible things in various possible arrangements and thus to represent to ourselves (or have represented to us) "states of affairs."[4] Though not all thoughts are directed to states of affairs, the mental condition in which, at some time, a state of affairs is represented to me is a thought. In these circumstances we may appropriately say that I have thought *of* the state of

---

[3] A main temptation to suppose that belief is exclusively an occurrent phenomenon and (thus) nondispositional arises from the fact that many of our beliefs are activated but once and very briefly, and many clearly exist only for the moment in which they are first activated, being immediately replaced by other and contrary beliefs. To see the former point, one need only pay attention to one's own conscious mental activity for a minute or two in the midst of a normal day and consider all the bits of information that are recorded and immediately forgotten, probably never to return to conscious experience. As an example of the latter phenomenon consider the case, mentioned by L. J. Cohen, of coming to believe that a gun has been fired and then immediately realizing that it was a car backfiring. But as Cohen points out, "such a concurrence, where it occurs, is a contingent, and not a necessary, feature" (ibid, p. 6). And his point can be phrased more broadly so as to apply to both sorts of case: there are possible worlds in which beliefs actually activated but once are repeatedly activated—I might have returned several times to the thought of a gun being fired before learning the real cause of the noise I heard, and the beliefs that have actually never returned to mind might very well have done so. (This last point is supported by the fact that an observer can never be sure, when the experience has vanished, that a qualitatively similar one will never arise, and would be prepared to grant, should this occur, that the same belief was revealing itself.) Thus cases of the sort in question tell us nothing about the nature of belief, which concerns what is *necessarily* true of it.

[4] "*x* represents *y*" expresses an odd relation, which we may accept as obtaining even when what is represented does not in fact exist: for example, a picture or a sentence or—our central concern—a thought may represent Santa Claus (children think of Santa Claus all the time) even if in fact there is no such individual. Individuals and states of affairs may also be *incorrectly* represented or represented in a *distorted* way by our thoughts: for example, I may picture my cousin as short when in fact she is tall; nevertheless, I have succeeded in representing to myself my cousin (if I say I am thinking of my cousin, I am surely not mistaken).

affairs in question. Otherwise put, the state of affairs is the *object* of the thought occurring at that time. For example, my cat chasing a mouse may at a certain time come to mind or be before my mind or be the object of a thought of mine in this way. Of course, this state of affairs, when I think of it, is not literally *in* my mind; it is *represented* to me by my thought.

This same notion of "thinking of" states of affairs seems to be involved when one uses the propositional expression "having the thought that." My meaning when I say that I just had a thought *of* my cat chasing a mouse appears to be preserved when I say instead that I just had the thought *that* my cat is chasing a mouse. But notice that to speak of "thinking that" instead of "having the thought that" results in a change of meaning. To have the thought that my cat is chasing a mouse is not necessarily to *think* that she is doing so. The latter expression we would use to refer to the *belief* that she is doing so, the former to refer to the coming to mind, in one way or another, and however briefly, of the state of affairs consisting in her being thus engaged. (The same notion is sometimes expressed in terms of "entertaining a proposition.") And this coming to mind can occur without belief, as in a situation where I notice my cat's agitation and rapid movements and mentally run through a list of possible causes without settling on any one of them.[5]

Because of the appropriateness of the propositional translation, we may say that to think of a state of affairs is to have a propositional thought. Thinking of a state of affairs *s* and having the thought that *p*, where *p* reports *s*, amount to the same thing. But notice that this identity holds only so long as we do not slip—as is easy to do—from the idea that the object of the thought is a state of affairs to the idea that it is a proposition. What one is thinking of here, what one's mind is directed to, is a possible arrangement of things, not a proposition indicating or representing or reporting that arrangement. When, upon hearing the dog bark, I have the thought that a car is turning into my driveway, I am thinking of a car turning into my driveway, not of the proposition "A car is turning into my driveway." (And this even though we may *describe* the mental event in question by saying that I had the thought "A car is turning into my driveway," thus making the proposition very explicit and directing attention to it. The circumstances of a thought's occurrence and the circumstances of its correct description can be very different.) That proposition, we may say, *expresses* my thought, and I may think of it when, at another time, I think of the thought; we can also say that it gives

---

[5] From the content of this paragraph it follows that one occurrently believes that *p* whenever one's thought that *p* is an *instance* of thinking that *p*; but although correct, this does not shed much light on the nature of belief!

the *content* of my thought (after all, it is a correct description which says that I had the thought "A car is turning into my driveway"), but it is not the *object* of my thought.

It follows from my description of propositional thinking that to have a propositional thought and to *consider* it—that is, to think *about* its propositional content—are different things. To think about a proposition in the most commonly used sense of that phrase involves giving reflective attention over a period of time to various facts or apparent facts concerning it—such as the fact (if it is a fact) that I believe that proposition, or the apparent fact that it is true or that it has such-and-such a probability—and obviously this involves more than just the coming to mind of the state of affairs reported by that proposition. Also, it cannot occur without one's thinking of the proposition: that is, without *the proposition* being at some point the object of one's attention.

Let us now see how these ground-clearing considerations can help us begin to understand what is going on when we experience belief. Suppose I wake up with a headache, and the thought flashes through my mind "It was the red wine." Clearly this can be a conscious experience of propositional belief: namely, the belief that the red wine I had last night caused my headache. Notice that when it is such an experience, I have the propositional thought that it was the red wine, but—or so it is initially tempting to say—I have it in a certain characteristic *way*. Here everything said in the paragraphs above can be applied. In particular, to believe that it was the red wine involves *thinking of* the red wine causing my headache or *having the thought that* it was the red wine. And this "thinking of" does not involve thinking about or forming any belief about the propositional content of the thought in question. (Whether events of these different kinds may nonetheless occur simultaneously I briefly consider later on.) It follows that, contrary to what philosophers tend to suppose, it is a state of affairs and not a proposition that is represented to me and is the object of my attention when I (occurrently or consciously) believe.[6]

It is natural to think that it is a proposition, in part because it is natural for us, when we seek to understand the psychological state of believing, to work backward from the way in which a belief is verbally expressed. If I believe that the red wine caused my headache, I may express my belief verbally by saying "That red wine caused my headache." Now this declarative sentence, as philosophers will say, expresses a proposition, so it is not unnatural to call my belief propositional. But is it belief *of* a proposition?

---

[6] It could be that philosophers are inclined to think otherwise because in their line of work beliefs about propositions are so common; as a result, it may be tempting to suppose that the object of belief is *always* a proposition.

Our discussion suggests that strictly speaking, it is not.[7] From the fact that my belief is expressed propositionally it does not follow that when I believe, I have a proposition before my mind and am directing some sort of affirming attitude toward *that*. And when we look carefully at what is actually going on in conscious belief, we can observe that this is in any case false: I am not, one wants to say, thinking of a proposition and under the impression that it is true; rather, I am thinking of a state of affairs and under the impression that it obtains. Though the proposition reporting that state of affairs may share something of the form of the state of affairs it reports, and is true when the state of affairs it reports actually obtains, the two—proposition and state of affairs—are quite distinct, and so are thoughts concerning them.[8] Another way of putting the point is to say that conscious believing is not *self*-conscious in the way it would be if one were taking note of the fact that what one was thinking of could be represented by a proposition of a certain sort, and considering one's response to that proposition. When I consciously believe that the red wine caused my headache, I am thinking of the state of affairs that proposition reports, and its apparent facticity fills my mind to the exclusion of thoughts concerning the proposition itself. A kind of *forgetfulness* with respect to the proposition itself is required for the concentration and focus and sense of facticity involved here.

Now in connection with my belief that the red wine caused my headache I may of course *also* experience beliefs in which states of affairs including propositions among their elements are represented to me. Having formed a belief concerning the red wine's causing my headache, I may later make the following response to someone else who verbally expresses the same belief: "What you have said is likely true." Suppose that I have a corresponding belief experience. This will then involve thinking of what we might call a *propositional* state of affairs: that is, it will involve thinking of the state of affairs consisting in "The red wine caused my headache" being likely true. Notice: when I have the relevant experience, I still think only of the state of affairs consisting in the proposition in question being likely true, not of *the proposition that* the proposition is

---

[7] Having said that, to avoid awkwardness in expression, I continue to speak of "believing a proposition" or "belief of a proposition" in some contexts. But when I do, it should be remembered what is meant here: a disposition to have, in some sense (yet to be defined), a thought of a state of affairs *expressible by* a proposition.

[8] Some would hold that a proposition is itself a state of affairs, since it is an arrangement of things of a certain special sort. There are various possible views on this, but here it suffices to say that a person who experiences belief has before her mind a state of affairs that is *not* a proposition, even if her belief may properly be said to be expressible by one that is. (This holds even when the former sort of state of affairs involves a proposition as one of its elements, as I go on to show.)

likely true, which is what many philosophers would say I have *expressed* in saying "What you have said is likely true," and so think of as the object of my belief.[9]

So much for what such beliefs as the belief that it was the red wine that caused my headache involve and do not involve on the thinking side, given the results of our earlier discussion. But as we have also seen, it appears that one can think of a state of affairs without believing. What is the "certain characteristic way" of having such a thought which brings us all the way to belief? I have alluded to an answer in the statements just made about being "under an impression" that the state of affairs obtains, or having one's mind filled with "a sense of its facticity." But these are really just place-holder expressions. We need to get much more serious now about clarifying the heart of belief: what it is that makes a believing thought a *believing* thought.

One's first inclination must be to find some suitable extra component. Perhaps, for example, in addition to thinking of a state of affairs, one takes it to obtain or to be real. But this idea is unhelpful for a variety of reasons. The apparent relevance of "taking it to obtain" stems from the fact that it is just a disguised (and vague) reference to belief, and so we are no further ahead. Moreover, it appears that insofar as it specifies a possible separate event at all, this expression refers to a voluntary action of a sort which, as we will see, is not appropriate to belief but is much more appropriate to faith. In the context of *belief* talk—for example, where we talk of taking the red wine state of affairs to obtain—"taking it to" expressions must be read as referring to something involuntary.[10] Now perhaps someone will say that the taking involved here is indeed a separate event, appropriate to belief: namely, the last event of a process of reasoning, the event of *concluding* that a certain state of affairs is real or obtains. But this is still not an act (that "last event" is just the formation of belief, which, again, occurs involuntarily—as I argue more fully later), and in any case, not all occurrences of conscious belief follow upon a process of reasoning. Finally, even if they did, the idea of "taking it to be real" (as already suggested above) is not very illuminating; it does not contribute to the phenomenological clarity we are seeking.

---

[9] A similar story is to be told about believing that a proposition is *true,* and it is clear that on my account, contrary to what many seem inclined to say, there is a difference between believing and believing true: the latter state does, but the former does not, have as its object a propositional state of affairs.

[10] There is a difference between climbing a fence and being *pulled* up by someone else. But someone, speaking loosely of the second case, might nonetheless refer to you as having climbed the fence—after all, you have got beyond it. This is analogous to what we find when it is said that in believing we "take" a state of affairs to obtain: it sounds like something we do, whereas it is really something done to us.

Neither is it helpful here to refer to the distinct event of consciously ascribing to a state of affairs the property of being realized, or to introduce a whole new extra component involving the experience of some feeling state correlated with the thought, or to emphasize the *absence* of certain mental events such as wondering or questioning. These options all bring with them problems of their own: they lack comprehensiveness, or are awkward or just inapplicable, or fail to do justice to the power of the belief experience (for some of this there will be more supportive argument later). In any case, a simpler and more illuminating account emerges when we set aside thinking about *how* something comes to mind in the experience of belief and instead think a little more deeply about *what* comes to mind, noticing when we do that we don't really need an extra component at all (or, at least, don't need a distinct event). The central point here is that although it seems that "having a thought of the state of affairs reported by *p*" must be the same for one who believes that *p* as for one who does not, and that some extra component over and above this common element is therefore needed to distinguish the believing from the nonbelieving case, this is in fact not so. The common description hides a pair of different meanings, and though on one of these meanings the cited expression does not yet articulate the distinctive nature of belief, on the other it does. For consider: what we mean when we say, in the case *not* involving belief, that someone has had a thought of a state of affairs involving the influence of red wine is only that the person has had a thought of *what it would be like* if the relevant arrangement of things were actual. (This is the sense of "state of affairs" we use when, though disbelieving in Santa Claus, we speak of the Santa Claus scenario as "a pleasant state of affairs.") But what we mean when we say in the case that *does* involve belief that someone has had a thought of a state of affairs involving the influence of red wine is that he has had a thought of the relevant arrangement of things *being* actual. (This is the sense of "state of affairs" we are using when we speak of some situation in which we find ourselves as "a fine state of affairs," or say of the Santa Claus scenario not that it *is* a pleasant state of affairs but that it *would* be one.) Here, in place of "a state of affairs involving red wine," we can read "a chunk of the world involving red wine"; the believer, when it comes right down to it, is simply *thinking of the world.*[11] (Notice that the world is real by definition;

[11] Nothing in this idea of "thinking of the world" implies that all (or any) of the elements of the conceived arrangement of things actually exist or that the arrangement actually obtains. To suppose otherwise would be to confuse the notion I am developing with the idea of one's mind lighting upon a state of affairs that *is* actual, which is not just a matter of thinking of the world but of thinking of it *correctly*. (This is not merely belief but *true* belief.) As pointed out earlier (see n. 4), the notion I have in mind here is one according

thus if *the world* is thought of by someone, there is no way for the question to arise whether he is not after all thinking of things in a detached way, perhaps in imaginative reverie, and thus in a manner implying or consistent with nonbelief.)

I suggest therefore that the expression "state of affairs" and the larger expressions involving it are not univocal in this context, and that this insight allows us to define belief by means of ideas already arrived at in the earlier, ground-clearing investigation, without further ado. Let us distinguish the two senses of "a state of affairs has come to mind," the belief sense and the nonbelief sense respectively, as *thick* and *thin*. Then we can say that to experience an activation of the belief that *p* is simply to have the experience of thinking of the state of affairs reported by *p*, *but in the thick sense*. And the disposition of belief itself? Well, utilizing our distinction, we can say that "*S* believes that *p*" is synonymous with the following proposition:

> *S* has a disposition such that (normally) it is only in the thick sense that the state of affairs reported by *p* comes to mind for *S*.

It seems to me that this formulation suffices, in connection with the surrounding conceptual material, to bring some illumination to the concept of belief. It is striking that what the experience of believing really comes down to is simply thinking of the world—no mention of property attribution or of assent or of an extra feeling component that so many (following Hume) have sought to put their finger on will seem tempting to the analyst, once it is seen that correctly identifying the *object* of the believing thought gives us everything we need. That elusive "characteristic way" in which the believer is supposed to be related to the object of her belief is nothing but a reflection of the object itself. But one or two more points about what is involved here will provide a somewhat deeper grounding for my definition and also generate one or two variations on it.

Consider first that the experience of the believer and our ability to arrive at an understanding of that experience are possible only because of a certain common feature of human existence, present early on: namely, the mental category or concept of what is *real*, as opposed to what is *not*

---

to which one's thought may not at all accurately depict the relevant part(s) of the world. Perhaps, for example, my belief about the wine badly misconstrues things. (Since it is *human* thoughts that we are talking about, we have to recognize that they will share in the limitations of human understanding; hence, how we conceive the world may fall well short of correctness.) Indeed, one's thought of the world, in the sense that is relevant here, may fail to capture anything of what there actually is in the world.

real—"just pretend," as children say, thus showing their possession of the concept. (Although on the broadest conception of reality even the objects of such imaginary play and the possibilities and states of affairs in the thin sense associated with them would count as real, we are dealing here with a more common and less generous conception of reality.)

This general concept or category structures all our experience and facilitates the exploratory process that is human life, which begins with primitive awarenesses about ourselves and our immediate surroundings and sensations when we are very young and, over time, moves much deeper, potentially discovering ever more of the complexity and richness of reality. We become much more discriminating in our use of the concept of reality, recognizing more and more clearly that not everything that *could* be *is*, which fuller recognition permits the free play of imagination and, more generally, acquisition of the abstract or thin understanding of states of affairs that we have just seen is at work when one has propositional thoughts without holding the corresponding beliefs. As intelligent beings equipped with the ability to represent such states of affairs to ourselves—and the basic concept of the real, as well as many related concepts, such as the concept of a *proposition*, and the concept of *evidence*—we find it easy to think of how the world would be if certain states of affairs were realized and to recognize evidential relations among propositions reporting them, relations pertinent to a correct conclusion as to whether the state of affairs reported by this or that proposition should be categorized as obtaining in reality (or, as we might now put it, whether a thin understanding of it should give way to a thick one).[12] Given these facts, as well as the ever present need to survive and to relate appropriately to others, and also our many consciously formed purposes (including, for some, the purpose to achieve knowledge of reality for its own sake), we are, whether consciously or not, constantly sorting and weighing propositions, and also *consciously experiencing (and reexperiencing) states of affairs as realized, or as belonging to what is real.* These latter experiences are of course the experiences that go with belief, to the essential nature of which I have sought to give a more precise formulation in terms of thought—in terms of thinking of states of affairs in a *thick* sense, thinking of the world.

But this involvement of the category of reality in the experience of believing does suggest an additional way of expressing what is going on in that experience. For we may say that conscious believing amounts to thinking *of* a certain way things might be or might be said to be (a state

---

[12] Of course, recognizing such a relation itself entails concluding that a certain state of affairs—namely, the obtaining of that relation—belongs to the world.

of affairs in the thin sense) *as* belonging to that category: that is, thinking of a certain way things might be or might be said to be as the way things are. It is important to be careful here. Clearly, I am not talking about consciously ascribing to a state of affairs, *thinly construed*, the property of being actualized or realized: that was ruled out above. What I mean is more like what you experience when, on the most natural interpretation, you think of the creature you saw stealing your chickens last night as a dog. You are not having the thought that the creature you saw *was* a dog. This would involve something like consciously thinking of a creature (as such) and of a dog and making a mental connection between the two. Of course, you may be disposed to have that sort of thought too, in appropriate circumstances. Such a disposition may even be *presupposed* by what we are talking about here, but that does not make it part of it. What we are talking about here has only obliquely to do with the *content* of the thought, as internally experienced, and rather more with an objective quality of it, one that might be referred to in a correct external description of the thought while yet not registering with you at the time: namely, that the creature putting in an appearance in your thought is—as I shall say—"apprehended under the concept" *dog*. In reply to a question as to the nature of your experience, you will say something like "I just had a thought of the dog I saw last night," but not "I just put it together that the creature I saw last night was a dog." The objective truth reflected in what you do say, on the relevant understanding, is something like this: that your possession of the concept *dog* so colored the experience in question, was so determinative of its subjective phenomenology, that it did not even occur to you that the creature could have been something other than a dog—indeed, that everything in your total (conscious) psychological state at the time was in perfect harmony with that concept being applicable to the remembered creature.

Applying to the nature of belief this idea of something x being apprehended under the concept y, we may say that my experiencing a belief amounts to my having a thought concerning what is objectively a way things might be (or might be said to be) in which that item is apprehended under the concept *reality*: that is, having a propositional thought so colored by the concept of reality, one whose subjective phenomenology is so completely determined by the concept of reality, that it does not occur to the thinker at the time that the state of affairs with which she is communing in thought could be anything but realized. Generalizing the result, and remembering that belief itself is a disposition, we may therefore say that "S believes that p" is also synonymous with the following proposition:

S is disposed to apprehend the state of affairs reported by *p*, when that state of affairs comes to mind, under the concept *reality*.

Acceptable variations on these definitions exist. We may again note that, on the view I have here developed, a believing disposition is activated whenever one thinks of the world. Say that to have the latter experience is to experience a token of the thought type *w*. Then we can put the essential point this way: *S* believes that *p* if and only if *S* has a disposition such that instances of the thought that *p* are, for *S*, normally tokens of the thought type *w*. Call the sort of thought one has when one thinks of a state of affairs in the manner of conscious belief a "world-thought." Then we may also shorten our offering and simply say that the distinctive fact about the thoughts involved in belief is that they are world-thoughts. In what follows, I move freely among these various characterizations of the believing state.[13]

2. A Contrary View: Belief as Confidence

An obvious feature of all the defining and explicating we have done is that the idea of feeling has been left entirely out of account: on the view that I have been developing, a belief is not a disposition to have a certain kind of feeling but rather a disposition to have a certain kind of thought. This clashes with a common view, given expression, for example, in the work of L. Jonathan Cohen, who says that believing that *p* involves a disposition to "feel it true" that *p*.[14] The common view apparently involves thinking of the feeling state referred to here as the intellectual feeling of *confidence*. We find a reference to the latter, for example, in William Alston, who incorporates Cohen's point into his own larger account (more on this

---

[13] Believing, on the view here developed, involves focusing on some particular state of affairs. But the larger context need not be ignored. We might compare the thought of conscious belief to the photograph appropriately characterized as a photograph of Banff National Park but in which only Banff Springs Hotel appears. In thinking of the world this way, one's mind is seeking to "zoom in on," or get a close-up view of, some part of the world, but it also gives such a snapshot a context. That is, even when I focus on one or another state of affairs, it tends to be seen against the backdrop of others, which, as I experience things, are similarly privileged to share existence with me and to contribute to making up the world. Here imagine a large collage or a bulletin board bristling with overlapping photographs. One might focus on one element of the collage or on one photograph while never ceasing to see that it is *one* element of a larger whole or *one* photograph in the midst of others. (By contrast, imagine a puzzle piece mistakenly thought of as a tiny, unframed, and irregularly bounded abstract painting.)

[14] Cohen, *Essay on Belief and Acceptance*, p. 4.

below) in these words: "If *S* believes that *p*, then if *S* considers whether it is the case that *p*, *S* will tend to feel it to be the case that *p*, with one or another degree of confidence."[15]

Now it may indeed seem that a feeling of confidence must in some way be bound up with the nature of belief, and that the experience of believing is therefore (as Alston's words suggest) a matter of degree. After all, we do speak of feeling or being confident that *p*, and it seems clear that one's confidence with respect to a proposition may be more or less firm. And it can seem equally clear that what we are speaking of when we speak of such things applies to belief. Two examples help to bring this out. Consider first what it is like to lose the belief that Santa Claus exists. Typically, this loss occurs over a period of time. One may begin with complete and unquestioning confidence with respect to the proposition "There is a Santa Claus," and then, after a series of intellectual or emotional events (often involving parents or siblings) which shake one's confidence, find oneself altogether without belief and saddled instead with uncertainty or doubt—the state of believing neither that proposition nor its denial. This is only a sketch of a certain process, but already we appear able to infer that what is lost when the former believer arrives at nonbelief is intellectual confidence. Now we have focused on *felt* confidence. But the term "confident" appears to apply to the believer even when her confidence is not occurrently felt or expressed in this way. If someone were to ask concerning the child who believes in Santa Claus whether she is confident that there is a Santa Claus, the correct answer would surely be "yes" even if she were at the time thinking about other matters. (What we have in mind when we give this answer is something like the following: the question whether it is true that there is a Santa Claus could come before her mind repeatedly, perhaps randomly, over a period of time, and always her response would involve that feeling of confidence.) Confidence, in other words, is dispositional too, and the various experiences of felt confidence one may have are merely activations of this disposition.

Consider next a religious case. Suppose one is faced with serious questions about God's existence. When these arise, the believer may not cease to feel confidence, but her positive inner response will probably be

---

[15] William P. Alston, "Belief, Acceptance, and Religious Faith," in *Faith, Freedom, and Rationality,* ed. Jeff Jordan and Daniel Howard-Snyder (Lanham, MD: Rowman & Littlefield, 1996), p. 4. Some of Alston's comments suggest that he might be sympathetic to the sort of account I have developed—feeling it to be the case that *p* is "a matter of one's being *struck by* (a sense of) how things are"; "feel" is a "broad enough term to range over a great variety of inner experiential states"; "I must confess to some uneasiness about the whole notion of degrees of belief" (pp. 5–6). But in the end he throws in his lot with the common view, and I shall respond to him accordingly.

more muted or sullied: it may become a "yes, but. . . ." She does not cease to see the world as a creature, but upon reflecting, for example, on the horrible suffering undergone by some of *its* creatures, she may entertain alternatives to her belief that the world has a benevolent creator. The doxastic and epistemic situation she is in may start to look much more complicated and messy, and projects she needs to undertake to properly and responsibly negotiate her way through to the other side of what is fast becoming a crisis of belief may suggest themselves to her, with the result that she may stay home and read philosophy or theology books instead of going to choir practice at church. The story could be developed; there are many endings. What seems clear is that the precious commodity the believer feels slipping away when she goes through the process of losing her belief is confidence, and that typically it *is* a process, which suggests both that believing is bound up with confidence and that it admits of degrees.

Such examples can seem very convincing, but I submit that they do not prove the identity of belief and confidence. Believing is indeed, as the second example almost admits, a matter of how one *sees* the world, not of how one *feels* about it, and this or that degree of confidence is indeed, as the Alston condition cited above almost says, something that tends (contingently) to appear *with* (i.e., alongside of) belief. Degrees of felt confidence should not be confused with degrees of belief (in general, feeling is not the important thing). The experience of activated belief is instead "all or nothing," for either my thought that p is a world-thought, or else it is not. Either I think of a state of affairs in the thick sense, or I do not. Either I apprehend some state of affairs under the concept *reality*, or I do not. The feeling of confidence comes into play only when one experiences the further, *proposition-directed* thoughts mentioned earlier—in particular, when I think about the *epistemic status* of the proposition I believe. And so I may ask myself whether indeed it is true that the red wine caused my headache, or how likely it is that this is so, instead of just having the thought that the red wine caused my headache as a world-thought. If I do, I will certainly find myself with a mental feeling that is a matter of degree, for then I will feel more or less confidence with respect to the proposition in question. But I repeat: this occurs only when thinking about the epistemic status of the proposition that my original believing thought expresses. Thus what we see here is really the activation of a different disposition—a disposition to experience felt confidence when thinking about such a proposition. Belief and confidence, then, are different things, dispositionally and otherwise, though they may occur together and causally interact (for example, when my degree of confidence with respect to p reaches a certain level, I may suddenly start to have the thought that p as a world-thought; and when it falls below a certain point, I may suddenly cease to have the thought that way), and so talk of degrees of confidence does not apply to belief proper.[16]

But how then are we to deal with the plausibility of examples such as those described above? Well, the facts they cite, if reported in a non-question-begging way, can easily be accommodated by my account. In particular, we might expect a steady weakening of confidence often to coincide with the period of one's critical investigation of a belief, and we might expect the complete loss of confidence to accompany the loss of belief if such is the upshot of the investigation, even if the experience of belief during all this time is phenomenologically the same and not in itself a matter of degree. (It is, after all, an *investigation*, in which one is *thinking about* one's belief.) And the latter state of affairs, when we look more closely, is precisely what we seem to find: even after confidence with regard to the existence of Santa Claus or God has taken a serious beating, and feelings of confidence are weakened, the individual may from time to time experience, in the manner of belief, a conscious thought of there being a Santa Claus or of God existing; only if *this* no longer occurs will she say that she no longer believes. Now she may at what seems the very same time experience a surge of confidence, no doubt in part caused by the belief experience, but the two states are not to be identified. Part of the problem here is that thoughts about the status of a proposition and our feeling responses thereto are phenomenologically so intertwined with thoughts activating belief of a proposition that it is easy to confuse these things. The former can, as it were, cover up the latter, with the result that we find it difficult to detect the true nature of belief, even upon careful in(tro)spection. Indeed, many mental states meet and cross here and can therefore easily be confused with one another.

Now it does not follow from anything I have said that there are no degrees of belief; indeed, it appears that there are. But this notion applies less to the conscious experience of activated belief, or subjectively, than

[16] Perhaps it is because of the exigencies of life that thoughts will be experienced as world-thoughts before we arrive at certainty concerning them. In any case, a sense that the weight of evidence is in favor of some proposition (this will be called a preponderance of probability by those who possess the latter concept) seems sufficient to effect the transformation that is the beginning of belief. With this the balance tends to tip, and the shift occurs. So what we believe probable we normally just plain *believe*, too. (This does not always occur. For example, contrary desires may block or prevent or at least delay the latter event in some cases.) And though a thought may continue to be experienced as a world-thought after we sense that its probability is diminishing, it is in the process of, as it were, being pried loose. It is embattled and may ultimately succumb to an alternative view of things, at which point we will no longer believe (more on this below).

objectively to the *disposition*, which may be weak or strong. Let us explore this notion a little further. One sense in which it might be said that there are degrees of belief does apply to the activation of belief itself, though not at all in the way that a proponent of confidence-belief identity would envisage it. Think of perception, where one's noting of an object may be more focal or more peripheral. Similarly here: the extent to which a belief is dislodged from its dispositional state can vary. In fact, at least for perceptual beliefs, these two things overlap: I was, a few moments ago, observing the pen beside my computer only peripherally and so only peripherally *believed,* in the occurrent way, that something was there, and when, seconds later, I focused my vision fully on the flag flying outside, my belief about it was, as it were, fully dislodged or exposed.

Another and more obvious and important sense in which we may speak of degrees of belief applies to the belief disposition. We can say that one disposition is weaker than another, or that the same disposition has different degrees of strength at different times. This can be determined by sensitivity to objections, how much is required to lose the belief, how much surprise is felt when it turns out to be mistaken, the regularity or constancy with which the thought in question is experienced as a world-thought. Even more specifically, we might pay attention to such things as the amount of time spent reflecting on the status of a proposition one believes before the relevant world-thought is experienced, or, contrariwise, how swiftly one turns from what we have called thinking *of* (in the context of a world-thought) to thinking *about,* and judge a belief disposition to be the weaker if the first number is high or the second low and stronger otherwise. But notice that there does not need to be a corresponding set of gradations of "strength" in the activated state of belief: either one has the relevant thought or one does not, and this whether the disposition is weak or strong.

It is useful to observe here that many belief experiences that seem weak may really be experiences of probability beliefs. With reflective activity come tendencies to believe in a different, more qualified way. So perhaps in some circumstances I occurrently believe that it is probable that my headache was caused by the wine (I have before my mind the state of affairs consisting in this being probable), but I do not flat out believe that it was thus caused. A relevant factor is that probability beliefs can have much the same effect on our action as unqualified beliefs, but it does not follow that the former are versions—perhaps somehow weaker versions—of the latter. Similarly for the experience that is sometimes described as a "suspicion" that *p.* This should be read not as a very weak experience of belief that *p,* but, if in terms of belief at all, as the (nondegreed) experience of the belief that *p may* be true.

Here we should also return to a question postponed earlier: Can one experience belief and confidence simultaneously? I would say that one can. Or at least it is not obvious that one cannot. I experience a world-thought in which today being Super Bowl Sunday figures prominently; then I think about my evidence and feel a rush of confidence with respect to the corresponding proposition; and when a moment later I turn from thinking about evidence and experience my belief once again, it does not seem (on the basis of what I later remember) that the feeling of confidence just disappears when the belief is activated. But it seems that one cannot—or at any rate cannot fully—experience the thought that activates belief that p and the thoughts *about* p that are *productive* of this or that degree of confidence simultaneously. One has to try to build a sort of hierarchy of thoughts here, and at least when considering what can be simultaneously activated and fully activated (that is, fully dislodged from a dispositional state, in the sense earlier discussed), one does not get very far. This is so not only because of the difficulty of holding more than one thought fully before one's mind at the same time but because of the distinctive sort of *shift* that must occur when one moves from a believing thought to a thought *about* that thought. Consider my occurrently believing that there is a tree before me and then experiencing the higher-level belief that I believe that there is a tree before me, or that the content of my belief that there is a tree before me is overwhelmingly probable. The "and then" here does seem of necessity to indicate a sequence in time that prohibits the simultaneous occurrence of these thoughts: to experience the second or third I must leave the first behind. The experience of belief thus occurs without being tainted by any other thought, and so also without thoughts of evidence concerning itself of the sort that produce more or less felt confidence. Belief may of course in a sense coincide with such thoughts, for it is in itself a disposition, but *occurrent* belief cannot.[17]

Or is this mistaken? I seemed a moment ago to be consciously believing that Regina was painting in her studio, and subsequent thinking about this proposition and its status did not seem to erase that conscious experience of belief. But there seems to be a subtle switch to thinking of the proposition *as* a proposition in such situations which one can fail to notice (and indeed much switching back and forth). The sort of switch that occurs here can even be visually represented—it may, for example, be a switch from mentally beholding the state of affairs someone might describe by saying "Regina is painting" to mentally beholding one expressible as "'Regina is

---

[17] Perhaps we could also say that in such circumstances of fleeting thoughts, the *memory* of a preceding thought may in some way be experienced even when the thought itself has been replaced by another.

painting' is extremely probable."[18] Another example: the thought flashes before my mind that my minister brother will be too busy to write me today, given that today is Sunday, and it does so in the manner of belief. But this time when I consider objections that diminish my confidence, my awareness of the aforementioned believing thought seems to disappear and to be replaced by thoughts of evidence, while *other* occurrent beliefs—such as the belief that it is at most probable that my brother is too busy to write me today, for the given reason—take turns occupying my mind. So do I perhaps no longer believe that he is too busy? Was my disposition to have that experience so short-lived? I do, after all, still think the proposition in question to be probable. But it seems that to experience occurrent belief of *that* proposition, I need to be once again caught unawares, with none of the reflective considerations *about* it in the vicinity; and that this does occur—since it just now did!

Perhaps, after all that I have said in the last few pages, it will still seem implausible that the experience of belief is not itself a feeling. Don't we sometimes express belief by saying "I feel that *p*," and don't others ask us what we feel about *p*, meaning what do we *believe*? I might, for example, say that I feel it was the red wine that caused my headache, or my wife may ask me whether I feel that it was the red wine. Wouldn't everyone know we were talking about belief? My answer to this objection is fourfold. First, there is a sense in which one does feel activated belief, even though it comes in the form of thought, for there is a sense in which to speak of feeling something mental is just to speak of *experiencing* it, which is something that may correctly be said of any such state. And it may be that sometimes when the "feel that" expression is used, this more general notion is all that is intended. Second, confidence and belief are, as we have seen, quite closely related, both causally and functionally. Normally, an expression of confidence may be taken to have many of the same concomitants as an expression of belief, and so we may fall into using interchangeably terms appropriate to the two states. (And there is also the fact that many may—mistakenly, in my view—think that it is literally *correct* to do so.) Third, the experience expressed by "feel that" may be one that includes belief in conjunction with certain *emotions* that attend it. It is interesting to note how rarely anyone uses this expression when reporting a belief that does not matter to him. (This, it seems to me, is why the "feel that" expression as applied to my red wine belief, though possible, does not make for a very

[18] It might seem that the first experience persists in the second, which simply *adds* something to what came before. But we are here misled by seeing the same words—"Regina," "is," "painting"—in the two descriptions. In the first experience I am mentally beholding the *state of affairs* those words may be used to describe; in the second I am beholding (among other things) the *proposition* they may be used to express.

convincing example. Neither, for the same reason, does "I feel that grass is green"; compare "I feel that what she said was insulting.") Fourth, it seems that often the "feel that" expression is an oblique reference to the *source* of the belief—namely an intuition or "gut feeling" or inarticulable "sense." (Perhaps this would apply in the red wine case.) Think, for example, of "I feel that our obligations are more demanding than your theory suggests." Among them, it seems to me, these four replies are quite capable of defusing the foregoing objection.

I now briefly introduce some further points in favor of distinguishing between belief and feelings of confidence, as I am doing, which may suffice to convince those who are still doubtful. First notice that our various believings generate what is sometimes called our picture of the world. And when thoughts of states of affairs enter our heads, either those states of affairs will seem to "fit" into our world picture or not (they may find a place in it immediately, or only upon investigation; or else it will be apparent—immediately or in time—that some contrary state of affairs fits). If they fit, they will, as it were, merge seamlessly with our world picture. And what is this if not coming to believe? But notice that it seems to have very little to do with a feeling of confidence.

Consider an example. I hear a sound and wonder what it is, realizing it is something familiar but encountering a lag between hearing and recognition. A second later I find myself with the belief that it is a seagull. What is going on here? I hear the sound of the gull before identifying its source. I do have certain related beliefs even then: I believe that I am hearing *something*, and that it is something familiar. But only later do I believe that it is a gull I am hearing. Only when the source of the sound comes into focus do I have the relevant belief (earlier I am at a loss about what it is, and perhaps even if the proposition "It is a gull" were to come before my mind, it would not be enough to unstick me psychologically). When this belief is formed, something, as it were, clicks into place; this event of hearing, about which I already have beliefs, is more completely filled in on the map; my world picture has a new part. Now this clicking into place involves an immediacy that might seem related to an immediate, spontaneous feeling of confidence, but when examined closely it seems prior to it and independent of it, especially when one considers that confidence is a matter of degree. The experience here is most naturally expressed in terms of how one sees the world or, more literally, in terms of how one *thinks* of it, which does not appear to be a matter of degree.

Consider another example. Suppose that when driving down the road I successively ask myself concerning the car in front of me, "Is it more than 11 feet long?" "Is it more than 10 feet, 11 inches long?" "Is it more than 10 feet, 10 inches long?" and so on down the line. It seems clear that there comes a point when I *believe* that the car has a length greater than that specified in the question, even though the moment before, I did not. When this occurs, it seems apt to describe my transformed psychological state in terms of my now experiencing the thought of a certain state of affairs as a world-thought, whereas earlier I did not. There is no gradual buildup to this point such that I want to say that my belief starts with an almost imperceptible degree of confidence and grows from there; nor do I want to say that my *belief* changes in any way as I consider even shorter lengths and feel my *confidence* increase. There is something that, once the transformation has been effected, remains the same through all such accompanying changes in confidence: namely, my basic picture of how things are in this respect. And here, surely, is where we ought to locate my state of belief.

A central argument in favor of my way of carving up this conceptual terrain claims that whereas confidence of the sort that has been mentioned entails belief, belief does not entail confidence; thus the two states cannot be identical. An anxious personality, feeling doubts and thus lacking anything like the sense of intellectual safety or security or assurance that must go with confidence, may still hold beliefs. A fearful flyer who is also a frequent flyer, for example, believes that the airplanes she boards will arrive safely at their destinations—otherwise, she surely would not keep getting on planes—but certainly she cannot be said to feel *confidence* when considering that proposition! What she does experience when she considers her belief may elicit the following sort of thought: "This is how it *really* is even though I don't *feel* it to be this way." Thus it appears that belief cannot be any sort of feeling disposition like confidence.

It may seem that this example and argument can be dealt with by paying more careful attention to the dispositional nature of belief. A disposition may exist even though it is not always activated in the relevant circumstances, and so a disposition of confidence can exist even when it is not activated as we might have expected it to be. Indeed, any number of psychological factors may serve to block the normal feeling of confidence in certain circumstances, but if that feeling remains an individual's normal response, surely her disposition of confidence persists through these lapses. Hence, even if anxiety blocks the fearful flyer's normal feeling of confidence, we may not infer that she lacks a disposition of confidence with respect to the proposition in question. And so it remains possible that the belief I have referred to *is* just this (continuing) disposition of confidence.

There are at least two problems with such a move. First, it seems that the belief our fearful flyer possesses, based on all the evidence that is commonly (but usually unsuccessfully) adduced to assuage the fears of fearful flyers, may be occurrently experienced even while all confidence is absent. It seems quite coherent to suppose that someone in the air might, throughout the flight, lack confidence that the plane will arrive safely and yet—perhaps because of intense efforts to clear and calm the mind—periodically experience as a world-thought the notion that the plane will arrive safely. (Although it would have to be said, even on my account, that confidence is normally caused by such a thought, together with recognition of its evidential underpinnings, we may imagine that in the circumstances I have described this is in each case prevented by, say, yet another lurch of the plane.) But in that case the two experiences—of the thought in question and of some degree of confidence—can, as it were, come apart, and we are forced to decide with which, if either, we want to identify occurrent belief. Though it would be question-begging here to assume that one should pick the former, simply the description of the situation and reflection on all its elements (including especially the fact that our fearful frequent flyer would surely not continually be on planes if she lacked the belief in question) may suffice to convince us that that is the proper choice.[19]

The second problem intensifies the first, making the aforementioned choice seem even more obviously correct. It is that the individual of our example may not *normally* feel confident either. Some fearful frequent flyers, even if normally (i.e., when on the ground) given to thinking believingly of the planes on which they travel arriving safely, will, however irrationally, feel discomfort or agitation about flying consistently enough to be prevented from normally experiencing anything plausibly called confidence. Thus we are committed to denying that their belief entails the latter state.

3. *Thought-Plus?*

So much for my defense of the view of belief as a thought disposition against views emphasizing confidence. I turn now to arguments suggesting that such an account must still be incomplete—that we ought to add

---

[19] It may be wondered what we are to do with the fact that the fearful flyer may not only seem to lack belief that she is safe but also to *possess* the belief that she is *not* safe. When she screams "We're all going to die!" what else are we to think? Well, perhaps what she is saying is only to be understood as an expression of fear. If we think the fear presupposes belief that she is in danger, we should notice that in such cases *both* beliefs may be possessed at the same time (at any rate for the duration of the flight)—though of course they cannot both be activated at the same time. Note that the confidence view needs to be able to deal with this issue too.

to our definition of belief certain other elements. William Alston, for example, says that belief may also include at least some of the following tendencies: to affirm the proposition believed when asked about it; to believe what one supposes to follow from it; to use it in theoretical and practical reasoning where applicable; to be surprised if it turns out to be false; and to act in (other) ways that would be appropriate if it were true, given the believer's purposes and other beliefs.[20]

This claim of Alston's resembles the claim made on behalf of a tendency toward ultimization in the early going of Chapter 1. There I sought to show that even if ultimization is not universally to be found in religion, a *tendency* toward it arguably is. Must we accept Alston's claim here, having utilized a similar one ourselves? I suggest that the answer is no. The tendencies mentioned by Alston, though they may be natural and expected *accompaniments* of believing, are not plausibly viewed as *part* of it. For if they were, then belief could not exist without them, and this seems false.[21] Perhaps we should think here of someone or something whose constitution includes no capacity to speak or act in the relevant ways at all. Might not such an individual for all of that be quite able to form a mental picture of how things are, and would we not be inclined to apply the concept of belief in understanding this capacity? Perhaps instead we should think of someone who starts out with each of the tendencies in question but then has all but one undermined by a scientist who fiddles with the brain chemistry supporting those tendencies. If that one tendency were a tendency or disposition to have world-thoughts, would we not say that the power of believing had been retained? We might also expand the previous example to include the implanting of *opposing* dispositions: if because of the scientist's activity I have all the dispositions (apart from the thought disposition I am emphasizing) that a defender of Alston's view would say are bound up with believing that not-*p*, I cannot at the same time have those that go with believing that *p*, and yet it seems that in this situation I might still believe that *p*.

We can illustrate the same general point without indulging in science fiction. For example, I may cultivate and over time acquire dispositions to speak and act in ways appropriate to the belief that my terrorist captors, who have kidnapped me, are not misguided, all the while secretly believing that they *are* misguided. But if I have the former dispositions, I cannot at the same time have dispositions to speak and act in ways appropriate to

---

[20] Alston, "Belief, Acceptance, and Religious Faith," p. 4. A similar list appears in H. H. Price, *Belief* (London: George Allen & Unwin, 1969), pp. 20, 294.

[21] Cohen makes a similar point in defense of his own one-dimensional concept of belief, in *Essay on Belief and Acceptance*, pp. 10–11.

the latter belief. Hence I can have the latter belief without those dispositions. Since such arguments as these are available and seem forceful, and since we can accommodate the various psychological and behavioral tendencies to which Alston refers by saying that they are often (even if not always) *caused* by belief, it does not seem we should say they are part of it.

One way of being misled into thinking otherwise which may be worth mentioning here (I am not saying it is found in Alston's thinking) involves failing to distinguish between the question of what belief is and the question of how one comes to *know* of its presence. These are different questions. Perhaps the various tendencies involved would be mentioned by an answer to the latter question, but it does not follow that they must be referred to by an answer to the former. A problem here is presented by the word "manifestation," often used in this context as a synonym for "activation": we may speak, for example, of a world-thought as an activation of belief *or* as a manifestation of it. "Manifestation" is much more naturally construed as an epistemological term, useful in speaking of occasions where something is *shown* to be the case or to exist. "Activation" serves better when one wants to express the real existence of something in an active as opposed to a latent state.[22] But since the former term is sometimes treated as synonymous with the latter, these two distinct concepts can easily be confused. If we separate them carefully and use the relevant terms more appropriately, we will, I think, see that belief is only *manifested* by such behaviors as are mentioned by Alston (that is, shown to exist, since it normally accompanies them) and can be activated (that is, realized in an active as opposed to a latent state) without them.[23]

Now it is true that we commonly deny that someone really has a certain belief that he claims to have on the grounds that he hasn't acted in ways one would who did hold that belief.[24] And even if such a denial is in this or that particular case false because one *could* hold the belief in question without the particular actions cited, the behavior it represents, Alston might say, still suggests (or will be taken by many as suggesting) that according to our ordinary concept of it, belief entails a tendency to act in

[22] That term too, however, because of ambiguity, fails to serve perfectly: we must be careful to note that by "activate" we mean not "start" or "set off" (as in "activate a bomb"), which allows for the activating event or state to be something *extrinsic* to what is activated, but rather "realize in an active as opposed to a latent state," which closes off that possibility.

[23] The conceptual situation here is complicated by the fact that it is possible for a state to be manifested and activated by the same event. My giving you $1,000 when you are down and out, for example, may activate a disposition to be compassionate and also (if observed) manifest it. Alston may say that his tendencies have this status, but for the reasons given I do not think this is the case.

[24] As William Alston has reminded me.

ways that would be appropriate were the believed proposition true (given the purposes and other beliefs, etc., of the believer)—contrary to what I have claimed. My answer makes use of the distinction just mentioned between the activation and the manifestation of belief. Because of relevant causal connections between it and other such things, belief may (typically) be manifested—that is, shown to exist—by actions done by the believer, even if it is possible for it to be activated without any tendency to perform them. The fact that belief is typically thus manifested is enough to generate (and also, often, to justify) the use of statements of the form that are taken by the critic as suggesting and supporting the entailment view. Recognizing that belief is manifested in action, someone might well issue just the sort of denial referred to (notice that the weaker, causal view is all we have to assume to make sense of particular instances of such a denial in ordinary language, and sometimes it is the more plausible of the two: e.g., "She just up and left him; that's not what people do who believe that their kids come first"). Since this alternative interpretation is available and plausible, the force of the common linguistic behavior cited by the critic as evidence for the view Alston favors is diluted: we don't need to suppose that a tendency to act in certain ways is—or is thought to be— part of the very *nature* of belief to account for this behavior. And in my view, given the independent reasons supporting a trimmer notion of belief, we should not do so.

Another question worth considering at this point is whether the disposition of belief I have been exploring in some way includes a *contrastive* dimension. Is it woven into the texture of the experience of believing that one gives the proposition one believes a higher rating than some other proposition(s)? Richard Swinburne thinks so, and if he is right, then we need to fill out our account accordingly. On Swinburne's view, "one believes this proposition as against that alternative proposition."[25] A proposition p may be contrasted either with its negation or—less commonly—with a variety of alternatives considered in a certain context (think here of doxastic situations arising from such things as horse races, football competitions, or religious pluralism). In the former case, to believe that p is to believe it more probable than not; in the latter, it is only to believe p more probable than each of its alternatives. (Notice that believing p more probable than each of its alternatives is quite compatible with not believing p more probable than its negation, which in such a case one would do only if one believed p more probable than the *disjunction* of the alternatives.) According to Swinburne, the contrastive element also enters into our identification

[25] Richard Swinburne, *Epistemic Justification* (Oxford: Clarendon Press, 2001), p. 34.

of degrees of belief: "I believe p strongly [in the more common case] if I believe that it is a lot more probable than its negation, weakly if I believe that it is only a little bit more probable than its negation."[26] In short, the strength of one's belief depends on the strength of one's contrastive attitude.

What should we say about this? Well, clearly the denial of Swinburne's view follows from my earlier analysis—especially from what was said about the common confusion between the content and the object of belief. So any plausibility attaching to the latter will make his view correspondingly less attractive. But let us attempt a more specific response to his points. Consider: someone asks me how I feel today, and I say, "Happy." Presumably, the propositional thought that I am happy is a world-thought for me. But I need not have given any thought at all to the alternative "I am unhappy" to have that world-thought. Though the possibility of my being unhappy may *objectively* be a condition of my believing that I am happy (for one thing, I may come to understand the latter proposition's meaning in part through experiencing the contrast in question), this possibility need not enter into my *subjective awareness* when I consciously hold the belief in question. Even if I take a look at my situation to determine the correct answer, I need not at any time compare the epistemic status of "I am happy" with that of "I am unhappy." Perhaps my happiness is immediately apparent; overwhelmed by that positive fact, the negative possibility does not so much as come into view. All of this, it seems, is just as we might expect it to be, given that my belief *is* the belief *that I am happy*, not the belief that my happiness is more likely than my unhappiness.

Certainly there may be cases where we are initially unsure what to believe and so investigate our options; in such circumstances alternatives and their relative probabilities will naturally come to mind. But we are not always in such circumstances when believing, and even when we are, the formation of belief takes us past the comparative stage to the endorsement of one alternative. It is also true that the belief-worthiness of "I am happy" entails that "I am unhappy" is not worthy of belief (at least not here and now, for me). But we do not need to be consciously aware of the entailments of a proposition to believe it. The notion that a contrastive element is built into the very texture of believing seems therefore to be unsupported and mistaken.

---

[26] Ibid., p. 37. Swinburne recognizes that not just any believer will have a well-developed concept of probability, but his emphasis on the contrastive attitude here leads him to insist that all of us, even young children, have at least "a vague and primitive form of a belief about relative probability."

But what about Swinburne's second sort of case, where p is alleged to be believed in the context of a variety of alternatives? Wouldn't a comparative judgment be part of believing p then? It seems not. Although a comparison is made here, it still does not follow that it enters into the very state of believing that p; the relevant probability judgments might, for example, *cause* one to believe that p instead of being part of the very fabric of the latter state. But a deeper problem is that what we have just been assuming for the sake of argument—that Swinburne's second sort of case is indeed a case of believing that p—seems false. An individual, S, understanding the logic of his situation, might very well hold the comparative beliefs in question—where the alternatives are q, r, s, etc., he might believe p more probable than q, and believe p more probable than r, and believe p more probable than s, and so on down the line—without believing that p, for he might be in a state of uncertainty as to whether the disjunction of q, r, s, and so on, is false. Given such uncertainty, S can hardly believe that p. That p is more probable than q, and more probable than r, and so on, will be no consolation to him and will not produce belief *that p* if p cannot be judged to be more probable than not-p.

Another argument against Swinburne's view here does not depend so much or in the same way on intuition. If S's believing p to be more probable than each of its alternatives in circumstances like these entailed believing that p, then any possible world that contained the former state of affairs would contain the latter as well, but this is not the case. Indeed, there is a possible world in which the state of affairs consisting in S's believing at a time t that p is more probable than each of its alternatives is realized in conjunction with S's believing at t that p is *improbable* (for one may hold a proposition to be significantly more probable than each of its alternatives, and yet because of the *number* of alternatives and the results of applying the Addition Theorem of the probability calculus to their disjunction, rationally view it as probably false).[27] Surely *this* is not a possible world in which p is believed by S at t! Rather, it is a world in which S believes at t that not-p. Swinburne himself is committed to this conclusion, for he holds that viewing a proposition as improbable entails disbelieving it. Given these points, the only way one could avoid relinquishing the view that the putative entailment holds is by arguing that it is possible to believe that p in one sense while believing that not-p in another. But this must, at best, be a strained response that fails to do justice to our use of the language and to our intuitions about belief. I suggest, therefore, that we may safely leave the contrastive understanding of belief behind.

[27] See J. L. Schellenberg, "Pluralism and Probability," *Religious Studies* 33 (1997): 143–159.

4. *The Involuntariness of Propositional Belief*

Before moving on to the apparently nonpropositional notion of belief-*in*, I want to address the question of whether propositional belief or belief-that, construed as I have construed it, should be deemed involuntary. Our attention to this question may be brief because my analysis of belief carries an affirmative answer to this question on its face. Here I simply add a few examples in support of this answer and tidy up some rough conceptual edges.

Various plausible arguments can be and have been given for the view that belief is involuntary—which I interpret as the view that belief is not under our direct voluntary control, that one's beliefs cannot be changed just by trying. If we construe belief in terms of my earlier analysis, these arguments must surely be correct in their conclusion. For although one might *imagine* (and thus think of) a state of affairs being actual just by trying to do so, nothing similar is possible where the sort of thought of the world I have been discussing is concerned. One can check this impossibility through experimentation. If belief were voluntary in the suggested sense, then we should be able to drop or add any beliefs we liked just like that—but we cannot. Though its rays no longer dance on my keyboard, the sun is turning the distant ocean to gold, and I can feel its warmth through my window. Try as I may, I cannot cease, just like that or even given a bit of time, to hold these beliefs. And similar experiments reveal that beliefs whose propositional content I would consider less probable (such as my belief concerning the red wine) cannot be got rid of just like that either. Certainly I can *entertain* the denials of these propositions—I can even say to myself "There is no sunshine today" or "My headache has nothing to do with red wine"—but that is not the same as believing them. And I imagine it is possible and perhaps even likely that by focusing only on evidence against some of these propositions, and by consorting only with persons who disbelieve, and by employing certain other, more colorful strategies that come to mind (such as hypnotism), I *may* lose the relevant beliefs over some extended period of time. But that is a long way from exercising any sort of direct voluntary control over the content of my beliefs.[28]

It may be useful to recur to a religious example. If belief were voluntary, then surely many people experiencing the loss of theistic belief would quickly regain it. It can be a painful experience to lose such belief,

---

[28] See William Alston's "The Deontological Conception of Epistemic Justification," in his *Epistemic Justification: Essays in the Theory of Knowledge* (Ithaca: Cornell University Press, 1989).

and though some, on account of the dishonesty involved in believing against what one takes to be undermining evidence, might refrain from doing so, others surely would take advantage of the "quick fix" available to them and blissfully go back to believing just as they did before. That they do not indicates that in the relevant sense they cannot.

It may be replied that religious persons *often* employ a method for resolving crises of belief that involves believing against the evidence: it is called self-deception. But although the phenomenon of self-deception is familiar enough, that it is always or typically present where crises of theistic belief are resolved—and in particular, where one returns to belief after having been in a situation of doubt—is not obvious. Whether theists who have resolved crises of belief of the relevant sort have deceived themselves as opposed to uncovering answers that they honestly (even if sometimes mistakenly) consider convincing is an empirical question, and it is not at all clear that it has been adequately answered in the affirmative. And it is not at all clear either whether self-deception of the sort that would be relevant here always or often involves the *removal* of troublesome beliefs concerning the evidence and *reinstatement* of the belief that has been lost—as opposed to the suppression into unconsciousness of the troublesome beliefs and the acquisition of the *belief* that one believes theism (which is very different from believing theism).[29]

Even where the former state of affairs does obtain, it does not seem appropriate to look upon it as the result of exercising direct voluntary control over one's beliefs; it seems rather to be because we lack such straightforward control that the complexities of self-deception are (sometimes) entered into. And if the objector now suggests that it is to avoid the intolerable consequences of facing one's dishonesty that an individual may opt for self-deception of this sort instead of brazenly choosing to believe differently, and not because she cannot do so, we may reply that this still leaves us without evidence of the voluntary control in question. Indeed, given the distinction (between self-deception and voluntary belief) that it concedes, such a suggestion involves the withdrawal of what was *said* to be evidence of this capacity. In any case, it is not at all clear why, if we have direct voluntary control over our beliefs and a believer wishes to use it to resolve a doxastic crisis, she should wait to do so until the belief she wishes to preserve is lost. It seems, therefore, that our claim concerning the support afforded for the involuntariness of belief by the phenomenon of the loss of theistic belief can be adequately defended against the present objection.

---

[29] See Cohen, *Essay on Belief and Acceptance,* chap. 5 for a discussion of various interpretive possibilities relevant to such a case.

It should also be noted that in a typical case of the loss of belief, belief ceases to exist because of the undermining or rebuttal of what is taken as evidence supporting that belief. Such belief seems therefore to *depend* on evidence (or, at any rate, on apparent evidence) and not on some decision made by the believer.[30] But if so, then belief cannot be brought about through the believer's (or would-be believer's) decision. In a word, it is involuntary.

5. *A Distinct Impression: Affective Belief*

Sometimes, when we might just as well have said that we believe (or that someone else believes) *that* something exists, we say instead that we (or they) believe *in* it. We may, for example, speak of someone believing in Santa Claus, meaning only that he believes that there is such an individual as Santa Claus, or that Santa Claus exists. The existential proposition lurking in this neighborhood is easier to see where the idiom is slightly altered and reference is made to belief in the *existence* of the individual in question. For example, it is very common, even in philosophy, to find references to belief in the existence of God. All such expressions are no more than disguised references to belief-that.

If every instance of propositional belief involved an existential proposition, it would follow that, at least in one sense, belief-in just *is* belief-that. But it may seem obvious that this is not the case. How, for example, is the proposition that the red wine caused my headache to be construed as an existential proposition? There is, however, something close to an existential proposition nearby, which our earlier analysis helps to bring out: namely, that there obtains a state of affairs consisting in the red wine's having caused my headache. So can we say that my believing that the red wine caused my headache is the same as believing in the obtaining of the state of affairs consisting in the red wine's being the cause of my headache—or, equivalently, in the red wine's being the cause of my headache? And is believing in God, in the manner referred to above, perhaps describable in terms of believing in the obtaining of the state of affairs consisting in there being a God, or in terms of believing in there being a God? Though it might seem odd to express one's own belief in such terms, and though the sentences involved in thus describing or

[30] For an interesting argument for the conclusion that this dependence is a logical one and not just psychological, see Richard Swinburne, *Responsibility and Atonement* (Oxford: Clarendon Press, 1989), pp. 165–166. See also Bernard Williams, *Problems of the Self* (Cambridge: Cambridge University Press, 1973), pp. 147–149.

expressing beliefs are often clumsy ones, there does not seem to be anything *conceptually* wrong with them. But then it is indeed the case that in at least one sense, "belief-in" is coextensive with "belief-that," for every case of belief-that can be cashed out in terms of believing in the obtaining of some state of affairs.[31] Notice how nicely this result dovetails with our earlier conclusion that what believers have before their minds when they occurrently believe is a state of affairs, not a proposition, and that their thinking of it is an instance of thinking of the world. Expressions involving the term "belief-in," in the sense I have been considering, are better suited to capturing these facts (though also more complicated and less elegant) than ones involving the term "belief-that."[32]

Be that as it may, it is evident that there is more to belief-in than just such a connection to belief-that, and it is this "more" that I want to focus on here. Unlike "belief-that," which appears to be univocal, "belief-in" has more than one meaning, and in the extra meaning we find new facts relevant to the ideas of religious belief and disbelief. The second sort of belief-in H. H. Price has described as "evaluative" (as opposed to propositional, or, as he says, "factual"). This label is a bit weak, however, given all that must be included under it; "affective" might be better. Indeed, if a positive evaluation were all that this sort of belief included, then we would not really have left propositional belief behind; we would merely be focusing on a specific sort of *content* for such belief: namely, evaluative content. (Belief in *x* would then simply amount to believing that *x* has value or is worthy of approval.)

To sort out these matters, we must look at examples, and the first thing that should strike us here is the great variety of things we believe in. Just about anything can be the object of this second sort of belief-in. As Price observes, a blind person may believe in her guide dog, a gardener in his chrysanthemums, a mariner in the sea, an embattled nation in victory. We may believe in our school, in penicillin, in cold baths, in abstaining from alcohol when driving, in equal pay for both sexes, in all kinds of causes and theories. To these examples might be added belief in foreign language study, in regular exercise, in affirmative action, in free enterprise, in the triumph of democracy, and in the victory of good over evil.

---

[31] The possibility of saying so for the reason given appears to be missed by H. H. Price in his otherwise admirable treatment of "belief-in." See his *Belief,* series 2, lecture 9.

[32] That "belief-that" expressions are nonetheless more commonly used no doubt owes something to the awkwardness mentioned but is perhaps also in part due to the fact that when discussing a belief we tend to focus on the proposition that expresses it. Think especially of criticism of belief in this connection. Beliefs thus become associated with propositions. (It could also be that the predominance of "belief-that" over "belief-in" in this region of discourse is linked to a wish to avoid confusing the meaning given to it with the broader meaning that "belief-in" carries when used in its *other* sense, yet to be discussed.)

Evidently, the range of this sort of belief-in is very wide. But it becomes apparent through reflection that in each case of belief-in, what figures prominently in addition to the evaluative belief is a *feeling* component (Price speaks of "warmth"), which, given the nature of the evaluation, results in a positive affective or emotional state.[33] This latter state appears in all cases of belief-in to involve the emotion that typically *attends* approval or a positive evaluative belief—sometimes this will be, more specifically, affection—blended with such emotions as one commonly finds in connection with trust and loyalty.[34]

Consider the cited examples: one can indeed detect such an affective element, present in one degree or another and varying only with the precise content of the evaluative belief, in each of them. The blind person, for example, feels affection for her guide dog and also emotions of trust and loyalty: she is *moved* in a certain characteristic, positive way—a way that often goes with trust and loyalty—when she considers whether he is dependable and whether she would easily give him up for another dog. And the one who believes in equal pay for both sexes, though affection for what she believes in may not be quite what she feels, nonetheless can be said to approve of it in a sense that involves more than just thinking it to be a good thing; what we see in her case also involves the sort of positive emotional state that commonly accompanies such thinking. And beyond this she too has emotions of trust and loyalty: she can easily get "worked up" about the importance and helpfulness of this social change in addressing human need and feel stubborn allegiance to policies supporting it which others deride. The presence of such an affective element as we see here, together with the fact that here too we are in contact with something dispositional (one may be said to believe in democracy or affirmative action or whatever even when one is not thinking about it), suggests that "*S* believes in *x*," in the distinctive sense at issue, is synonymous with the conjunction of the following propositions:

(1) *S* believes that *x* has value or is in some way a good thing.
(2) *S* is disposed, when *x* comes to mind, to experience a feeling state that, when conjoined with the fact represented by (1), produces a blended experience of approving, trusting, and loyal emotions toward *x*.

---

[33] Note that the feeling by itself is not yet an emotion; emotion, I assume, is more complex, involving belief as well (here an evaluative belief).

[34] For convenience I sometimes refer to these as trusting and loyal emotions or emotions *of* trust and loyalty, but I underline that I am referring only to emotions that *commonly attend or accompany* trust and loyalty, making no assumption that such emotions *constitute or essentially belong to* trust and loyalty. As we will see in Chapter 5, at least for trust, the latter assumption appears to be false.

My aim here is not to work out exactly what forms the evaluative belief and the affective content of belief-in may take and in what circumstances (it will be better to look at such details with regard to pertinent religious and nonreligious examples, in the next chapter).[35] Rather, my aim is (a) to show that it *is* primarily an affective state that we have got hold of and to identify certain corollaries that concern other states in the neighborhood, and (b) to consider the relation between belief in something and the propositional belief *that* it presently exists (or at some time will exist).

Belief-in is often thought to entail, in addition to the evaluative and feeling components I am emphasizing, a variety of action dispositions (in philosophical discussions of belief in God, for example, such things as commitment and obedience are commonly mentioned). In part for this reason, it is also often thought to be identical to *faith*-in. I think these views are mistaken. Consider first the reasons for emphasizing feeling here instead of action. We are not just information processors; we become *attached* to things in the course of making our way through life, in pursuing our goals, forming and preserving our identities, and seeking to flourish and to help others flourish. We become attached to persons, of course, but also to cultural entities with symbolic value, to our goals and ideals, to certain ways of pursuing them, and as well to general practices or policies, nonhuman animals, and even machines. It is in and through such attachments that we move beyond mere belief-that (or any belief-in equivalent thereof) to the sort of belief-in I am talking about, with its approving, trusting, and loyal emotions. According to Wilfred Cantwell Smith, "to believe" originally meant "to hold dear" or "to love" (the German *belieben* still has this content).[36] We might therefore expect that traces of this denotation may still be found in our language, and I am suggesting that a close look at "belief-in" will show where they are.

Now it may seem to some that action dispositions are of necessity *also* present. But consider a counterexample provided by the sympathetic husband who asks his wife, thinking of embracing some cause that will make demands on the family, "Do you really believe in it?" and who, upon receiving an affirmative answer, says, "Well, then, perhaps we should do it." Here it appears that emotional dispositions and action dispositions are sharply distinguished, and belief-in is identified with the former. The husband, notice, might just as well have asked, "Do you

---

[35] Hereafter, when I use the term "belief-in," it should (unless otherwise indicated) be understood as referring to the second form of belief-in: that is, to the affective state here discussed.

[36] See Wilfred Cantwell Smith, *Faith and Belief* (Princeton: Princeton University Press, 1979).

really feel strongly about it?" He might even have used the two expressions together and *explicitly* separated any determination as to their application from talk about action dispositions: "Let's first see how strongly you feel about it: Would you say that this is something you really *believe* in? . . . Well, then, in light of that, perhaps we should do it." It seems clear that we would not and should not think the husband conceptually confused were he to interact with his wife in this manner. And yet he *would* be conceptually confused were the view under consideration correct. Belief-in therefore seems not to entail action dispositions but to be primarily a matter of emotion.[37]

Here we might also consider the common expression "fighting for what we believe in." If action dispositions bound up with emotions were part of belief in *x*, then why distinguish the belief-in from the actions involved in "fighting for" *x*? Someone may reply that the proper answer is not the one I am looking for but rather the following: "Because belief-in is not identical with the action dispositions involved in fighting for *x*, and one who uses the 'fighting for *x*' locution wants to emphasize what follows conceptually from belief-in." This reply is unconvincing, however. Even if belief-in is not identical with the action dispositions referred to, on the view defended by the critic the latter *are entailed*, and so one would not expect someone whose locutions reflect this view to distinguish the two in the manner indicated: by doing so he would generate something (roughly) translatable as "fighting for what we feel strongly about and are disposed to fight for." The oddness becomes even more extreme given certain plausible ways of filling out the cited expression: "Why don't we fight for what we believe in?" (translation: "Why don't we fight for what we feel strongly about and are disposed to fight for?"); "You *should* fight for what you believe in" (translation: "You *should* fight for what you feel strongly about and are disposed to fight for"). What would be the point of such questions or admonitions if it were already agreed on all sides that a disposition to fight is *part* of belief-in? The critic may say that they are utilized to provoke an *activation* of the

---

[37] Extending the conversation still further, suppose the wife said, "Now don't get carried away, honey; for crying out loud, I only said I believe in it!" Surely the husband would have reason to think his wife conceptually confused in such a case. (I owe this objection and also the one considered next in the text to Daniel Howard-Snyder.) But although the wife's response might be *odd*, I do not see that it is conceptually confused—at least not in a manner relevant here. It is odd and perhaps also confused because the wife may be expected to be aware of the fact that belief-in often provides a reason for action, whereas the response evinces no such awareness. And note that the proper result of filling this lacuna would not (as the objection assumes) be acceptance of the view I am disputing, for we are often aware of reasons for action without having a tendency to act accordingly generated thereby.

relevant disposition in *particular circumstances*. But then an interpretation according to which the admonition, say, refers to the *need for* a fighting disposition would be unnatural, and it is not. (May it not be precisely when one is lazy or complacent or timid rather than in a fighting mood that the admonition is issued?) More generally, in contexts where locutions of the sort in question are used, the speaker is not naturally interpreted as reminding hearers of what they are already disposed to do. A much more natural interpretation is that he is seeking to *rouse* them to such a disposition by pointing out that their belief-in—an affective state—gives them a *reason* to act in support of its object. And this interpretation does not fit the critic's position at all.

Now as we already begin to see here, action dispositions of various sorts may often be *caused*—at least in part—by states of believing-in, and perhaps causation can run in the other direction too. Belief in penicillin would normally cause one to take it if it were prescribed for relief of an illness, and the disposition to follow a doctor's order to take penicillin may over time lead one to believe in the drug. Also, it may sometimes be through observing an individual's actions that his state of belief-in is most easily *detected*: maybe it is through observing the gardener's loving attention to his chrysanthemums that we most readily learn of his belief in those flowers. But these things do not add up to a connection of entailment between belief-in and such action dispositions. Moreover, the idea of an entailment here is strongly countered by the fact that if we saw someone positively evaluating the penicillin or the chrysanthemums (or her dog or car or affirmative action or her friend) and noticed that she was disposed to respond to the penicillin or the chrysanthemums (or her dog or car or affirmative action or her friend) with the relevant warm emotions, *we would already find it natural and appropriate to speak of her as believing in these things*. We would not need anything else to bring us to this place.

What all of this strongly suggests is that belief-in is not at all the same as *faith*-in, which, apart from having its own name (something that might already prompt one to look for a conceptual distinction), is naturally viewed as a matter of how one is disposed to *act* in the face of *risks* of various kinds.[38] By emphasizing the affective character of belief-in, we can do justice to this distinction. A glance at the foregoing examples shows support for distinguishing belief-in from faith-in in this way. Although we speak perfectly appropriately of believing in affirmative action or in

---

[38] In my view, faith—of every sort—appears on the voluntary, action-oriented side of things, while belief—of every sort—belongs on the *in*voluntary side. (There is much more on faith in Chapters 5 and 6.)

abstaining from alcohol, to cite just two cases, it sounds decidedly odd (or, at the very least, it seems that a new meaning is being introduced) when we speak of having *faith* in abstaining from alcohol or in affirmative action. And although we may speak of fighting for what we believe in, it sounds decidedly odd (or, at the very least, it seems that a new meaning is being introduced) when we speak of fighting for what we have *faith* in.[39] Even if these seemingly different notions could somehow be shown to overlap significantly, I would argue that for clarity's sake and to do justice to the various linguistic facts and intuitions mentioned in this section, it is best to treat "belief-in" and "faith-in" as representing distinct concepts. (We will see later that it is also *useful* in philosophy of religion to arrange a sort of conceptual division of labor here.)

As to (b) above, the relation between belief in *x* and propositional beliefs concerning its existence, it appears that to believe in *x* one need not believe that *x* exists at present (consider belief in the complete triumph of good over evil, for example).[40] But it is sometimes claimed that belief in *x* nonetheless presupposes the present existence of *x* whenever *x* is an *entity* (as opposed to, for instance, an abstraction such as an ideal state of affairs). Is this the case? It seems not. It seems that I can believe in entities I know do not exist; I might, for example, believe in my unborn children, and someone distressed by the mess we humans have made of things might believe in members of future generations. Perhaps we should say, then, paying attention to the peculiar nature of these examples, that in the case of belief in entities one must at any rate believe that the entity believed in *will* exist at some time and so, more generally, that to believe in *x* (for any *x*) one must believe either that it presently exists or that at some time it will exist.

To this claim I can imagine the following sort of objection. Something that is not present may *appear* as present because of the manner in which, in imagination, we relate to it. What makes oppressed citizens believe in victory despite not believing that it is present is not that they believe it someday *will* be present but that on account of their manner of relating to it, they can, as it were, *touch it and taste it right now*. The same goes for belief in unborn children, and so on. We should therefore say, even more generally (and thinking of this as applicable also to entities), that some of the things we believe in we believe to exist or to be such as

---

[39] As shown in later chapters, the oddness or difference here is due to the fact that when one has faith in *x*, one acts on the view that a certain result will be forthcoming in relation to *x*, when there is some reason to think it will not be so. Nothing of this sort is part of belief-in.

[40] For convenience in this discussion I use "exists" fairly broadly to cover, inter alia, the obtaining of states of affairs.

will exist, and we approve this state of affairs and come to feel emotionally connected to these things; others are such as may not ever exist and such as we may not believe will ever exist, but we approve the thought that they should exist and come to feel emotionally connected to that possibility and also to *them,* insofar as they come to occupy our thoughts in a present-tense sort of way.

I do not find this objection persuasive. It does not seem that in the cited cases one would have the present-tense *feeling* without the future-tense *belief.* And when one looks at examples where both a present-tense and a future-tense existential belief are absent, a different analysis (already implicit in the preferred approach of the objection) suggests itself. Consider someone who, though not believing that there is or that there ever will be an afterlife, considers it possible and builds her whole life around this possibility, writing books that explore the concept and seeking to find evidence that it is realized. Does this individual believe in the afterlife? And consider the same question phrased in terms of someone similarly (i.e., also without the relevant beliefs) investigating claims as to the existence of the Loch Ness Monster—an entity if ever there was one! It seems that the answer to the question must in both cases be negative. For here we are merely inclined to add to the list of *existing* things that can be believed in a couple of extra items: ideas and possibilities. What the individuals in our examples believe in, one wants to say, is not the afterlife or Nessie but the *idea or possibility* of an afterlife, or the *idea or possibility* of Nessie. Notice that this connects nicely with an emphasis on the future-oriented nature of those previously mentioned clear cases of belief-in, where one does not find belief that the object believed in presently exists. For part of what makes us want to say that the person in the afterlife example believes in the idea of the afterlife is that she believes that *something positive may yet come of this idea* (and experiences certain relevant emotional states bound up with that belief). And something similar holds for the Nessie investigator. I suggest, therefore, that the proposal to broaden our understanding of the idea of belief-in we have just been considering is inadequately supported, and that the original suggestion—that to believe in *x* (for any *x*), one must believe either that it presently exists or that at some time it will exist—stands.

Let us now consider how the resolution of these general issues concerning belief bears on the nature of beliefs directed to matters religious.

On Religious Belief and Religious Disbelief

At the beginning of Chapter 2 I spoke of wishing to color in the borders of the discussion by considering the "outermost" responses to religious claims—religious belief and religious disbelief—before analyzing other responses falling between them. But then we saw how even before that, we needed to become better acquainted with the belief element those opposites have in common. Now, with a better understanding both of religion and of belief in hand, we are finally able to approach religious belief and religious disbelief directly and with a realistic hope of illuminating their natures. I discuss them in that order, starting in each case with the relevant sort of propositional belief and then moving to consider its affective sibling.

1. *Propositional Religious Belief*

If the arguments of the previous chapter are correct, then for someone to believe that *p* is for it normally to be only in what I have called the "thick" sense that the state of affairs reported by *p* comes to mind for her, or for her to be disposed to apprehend the state of affairs reported by *p*, when it comes to mind, under the concept *reality*, or, equivalently, disposed to experience the thought that *p* as a world-thought. We must therefore take all this to apply to propositional religious belief as well: the thoughts bound up with religious beliefs are experienced by religious believers as world-thoughts. But questions lurk here that we have not yet satisfactorily answered. For example, what is the *range* or *scope* of religious belief? Exactly who are the religious believers? And which of their beliefs count as *religious* beliefs? (Presumably not just any belief held by a religious believer counts as a religious belief.)

I start with a small clarification concerning "religious believer." Although it may sometimes be tempting to read this term as referring to a believer who is religious, such an interpretation does not seem appropriate.[1] Intuitively, the category of religious believers is broad enough to include both those who hold certain relevant beliefs and have made the commitment that is part of being religious and those who hold such beliefs without having made the commitment. (Isn't someone who responds to those notorious Gallup polls with a sincere profession of belief that God exists to be counted as a religious believer whether or not he has involved himself in religious practice?) Even so, of course, it may plausibly be claimed that it is because the beliefs of the latter set of individuals are at least *appropriate or conducive* to the practice of religion—such as *do* guide the behavior of those who pursue a religious way—that we are inclined to call them religious beliefs. Religious believers, in other words, even when they are not actually religious themselves, may nonetheless be expected in some way or some respect to see things as a religious person *qua* religious person would or might see them. This expectation is in harmony with what we are inclined to say of beliefs in other categories—say, scientific or political beliefs: a scientific belief is a belief that, even though it may be held by nonscientists, could belong to the perspective on the world formed by a scientist *qua* scientist and inform her scientific activity; the same goes for political beliefs and politicians. And then there is the obvious fact that in their evaluations of propositional religious belief, philosophers are (among other things) considering it as a possible basis for a religious life; this means that our interpretation would be at odds with the needs of philosophy if it did not at least say that such belief must be appropriate to or conducive to the practice of religion.

I suggest, therefore, that we have reason to accept this notion as a guiding principle. So what sort of belief is appropriate to or conducive to the practice of religion? Since beliefs are distinguished by their content, we can answer this question by identifying the relevant sort of proposition. Perhaps we should introduce the notion of a *religious proposition,* clarify *its* nature, and then say that religious beliefs are all those beliefs whose constituent thoughts are expressible by religious propositions. But even

---

[1] A similar interpretation, also to be resisted, might lead to an understanding of "propositional religious belief" in which the more purely connotative aspects of "religious," which have to do with a special fervor and devotion and perhaps also proselytizing zeal, are highlighted. Something in some ways like this is part of affective religious belief, but that is another story.

though the first two steps of this procedure are important and need to be taken, the conclusion represented by the third step seems false. We will see why in a moment, but first let's take the other two steps.

It seems natural to reserve a category for religious propositions. (After all, we speak in a similar manner of political or scientific or juridical or philosophical propositions.) That there is such a category was assumed in previous chapters when I spoke of "religious claims." But how should this category be understood? Clearly, religious propositions or claims must have something to do with religion, since their subject matter is religious. But what? An obvious suggestion reminds us that a religious person takes the object of her concern to be metaphysically and axiologically ultimate as well as salvific ("salvific" here and hereafter is short for "a reality in relation to which an ultimate good can be attained"). Perhaps we should say then that religious propositions are all those that entail some reference to an ultimate and salvific reality. It is important to note that not just any old reference will do, however. Our first approximation to a correct understanding would be satisfied by a proposition *denying* that there is an ultimate and salvific reality, and such a proposition could hardly be appropriate to religious commitment. We seem therefore to be led in the direction of propositions *affirming* that there is such a reality (for it seems that commitments involving such propositions can be religious, and that commitments not sharing this characteristic cannot). Let us therefore revise our definition as follows: "*p* is a religious proposition if and only if *p* entails that there is an ultimate and salvific reality." Or, given what we have seen "salvific" to mean and the definition of "ultimism" at the end of Chapter 1: "*p* is a religious proposition if and only if *p* entails ultimism."

Is this adequate? In objection, it might be suggested that the conjunctive proposition "God exists, and we should resist God with all our might" satisfies the condition I have endorsed here but is manifestly not religiously adequate—with the consequence that our condition is not a sufficient condition in this connection, as my claim entails. What we need to find in religious propositions, if they are to be said to have the relation to the believer's commitment I have mentioned, is not only an admission of the existence of the reality in question but also (what we might call) a positive evaluation of it—or at least content compatible with such an evaluation. But I would reply that if "God" is taken in its religious sense, in which sense it refers to a reality that is ultimate and salvific, the relevant positive evaluation is expressed. Any proposition entailing the existence of such a reality ipso facto evaluates it thus: What could be more positive than to say of a reality that it embodies the highest possible value? So the proposed counterexample makes the positive claim in question. Of course, it makes a negative one too. Indeed, because of what "God exists" (in conjunction with certain relevant necessary truths) entails, the second conjunct of the proposed counterexample implicitly contradicts the first: if God exists and if God's existence would be the greatest good, and if, given the existence of God, human well-being lies in the pursuit of God, then we can pretty quickly deduce the negation of that conjunct.[2] Now if we accept such contradictory propositions as counterexamples, then it is impossible to state what a religious proposition is. (For then any proposed definition's conditions can be shown to be insufficient by a proposition satisfying those conditions conjoined with its negation.) But this is absurd. Therefore, we should not so accept them.

More difficult counterexamples are available, however. Consider "God exists and I hate God" or "God exists and I don't care." These do not seem contradictory; at least they will not seem contradictory if we suppose that it is possible to evaluate something positively and yet be warped enough to dislike it or be indifferent to it—and many will suppose this. There is also the problem that if ultimism were to turn out to be necessarily true, we would be required to say, given the definition above, that *every* proposition is a religious proposition, since every proposition would then entail ultimism.[3] But these problems are not insurmountable. Actually, the solution to them is staring us in the face, given the guiding principle we adopted at the beginning of this discussion: simply glean from that principle an extra condition for our definition of "religious proposition," saying that to be religious a proposition must not only entail ultimism but be such that anyone, whether believer or person of faith, who responds to it by acting on it in the relevant way—that is, ultimistically (here recall our final definition of "religion" in Chapter 1)—is properly viewed as pursuing a religious way. Let us say of any such proposition that it is *capable of informing a religious practice*. The reason that such propositions as "God exists and I hate God" and "God exists and I don't care" are problematic is that although they are apparently noncontradictory and entail that there is an ultimate and salvific reality, they are *inimical* to religious practice; and the reason that we would have a problem if ultimism were to turn out to be necessarily true is that humdrum propositions such as "There is a telephone beside me" would in that case count as religious, whereas they seem to have nothing to do with religious practice. But if we add to our definition the proposed new

[2] To avoid contradiction here, the objector would have to say that the individual in question does not conceive God in what I have called the religious way, perhaps thinking of God as an evil tyrant; but then the condition I have put forward is not in fact satisfied by the proposed counterexample, as the objection requires it to be, and so the latter fails for that reason instead of the one I am here emphasizing.

[3] I owe these last two points to Daniel Howard-Snyder.

condition, our problems seem to disappear, for how could "God exists and I hate God" or "God exists and I don't care" or "There is a telephone beside me" ever inform a religious way? Now perhaps if one acted on "There is a telephone beside me" *together with* certain other propositions such as, say, "God has decreed that the way to bliss requires helping others" and "Smith has just taken a heart attack in the next room," one could be seen as pursuing a religious way! But we can deal with this suggestion by clarifying what is implicit here anyway: that a religious proposition is *independently* capable—capable *on its own*—of informing a religious practice. I suggest, therefore, that we fill out our definition of "religious proposition" as follows: "*p* is a religious proposition if and only if (1) *p* entails that there is an ultimate and salvific reality and (2) *p* is independently capable of informing a religious practice."

Suppose, then, that this understanding of religious propositions is correct. Why does it not at the same time give us an adequate understanding of religious beliefs? Can we not simply say that religious beliefs are all those whose constituent thoughts are expressible by religious propositions? The answer is no: it is enough for a religious *proposition* to entail that there is a reality of the sort ultimism refers to and to be independently capable of informing a religious practice, but it is not enough for a religious *belief* that its constituent thought be expressible by such a proposition. The religious content of her belief must also be *recognized* by the believer. (This recognition need not be construed as entailing that religious belief is occurrently believed to be tied to the idea of ultimism whenever it is activated; "believed" is enough.) For, human cognitive limitations being what they are, any one of us may, *without even knowing it,* be holding a belief articulable by a proposition including the relevant content somewhere among its entailments. Thus, without our stipulation, we would have to say that literally anyone might turn out to be a religious believer. Yet it seems clear that there are individuals who are definitely not religious believers. A related point draws our attention again to the fact that religious belief ought to be appropriate or conducive to the practice of religion (even if it may be possessed by someone who is not practicing). Now it might be thought that this is assured if the proposition involved is independently capable of informing a religious practice. But given the point just made, the latter status might be possessed by a proposition someone believes even if she fails her whole life long to recognize the religious connection. The belief of someone like this does not seem in the relevant sense appropriate to or conducive to religious practice. To be such, it seems that the belief's connection to the idea of an ultimate and salvific reality must at some level be recognized or acknowledged by the believer. We may conclude, therefore, that propositional religious beliefs are all those propositional beliefs articulable by religious propositions whose religious character *is recognized as such.*[4]

Someone may now object that we have got it all wrong: what makes a belief religious is not the content of propositions abstractly determined to be appropriate to the practice of religion and the believer's recognition of that content for what it is but rather that practice itself. More precisely, any belief caused by one's religious commitment and the distinctive mental life and activities it engenders is to be regarded as religious. What we need, in other words, is a *causal* criterion, not a content criterion.

There is a certain initial plausibility to this proposal, but I suggest that it has implausible consequences. In brief, if we accept it, we are committed to regarding virtually any beliefs as potentially religious—even ones that on any natural construal would be said to be far removed from religion. Given the quirks of human psychology, many strange causal connections can obtain; virtually any belief *could* be rooted in religious practice. But we can see the implausibility of the suggestion even in more normal connections. Suppose you are religious and engage in conversation with a politician after church, hoping to befriend him and lure him back. And suppose that the politician, wily devil that he is, manages to effect a conversion of his own: you leave church convinced that Quebec should be granted sovereignty. Should this new belief of yours be regarded as a religious belief? Surely not. It is a *political* belief. (And if there is anything we have learned in centuries of fighting, it is not to confuse religion with politics!) Yet this belief was caused in the manner deemed appropriate by the causal criterion of religious belief. Hence that criterion is inadequate.

Another reason for supposing so is that the causal criterion prevents us from saying that persons lacking the degree of personal involvement our definition requires may nonetheless be religious believers. As we have seen, it would be very strange to deny of someone who believes that the God of classical theism exists, though doing little or nothing in response to his belief, that his belief is religious in nature. Yet this is what the causal criterion requires in insisting that only beliefs caused by actual involvement in religion are religious. (Notice: it also requires that, should the individual in question take up religious practice in response to his belief, it is *still* not to be considered a religious belief because not caused in the right way.)

---

[4] This definition might seem too restrictive, excluding from religious belief certain unsophisticated individuals, if we forget that (as spelled out in Chapter 1) it is possible to take a reality to be ultimate, both metaphysically and axiologically, and a good to be ultimate, and so on, even if these words (and configurations of words) are not part of one's vocabulary, since one may nevertheless clearly possess the *concepts* denoted by these terms and consider them to be realized. I therefore remind the reader of these facts.

The content-based approach we have settled on therefore seems preferable. Accordingly I suggest that, where all relevant points are incorporated, "*S* possesses (propositional) religious belief" will be taken as equivalent in meaning to the conjunction of the following:

(1) *S* is disposed to apprehend the state of affairs reported by a certain proposition *p*, when that state of affairs comes to mind, under the concept *reality*.

(2) *p* entails the existence of an ultimate and salvific reality.

(3) *p* is independently capable of informing a religious practice.

(4) *S* recognizes the religious character of her belief.

Given this definition, many instances of belief we would naturally view as religious clearly do count as such, and many others we might not have been sure about may now be determined to be religious or not. Such beliefs will of course include beliefs to the effect that there *is* an ultimate and salvific reality but much else besides: beliefs about the *properties* of this reality (for example, that it is exclusively personal or that it is nonpersonal or that it is suprapersonal—i.e., that is includes but also transcends personality)[5] and about the *relations* between this reality and other things, in particular the events of one's own life (for example, that it is distinct from oneself or not distinct; that one will be in some way related to it in an afterlife or that the relationship is terminated at the time of physical death), and many other, similar beliefs all count as religious. And such beliefs are of course religious beliefs whether the believer is a religious practitioner or not.

Having thus answered the question concerning the range or scope of propositional religious belief, we may turn to some of the latter's paradigm manifestations, making note of some important features and connections to other aspects of the believer's psychic life that we have so far neglected. When we speak of matters concerning the "nature of religious belief," we mean of course such definitional matters as have already been discussed, but in a broader sense we may also (and naturally) be indicating an interest in the *impact*, or *causal power*, of such belief. For example, it is important to observe how *world-defining* and *mind-embracing* such beliefs

---

[5] Notice here that if one's belief were only that *should there be* an ultimate reality, its properties would be of such and such a description, one's belief would not count as religious by our definition, because the proposition involved is not of the relevant sort. To be relevant, it would have to say that there *is* such a reality and that its properties *are* of such and such a sort. (The former belief and proposition we would call *philosophical* as opposed to religious.) That all of this is just as, intuitively, it seems it should be provides additional confirmation for our definition.

typically will be. Here we do not see only a momentary response to some passing bit of information, recorded and then forgotten or replaced. Nor do we see belief concerning some small corner of reality without ramifications for larger tracts of it or for the whole. No, religious belief tends to be experienced as putting one in touch with overwhelmingly important facts, facts that have consequences for one's whole life (this is so especially when it first arises in someone, but also when it is reexperienced or renewed after a period of doubt, and certainly on a more ongoing basis in those believers who are religious).[6] Here, indeed, we find precisely those beliefs that contribute the most, for those who hold them, to an overall picture of how things are. They will, the more deeply they become embedded in the believer's doxastic system (and of course they will tend—especially in the lives of the religious—to become very deeply embedded), penetrate and affect the color of ever more of what she believes on other matters given her implicit or explicit awareness of the relevant entailment relations.

We have made reference to the belief that there is a God, and we may continue to use this paradigm case of propositional religious belief for illustrative purposes. One who is disposed to experience the thought of there being a God as a world-thought will tend to see things very differently from one who is not thus disposed. She will have the sense of an infinite presence that lights up the world. And literally everything must appear differently in that light, for it is obvious that if God exists, the whole of creation *is* a creation, owing its existence and character to the activity of God. The basic particles of physics will not be seen as swimming alone in the universe. Prospects for oneself and for others will be radically differently perceived. The meaning of history and the likely course of future events, what one can realistically undertake to do or ought to forswear, the very ground one treads and the other creatures with whom it is shared, whether human or nonhuman—all will appear very different for one who believes in the existence of a God who is creator and sustainer and redeemer of all things.

Someone may now object to this by saying that what I am talking about will be found not in every case of religious belief but only in cases of *confident* belief (that is, belief accompanied by a disposition of confidence of the sort I distinguished from belief itself in the previous chapter). And, pointing to my repeated reference to religiosity, the objector may add that it is also really only in those who are acting on their religious belief,

---

[6] The whole point of many religious activities, whether solitary or communal, is to reinforce a sense of the importance of what is believed—to "bring alive" for the believer the significance attaching to the content of her belief.

engaged in religious practice, that the effects to which I have drawn attention can be observed. Finally, taking a page from religion itself, he may say that even this is not sufficient: that while the transformed perspective on the world to which I have referred is one to which a religious person will naturally seek to be alive, human nature and the omnipresence of more local concerns are such that even in the religious it may (quite irrationally, to be sure) fade to the background and lose its luster, which is one of the reasons why special spiritual disciplines are advocated. The light of ultimate things, in short, may be a much dimmer light in the lives of religious believers than I am suggesting.

Any reminder of human limitations in this connection is of course salutary and well-taken, but I would point out in response that I have spoken of what is normally or usually or tends to be the case for one who holds a religious belief, and of the intellectual effects that such belief *typically* will have. I have also restricted myself to observations concerning how the world is seen by a religious believer; whether she acts upon what she sees may well be influenced by mundane factors of the sort to which the objection alludes, operative when a believer's belief is not being activated (which of course may be a fair bit of the time), with the result that her *life* is not transformed. After all this is taken into account, however, it must still be said that when a person who is a religious believer does turn her thoughts fully to what she believes, she must see the world very differently from one who lacks religious belief. Indeed, I suggest that instead of thinking of the "loss of luster" to which the objection refers as implying an absence of intellectual influence on the part of religious beliefs or a diminished awareness of their presence on the part of believers, we should try another possible interpretation of this phrase and note how rather commonplace and *ordinary* apparent religious facts can sometimes come to appear to religious believers, how taken for granted. (A light that is always thought to be present, though its presence may not cease to be noted, may come to seem unremarkable.) No doubt when this taking-for-granted occurs, it is also in a sense "irrational," and it is also due to human nature, but apparently what we have here is not the phenomenon appealed to by the objection, and its prevalence is quite compatible with the realization of the intellectual effects referred to above.

What of my references to religiosity? Here I want to confirm that, as indicated earlier, I see the category of religious believers as broad enough to include both those who hold certain beliefs about an ultimate reality and have made the commitment that is part of being religious *and* those who hold such beliefs without having made the commitment. (This interpretation is related to the distinction above between the transformation of one's perspective and the transformation of one's life.) There is a possible confusion between (1) a state of believing that is an attitude with content expressible by religious claims, an attitude *appropriate or conducive to* the practice of religion, and (2) a state of believing that is *part* of a religious life—a confusion that must be avoided here. That having been said, we have also seen that, in their evaluations of religious belief, philosophers often consider it as a possible basis for a religious life, and so it is appropriate, when examining the nature of religious belief, to give some special emphasis to how it may be expected to function in the life of a religious person. And this, as I see it, is the most that can be observed in my comments above.

One important effect that propositional religious belief can have which we have not yet touched upon is an effect of which we are reminded by the reference to human nature in the objection just discussed. It takes us beyond the obvious, more general implications noted above of propositions expressing the belief that there is an ultimate and salvific reality and their already dramatic impact on how the world as a whole will be experienced. This new effect is sponsored by the natural human desire to *fill out the picture completely*. Propositional religious belief, whether it is initially general (say, the belief that there is some reality that is ultimate and salvific, together with certain associated beliefs) or fairly specific (say, the belief that the way to "superconsciousness" proclaimed by a certain New Age guru is reliable, and certain other beliefs that will seem supported by it), naturally attracts even more specific beliefs of the same sort as partners in the business of securing a comprehensive and comprehensible intellectual environment. If you have even one belief entailing that there is an ultimate and salvific reality, you will, as suggested above, suppose the rest of reality to bear its stamp as well and thus be on the lookout for the missing religious details.

This phenomenon, together with the intellectual desire mentioned earlier, is one reason why people seldom have just a single religious belief or only a few, why it is much more common to find a whole network of beliefs providing a more or less complete and fine-grained religious interpretation of the nature of things. If now we combine the latter fact with the fact that such interpretations tend rather obviously to entail the falsity of a whole ream of propositions expressing the beliefs of *other* people, both religious and secular, and remind ourselves of the point made above to the effect that one's religious beliefs can come to appear commonplace and be taken for granted, we will see how the investigation-inhibiting effects of much propositional religious belief in the actual world can arise, and why they must always represent, at the very least, an intellectual danger to be associated with such belief.

2. *Affective Religious Belief*

I come now to a topic that does not loom as large in the discussions of philosophers of religion but which for all of that (and in part because of that) deserves our attention. Though propositional religious belief—religious belief-that—is what philosophers of religion are normally concerned with, it is evident that religious forms of belief-in are (1) of considerable importance in the overall economy of religion, (2) in various ways intellectually linked to propositional religious belief, and therefore (3) in need of careful consideration by philosophers hoping to determine the nature and intellectual status of the latter.

In the previous chapter we saw how diverse are the possible objects of belief-in. What are the possible objects of *religious* belief-in? Well, belief in the ultimate, construed thus generically, is not impossible to imagine, given that a positive evaluation could hardly be withheld from a reality in relation to which an ultimate good can be attained, and given that emotions of trust and loyalty and so on can be evoked by the belief that there is such a reality and meditation on the content of this belief. But perhaps more likely, and certainly more common in the actual world as it has unfolded thus far, is belief in realities of a more specific sort, the existence of any one of which would *entail* the existence of an ultimate reality—for example, belief in Jahweh, Christ, or Vishnu. Each of these gives to the ultimate a more sharply defined face, and it is perhaps easier to respond with belief-in to a reality with such a face than to a reality lacking one. Another form of religious belief-in would of course be belief in human individuals deemed to have a role in *mediating* the good bound up with the ultimate reality; within Catholicism, belief in the pope might provide an example. In a similar or extended sense, belief in one's fellow travelers on the religious way or belief in the religious way itself or success in pursuing it might also be held to belong in the religious category. In each case one finds a state of belief-in that begs to be described in religious terms, since at least part of the believer's reason for valuing the item in question is that she values the existence of an ultimate and salvific reality or, more directly, the good obtainable in relation to such a reality, if it exists. And it does indeed seem to be a state of belief-in that we see, since the positive evaluation is there and also—in connection with it and with its recognized content—approving, trusting, and loyal emotions directed toward the object of the state. I suggest, therefore, that "*S* possesses (affective) religious belief" may be taken as equivalent in meaning to the conjunction of the following propositions:

> (1) *S* believes that a certain item *x* has value or is in some way a good thing.

(2) At least a part of S's reason for valuing x is that S values the existence of an ultimate and salvific reality or, more directly, the good
obtainable in relation to such a reality, if it exists.

(3) S is disposed, when x comes to mind, to experience a feeling state
that, when conjoined with the facts represented by (1) and (2),
produces a blended experience of approving, trusting and loyal
emotions toward x.

Now religious belief-in, as we are understanding it, since restricted to
affective components, does not in and of itself represent a sufficient condition of religiousness; for that, as we saw in Chapter 1, certain action dispositions are required. Indeed, it is not even a necessary condition, given
our definition of "religion." But there is no denying that it is a part of the
life of many a religious person, as actually lived out in all its specificity. We
may even say, without altering any of our general definitions (for which
justifications have been provided), that the object and also the emotions
of religious belief-in may be determined or influenced by the activities of
the religious person and that the activities of the religious person may be
affected by these emotions, for there can be causal relations among phenomena conceptually distinguished in philosophical definitions. In the
actual living of life, many of these (conceptually distinct) phenomena are
in fact deeply intertwined. Let us focus now on one particular set of connections to which I have already alluded: namely, links between religious
belief-in and religious belief-that, where the latter is understood as
directed toward the existence of the former's object. There is first of all
the possibility of a *logical* connection, and indeed many would think this
more than a possibility: belief that the object of religious belief-in exists is
commonly viewed as necessarily presupposed by such belief-in. Is this view
of the matter correct?

Consider the representative objects of religious belief-in already mentioned—the ultimate (generically construed), Jahweh, Christ, Vishnu,
the pope, members of a religious community, and the religious way itself
(that is, one's form of religious life, whether Buddhist, Islamic, New Age,
or whatever) or success in pursuing it. Does belief in these items logically
presuppose belief that they exist? If by "exist" we mean "presently exist,"
then this certainly seems to hold for the entities on the list (as opposed
to, e.g., ideal states of affairs), for how could I believe in Christ or the
pope without believing that there is, right now, such a thing as Christ or
the pope? But there is reason for caution. As we saw in the previous
chapter, although individual cases of belief-in commonly involve belief-
that in the manner here considered, this connection is not inevitable or
necessary. And in evaluating the general criterion stating that belief in

entities always presupposes belief that those entities presently exist, we concluded that this criterion seems false. So does this rescue the idea, say, of believing in Christ without believing that Christ presently exists? Well, what we also saw is that believing in an entity x, where it is recognized that x does not presently exist, can occur only if it is believed that x will exist in the future; otherwise what we have is at most belief in the *idea* of x. And unfortunately, if Christ or Vishnu or the ultimate more generically do not exist now, they never will. It seems, therefore, that when it comes to belief in entities *of the sort that are most relevant to religion,* a belief that the entity in question exists (and exists right now) is logically required.[7]

Before turning our gaze to religious disbelief, let us consider one other point about connections between religious belief-in and religious belief-that. It is simply that among those who have the latter, the former may (causally speaking) not be far behind. This is because, while possible, it is hard not to respond emotionally to the object of propositional belief when it is truly religious in nature and when the implications of that fact are allowed to sink in. If, for example, you really believe that a personal creator who loves you and plans to bring you to eternal happiness is the deepest reality, and you spend any time seriously considering what this state of affairs involves, it will be difficult to remain aloof and untouched. Obviously, you will evaluate it positively, and, given the presence of other attributes typically possessed by human beings, emotions of trust and (in time) loyalty toward the creator may be hard to suppress. And why would you wish to suppress them? Are they not perfectly appropriate to the state of affairs you believe yourself to be in? What this suggests is that, at least in typical human beings, religious belief-that whose content is reflected upon has a tendency to lead to belief-in, which in turn—given the power of emotion we all recognize—suggests that the former has a tendency to become entrenched and may in time become quite resistant to rational attempts to assess the situation. Indeed, in the case of religion, given the belief that the *ultimate* reality is such-and-so, we might expect to find a loyalty about as strong as can be imagined. No doubt this at least partially explains the reputation for passionate irrationality that propositional religious belief seems to have won in many corners of the intellectual world.

[7] Should we grant that belief in the idea of Christ or the ultimate—that is, I suppose, belief in the *possibility* of truth in religious claims concerning such things—counts as affective religious belief? This may seem to be a borderline case, but nothing in our definition forbids it, since one who values such things may do so at least in part because she values the existence of an ultimate and salvific reality, or the good obtainable in relation to such a reality, if it exists.

3. *Propositional Religious Disbelief*

It will not be hard to guess what is coming under this heading, especially given my advertisement at the beginning of Chapter 2 that religious disbelief is "about as opposed, intellectually, to religious belief as anything could be." The notion of religious disbelief is derivative—defined by what it opposes. And so, since we have spent a fair bit of time identifying the nature of propositional religious belief, it will not take long to identify the nature of its opposite. We may sum things up as follows. If propositional religious belief is instantiated by all those propositional beliefs whose constituent thoughts are expressible by religious propositions and recognized as religious, then propositional religious *dis*belief is instantiated by all those propositional beliefs whose constituent thoughts are expressible by the *denial* of religious propositions and recognized as *non*religious. More exactly, and remembering that it is the nature of a generalized disbelief that we are seeking to capture, we can say that "*S* possesses (propositional) religious disbelief" is synonymous with the conjunction of the following propositions:

(1) *S* is disposed to apprehend the state of affairs reported by a certain proposition *p*, when that state of affairs comes to mind, under the concept *reality*.
(2) *p* entails the nonexistence of an ultimate and salvific reality.
(3) *S* recognizes the nonreligious character of her belief.[8]

Now it may seem that the recognition point—proposition (3)—is unnecessary in the case of religious disbelief. The main reason for adding it in the case of religious belief was that full conduciveness to religious practice could not otherwise be assured, but it would be going too far to suppose that there is some antireligious practice to which religious disbelief must be conducive. Religious disbelievers, so it will be said, need not be militantly antireligious or obsessed with the defeat of religion—indeed, they may spend very little time thinking about what their beliefs oppose. But to deal with this objection we might note that it is a *response to religious claims* that philosophers usually have in mind when they speak of religious disbelief. Thus some awareness of how it opposes such claims is naturally assumed to exist among those who exhibit it. Moreover, there is

---

[8] If *S* believes that there is no ultimate and salvific reality, recognizing this content for what it is, then clearly *S* will deny that any proposition entailing that there is such a reality is true; but in that case *S* will also be committed to the denial, more specifically, of any proposition entailing that there is such a reality *and capable of independently informing a religious practice*. Thus we need no separate indication of the latter fact.

the fact that—for reasons similar to those discussed in connection with religious belief—without the recognitional constraint we would have to say that just about anyone might turn out to be a religious disbeliever, and this result is unacceptable, since there seem to be individuals who definitely do not belong in that category.

Are there other parallels? Given that the two states share the element of belief, and that what religious disbelievers believe seems initially no less likely to be "world-defining" and "mind-embracing" than what religious believers believe, it might appear that there would have to be. But there are also objections to this line of thought. For religious disbelief is by definition negative, not about what there is but about what there isn't. Thus, or so it may be said, the positive content of the religious disbeliever's worldview cannot be expected to be given by her religious disbelief, and her belief can therefore not in any relevant sense be "world-defining." Moreover, a huge variety of intellectual possibilities are compatible with religious disbelief, and deep disagreements may be found in the camp of religious disbelievers. One will find there both realists and antirealists, both Marxists and capitalists, both modernists and postmodernists, both dualists and materialists, and so forth. Indeed, in theory it is possible even to find both individuals who deny that there is any supernatural reality and individuals who hold that there is a limited supernatural reality who is willing to confer on us some limited good—for the latter view too can be combined with the claim that there is no *ultimate* reality and no *ultimate* human good. Clearly, there are rather few commonalities of content here of the sort my view apparently presupposes.

But there are many deep divisions also among religious believers—as one can see simply by comparing, say, Christianity and Buddhism—and yet this goes hand in hand with common emphases at the most general level, emphases that have (to some extent) qualitatively similar effects. In any event, in saying that religious disbelief is commonly world-defining, we are not committed to saying that when it defines mental worlds, it does so in the same way in every case. So the second objection does not appear to have much force. As for the first, the conclusion that religious disbelief is not ever world-defining does not follow from the facts cited; indeed, it seems false. The positive and detailed content of the religious disbeliever's worldview may not be given directly by his belief, but some very general constraints *are* given, and these must very much affect the shape and color of the worldview that any typical religious disbeliever accepts. Someone's overall picture of things may be just as much influenced by what is excluded from it as by what it includes, for when one excludes certain possibilities, one's worldview is limited to what is compatible with such exclusion. And just as in the religious case, so here we must take account of the natural human desire to fill out the picture completely. If at a very general level you believe that there is no ultimate and salvific reality, and if you are reflective, you will suppose the rest of reality to bear *this* stamp, and be on the lookout for the missing *non*religious details. (And again, that you find different details from those developed by another religious disbeliever takes nothing away from the fact that your religious disbelief is world-defining.)

It should be noted that I am not saying that by excluding the epistemic possibility of religious truth the religious disbeliever must declare—as the only alternative—that natural processes alone govern the way things are and therefore develop a view based solely on natural law. For we have already seen that naturalism is a contrary of ultimism, not its contradictory. However a naturalistic orientation does commonly follow upon the former exclusion, given the way things actually are (and will most likely continue to be), for religion's critics tend as a matter of fact to associate just any form of supernaturalism with religion; the in-between possibilities—such as the possibility represented by a limited supernaturalism—are never heavily subscribed, given what seems to be a human tendency to adopt, in this context, an all-or-nothing attitude.

Even more significant among the corollaries of religious disbelief than those so far mentioned is the fact that any person who denies the truth of all religious claims will tend to see radically less *good* in the world than if he were a religious believer, and the good of which he thinks we humans are capable and which he thinks it appropriate to pursue, though perhaps still great, will be radically less great than what religious believers refer to. His worldview must necessarily be less optimistic than that of a religious believer. The facts of fruitless suffering and of vast tracts of unfulfilled human potential, however tragic and deeply regrettable they may appear, he will see as needing simply to be accepted.

Religious disbelievers may of course do much to *improve* the world and themselves within those limits and may derive much satisfaction from uncovering nature's mysteries. But it cannot be expected, if you are a religious disbeliever, that you will find within yourself much in the way of investigatory zeal when it comes to matters religious, not because you think you have found the religious answer but because you think there is none. The result is what we might call a reduced sense of the mystery of the world. Though he may see many exciting discoveries in, say, science as still lying ahead of us, the religious disbeliever will tend to minimize the significance of looking into the possibility of a mystery deeper and more profound than the natural world could represent, and he will commonly be inclined to dismiss talk of a truly ultimate reality as wishful thinking.

Of course, perhaps not all these things are *entailed* by religious disbelief, just as some of the things earlier discussed in connection with religious belief are not entailed by it. But it does appear that they all belong in any description of what one might reasonably expect to see in a religious disbeliever's form of life.

4. *Affective Religious Disbelief*

We have seen how propositional religious disbelief is really just a form of belief-that, denying what all religious believers in some way affirm: that there is an ultimate, salvific reality. The religious disbeliever *believes that* there is *no* such reality. Is there a form of belief-in that in a similar fashion opposes religious belief-in? I would suggest that there is, while also noting a disanalogy with the situation at the propositional level: this form of belief-in is not to be *equated* with affective religious disbelief as the relevant form of belief-that is to be equated with propositional religious disbelief. For affective religious disbelief we have to look in a slightly different direction. Why? Because belief-in entails a positive evaluation, and the evaluation of affective religious disbelief, properly so called, is negative. Furthermore, says H. H. Price, who speaks of the central attitude here as one of "disbelieving-in," we find in affective disbelief not positive emotions of approval and trust but rather emotions of "disesteem or distrust."[9] You will in this way disbelieve in your enemies (if you have any), in corrupt lawyers and politicians, in overeager insurance or automobile salespeople. Someone may disbelieve in affirmative action, in fad diets, in cough syrup, or in communism. And in a similar manner, one may disbelieve in religion, or in various symbols, goals, practices, policies, or people associated with religion. Here, it seems, is where affective religious disbelief, properly so called, is to be located, and it is evident that it is not to be identified with any state of belief-in. Let us pause now to tidy this up and state what we have arrived at a little more formally. "*S* possesses (affective) religious disbelief," I am suggesting, should be taken as equivalent in meaning to the conjunction of the following propositions:

(1) *S* believes that a certain item *x* has disvalue or is in some way a bad thing.
(2) At least a part of *S*'s reason for disvaluing *x* is that *S* disvalues the valuing of the existence of an ultimate and salvific reality or,

[9] See H. H. Price, *Belief* (London: George Allen & Unwin, 1969), p. 436.

more directly, disvalues the valuing of a good obtainable in relation to it, if it exists.[10]

(3) *S* is disposed, when *x* comes to mind, to experience a feeling state
that, when conjoined with the facts represented by (1) and (2),
produces a blended experience of disapproving and distrusting
emotions toward *x*.

Now, having identified religious *dis*belief-in, it is not at all hard to notice a
form of *belief*-in very close by. For the affective religious disbeliever may be
caused by his affective disbelief to evaluate *positively* the *anti*religious symbols, goals, practices, policies, people, and so on whose value is for him
bound up with the value of rejecting any idea of an ultimate and salvific
reality, and come to experience *positive* emotions—that is, approving, trusting, and loyal emotions—toward them. Such a state would certainly count
as belief-in and, like the state of religious disbelief-in we have identified,
appears to presuppose propositional religious disbelief. It has also not infrequently been realized in human history, especially recently: think of the attitudes of some Marxists, Freudians, evolutionary naturalists, and others of a
similar orientation who declare themselves opposed not only to theism but
to religion in general and who favor goals and policies that might allow people to transcend it, to move beyond it. So it does seem that there is not just
affective religious disbelief or religious disbelief-in but also a closely related
state of belief-in, in some cases caused by the negative state, which is positive
instead of negative. And it seems that both these states deserve consideration when religious disbelief and its potential impact are explored.

Granted, and as suggested above, propositional religious disbelievers
who also possess the states of disbelief-in and belief-in just mentioned
may not have a very clear idea of what they are rejecting or approving;
they may in any case not be thinking precisely of what I have called an
ultimate and salvific reality when they declare themselves opposed to religion. More common, perhaps, is a narrower sort of affective disbelief,
with corresponding affective belief, which opposes *specific* religious
ideas—such as the idea that the physical universe was Divinely created
only a few millennia ago, or that a God exists who will consign the larger
part of the human race to the flames of hell—and approves policies and
practices that may cause such ideas to wither away over time. But not a

---

[10] I do not say "disvalues the existence of an ultimate and salvific reality or of a good
obtainable in relation to it," not only because it would be hard to stare the idea of an ultimate and salvific reality or of an ultimate good in the face and disvalue it (more on this
below), but also because the alternative expressions capture what affective disbelievers
take—sometimes a bit scornfully—to be the *futility* of religion. In any case, the expressions
I use seem to cover the cases that need to be covered here.

few religious disbelievers are of the view, explicitly or implicitly, that *all* religious perspectives are bound up with such inadequate understandings of things. And so in rejecting the specific views in question they see themselves as opposed to *all* religion. Further, they would likely continue to affirm this (itself inadequate) understanding of things if presented with our more sophisticated characterization of the nature of religion. Thus a thoroughgoing form of affective religious disbelief (and corresponding affective belief) still seems possible.

But would not a fuller knowledge of religion, both actual and possible, ultimately lead *such states* to wither away? Surely someone who considered the generic idea of an ultimate and salvific reality and truly understood it could not remain valuationally opposed to it and to things bound up with it. Yet even this is not obvious: some religious disbelievers will think that this idea and any sort of positive response to it bespeak only human intellectual and/or psychological immaturity; others may be so psychologically and socially and intellectually invested in their antireligion as to lack any sense of meaning in life without it. Remember here the human tendency, affecting both religious belief and religious disbelief in their propositional varieties, to hold not just a single belief or only a few but to be enmeshed in a whole network of beliefs, which provides a more or less complete and finegrained interpretation of the nature of things. An individual holding propositional religious disbelief and reflecting this tendency may very well accept and retain, even in the face of considerable counterweights, at least somewhat positive evaluations of antireligious goals and policies and may experience at least low-level emotions favoring them. In other words, here too the propositional form of belief may well be linked to the affective.

Perhaps this linkage will be resisted on the grounds that propositional religious disbelief does not bring with it the same extravagant promises of reward that can be found in connection with religious belief. Because of those promises, it will be said, we might indeed expect a religious believer to become emotionally involved with the content of her belief in the manner of belief-in, but our reasons for expecting her to do so have no counterparts in the case of disbelief.

There can be more than one reason, however, for expecting an emotional response. There may be no promise of reward associated with propositional religious disbelief (and here it must also be remembered that rewards come in different forms), but we have already seen that there are other factors sufficient to prompt affective religious disbelief, as well as the associated form of belief-in, and likely to be operative in many cases. Given the power of emotion, already noted, this suggests that propositional religious disbelief too can become entrenched and lamentably resistant to rational investigation and assessment of the sort that might otherwise overturn it. All of this will also need to be borne in mind by philosophers of religion concerned with evaluating the diverse responses to religious claims identified in this chapter.[11]

[11] In addition to the generalized attitudes of religious disbelief explored here, there are of course also *particular* rejections of *particular* religious propositions or policies. One may, for example, not only disbelieve that there is an ultimate, salvific reality but, more narrowly, disbelieve that there is a personal God (which state is compatible with believing that there is an ultimate, salvific reality of another sort); and one may—as seen above—not only disapprove of practices and persons and ideas associated with the idea of the ultimate but, more narrowly, disapprove of practices and persons and ideas associated with a specific category of religious ideas (which state is compatible with approving things associated with the ultimate otherwise, or generically, construed). But for reasons emerging more fully in Chapters 7 and 8, having to do with the central tasks of philosophy of religion, I have here focused on the generalized forms of religious disbelief.

On Religious Skepticism

Once or twice already I have mentioned that there are responses to religious claims which fall *between* (propositional) belief and disbelief. The most obvious of these is skepticism. Everyone knows both that there are religious believers and disbelievers and that there are religious skeptics, and also that skeptics lack precisely what the believers and disbelievers possess: where believers and disbelievers in their different ways hold beliefs, skeptics are uncertain or in doubt. Here I want to get clearer about the nature of this skepticism. Now presumably we know a lot more than we did at the beginning of the book about the domain of religion and the nature of belief. And we all understand the concepts of "uncertainty" and "doubt." So what is left to say? A fair bit, as it turns out—though admittedly less than some previous topics have required. I begin with a few brief notes about the concept of "doubt" and then spend a little more time with some *types* of religious skepticism which it is important for philosophers of religion to distinguish.

1. *Doubts and Doubting*

Doubts or uncertainties are not the same as doubt or uncertainty (or doubt*fulness,* as the latter might also be called). Doubts or uncertainties are disruptive and typically troubling feelings caused by one's awareness of objections to a proposition one once confidently believed and the (consequent) sense that it may not after all be true—feelings that involve or result in a diminishment of one's confidence with respect to that proposition and threaten one's belief but do not necessarily result in a complete loss of belief. Doubt or uncertainty with respect to a proposition p, on the other hand, involves a complete absence of confidence with respect to p and also the absence of belief that p, given what appears to the doubter to be inconclusiveness in the relevant evidence. And precisely because of this apparent inconclusiveness, we do not find the belief that not-p being substituted for belief that p. What we have here instead is a state in which one believes neither p nor not-p.

Now doubt or uncertainty, in many cases, is what results from doubts or uncertainties wearing one's belief down to nothing, and so it may well share in the troubling and disruptive feelings that doubts or uncertainties represent. Something else that may go along with doubt is a restless and questioning attitude, one that prompts a continuing and deliberate investigation of the relevant issue and perhaps a defense of evidential inconclusiveness with respect to it (more on this in section 3 below). But it is important to recognize that these things *need not* accompany doubt. Doubt, it must always be remembered, is simply the state of believing nothing on some issue because of apparently indecisive evidence, and one may be in this state even if one does not want to be in it (and so even if one is not exactly inclined to defend evidential inconclusiveness), or has long since left the whole issue behind, or else has recognized alternative ways of resolving it that do not require the formation of belief.[1]

The concept of doubt I am exploring here may appear to be present in each of the following expressions: "I am in doubt about the existence of God"; "I doubt that God exists"; "I doubt whether God exists." But it is unambiguously present only in the first. Each of the others is quite naturally interpreted in terms of disbelief, together with some measure of confidence that God does *not* exist; this takes us past doubt of the sort with which we are concerned, which involves possessing neither belief nor disbelief and lacking confidence on either side.

Finally, it should be noted that doubt is not a voluntary state; it participates in the involuntariness of belief. Because one cannot affect one's belief states at will, one cannot voluntarily ensure that one does not land in doubt (this would entail *preserving* belief at will), and neither can one ensure that one gets out of doubt if one does land in it (this would entail *forming* belief at will).

Now, as suggested above, the term "skepticism" is in philosophy normally reserved for precisely the sort of doubt I have been discussing—for

---

[1] It is because doubt thus understood can go with so many other psychological states, and also because there is no doubt-related counterpart to the belief-that/belief-in and faith-that/faith-in distinctions, that this chapter yields less information than its neighbors about how the central state under discussion is linked to affective states and dispositions to act.

uncertainty, with respect to some proposition p, as to whether it is p or not-p that is true. Because of apparently inconclusive evidence the skeptic, so it would be said, believes neither. A *religious* skeptic, then, should presumably be in just this sort of doubt about some religious proposition. But although this is indeed one way of understanding religious skepticism, it is not the only one.

2. *Four Types of Religious Skepticism*

To more fully understand the nature of religious skepticism, we must consider the following question: What is the object of religious skepticism? In other words, what is a religious skeptic skeptical *about*? To what must doubt be directed in order to count as religious skepticism?

There is a clear sense in which someone who formerly believed a religious proposition or propositions but now is doubtful may be said to be skeptical about that proposition or propositions. And what else would we call this but religious skepticism? So (as noted above) there is a sense in which religious skepticism may be linked simply to doubt about this or that particular religious proposition or limited set of propositions. Often, in contemporary philosophy of religion, the proposition in question is the proposition "There is a God"—perhaps together with certain propositions logically connected to it. Persons doubtful about such propositions are commonly labeled religious skeptics. (Another term for skepticism specifically about the existence of God is of course "agnosticism.") Because this use of the term is well entrenched, and because thus understood it applies to rather a lot of people, let us call the religious skepticism to which it refers *common* skepticism.[2]

But surely we sometimes understand the term "religious skepticism" to mean something more than just "doubt about this or that particular religious proposition or limited set of propositions." Notice: there is nothing in theory to rule out the coexistence of the latter sort of skepticism with belief of other religious propositions not within its purview—which is to say that one could experience common skepticism while contentedly believing religious propositions.[3] And this does seem to jar with at least one way of using the term "religious skepticism," for isn't it often our

[2] A similar point might be urged for religious disbelief, as noted at the end of the previous chapter. But my sense is that, both in everyday life and in philosophy of religion, religious disbelief is more commonly viewed as general—as applying to all religious propositions—than is religious skepticism.

[3] As an example, think of someone who is skeptical about whether a personal God exists but who believes that there is *something* ultimate and salvific.

sense that a religious skeptic believes *no* religious proposition? But then how exactly should this more general skepticism be understood? Should we think of such a skeptic as one who is doubtful about *each* religious proposition? That doesn't seem right. For one thing, a skeptic who thought some religious claim was false while in doubt about the others would not on that account lose the right to her title. For another, there will always be religious propositions, actually or potentially believed by religious persons, that a religious skeptic does not even know about. So should we instead expect the religious skeptic to be doubtful about the *conjunction* of all religious propositions—the proposition saying they are all true? No, for any reflective individual will positively disbelieve such a proposition: it is impossible for all religious claims to be true at once (just try, for example, to conceive of reality as governed by a personal God and an exclusively nonpersonal force at the same time).

What is left? Well, perhaps a more plausible suggestion is that the more general religious skepticism we are seeking to understand involves doubt with respect to the *disjunction* of all religious claims—which is the proposition saying that one or other of the various religious claims is true. Religious skeptics, on this interpretation, are doubtful about whether *any* religious proposition is true. Put otherwise, they are doubtful about the proposition "There is truth in religion," which is equivalent to the proposition "At least one religious proposition is true"—which, as it happens, is equivalent to the disjunction mentioned above. Now an individual could hardly be in doubt about this while believing a religious proposition. So it is easy to see that religious skepticism, thus understood, will involve the complete absence of religious belief which was earlier identified as belonging to an important sense of the term. To highlight this aspect of its nature, let us call this sort of religious skepticism *categorical* skepticism.[4]

The view of categorical religious skepticism, as can be seen, concerns a proposition *about* religious propositions, about the whole class or category of such propositions: namely, the proposition claiming that at least one member of that class is true. This has an interesting consequence. Any categorical skeptic who accepts my definition of "religious proposition" ("a proposition entailing that there is an ultimate and salvific reality") and sees the relevant logical connections will also be doubtful about the following proposition: "There is an ultimate and salvific reality." For

---

[4] Some of those who are common skeptics—given their assumption that only the religious claim(s) concerning which they happen to be in doubt have any chance of being true—turn out to be categorical skeptics as well. So these two forms of skepticism can go together.

given that definition, if some member of the class of religious propositions is true, then there is such a reality; and clearly, if there is such a reality, then at least one religious proposition is true. In other words,
although "There is an ultimate and salvific reality" and "At least one religious proposition is true" are different propositions, they are *logically*
equivalent. And if we assume that the categorical skeptic sees this equiva-
lence, we may describe her skepticism as well in terms of the one proposition as in terms of the other. I make that assumption in what follows.

Our discoveries here have another interesting consequence as well
(alluded to earlier but needing to be clarified). It is that one may be a categorical religious skeptic while denying or disbelieving some or many religious claims. Just as one may be skeptical about whether an American
citizen was involved in the planning of the World Trade Center attacks
while—because of the obviousness of this proposition—believing that the
Reverend Billy Graham was not involved, so one may be skeptical about
whether some religious proposition is true (or in doubt about whether
there is an ultimate and salvific reality) while believing (for example) that
there is no perfectly loving God.[5]

We would, however, be closing off discussion prematurely if we
stopped at this point, for there is another, quite important object of religious skepticism. We can bring it into focus by noticing the possibility of
the following sort of question: Is the truth about whether there is or is
not something ultimate and salvific, or about the details of the nature
any such reality must possess, even *accessible* to human beings? Do human
beings *have what it takes* to make effective cognitive contact with such
matters, to discern the truth about them, instead of just ineffectually
fishing around, persistently missing the truth, getting reality (in those
respects) wrong?[6] Let us say that for us to have what it takes to acquire
such information is for us to be *capable* of doing so, and that if one has
done so, one has discovered at least some basic truths concerning religion. Then we can give a formulation of the proposition that is the
object of this new form of skepticism as follows: "Human beings are capable of discovering at least some basic truths concerning religion." Call
this "the capacity claim."

---

[5] It is also possible to have this combination: belief of ultimism and skepticism (though
now common skepticism) with respect to some *particular* religious proposition such as theism. None of this, of course, prevents belief, disbelief, and skepticism from representing
mutually exclusive classes when we are talking about belief, disbelief, and skepticism *with
respect to the same proposition.*

[6] Notice that determining what sort of nature an ultimate reality would *not* have would
not count as such an accomplishment, unless from a severely limited set of options we had
ruled out all but one.

That formulation is inadequate however, because it leaves us with the following question: By "capable," do we mean *at present* capable or *at some time* capable? More fully and accurately, do we mean that in our present intellectual, moral, psychological, social (etc.) situation at least some basic truths about religion are discernible by us, or that at some time in the total life span of the race—perhaps far into the future—they will be discernible by us? Clearly, the latter claim is the weaker, and skepticism about it the stronger. Let us say that when the capacity claim is intended to be taken in the latter way, the word "capacity" is being used in an *unqualified* sense; in the former way, in a *qualified* sense. And let us accordingly call the claim we have in the latter case "the unqualified capacity claim," and the claim we have in the former case "the qualified capacity claim." The disjunction of these two I continue to call simply "the capacity claim." Skepticism that involves doubt about one or other of the disjuncts may therefore be called *capacity* skepticism; the more specific forms that it can take, corresponding to the disjuncts, I call *unqualified* capacity skepticism and *qualified* capacity skepticism.[7]

It can be seen that the capacity claim, unlike the categorical proposition previously discussed, is not in the first instance about an ultimate and salvific reality but about our intellectual and spiritual qualifications. The two propositions are indeed not the same at all; neither are they logically linked, since either one could be true without the other being true. And yet it does seem that capacity skepticism should count as religious skepticism. Why? Well, perhaps part of the reason for our inclination to say so is that a categorical skeptic may be a capacity skeptic too, and the former sort of skepticism may indeed draw sustenance from the latter. That is, someone may be doubtful as to whether there is an ultimate and salvific reality precisely because he is in doubt about whether we are (in one or another sense) capable of discovering any basic truths about such a reality.[8] Indeed, *anyone* who is skeptical about our possessing this capacity is going to be skeptical also about whether there is such a reality as the one

---

[7] Here we may also acknowledge and countenance the extra connotation of *modesty* attached to the use of the word "qualified" in connection with capacity skepticism, but not in connection with the relevant capacity claim itself (as we have seen, the qualified capacity claim, attributing the relevant capacity to us *right now*, is in fact the stronger).

[8] We should notice here that even someone who goes beyond doubt to a denial of this capacity claim has a basis for no more than doubt about the existence of a reality of the sort in question. Perhaps because of this tendency for even the belief that the capacity claim is false to underwrite no more than doubt as to whether there is truth in religion, there is a tendency not to distinguish sharply between doubt about that claim and its denial, and a tendency to assimilate even the latter to skepticism about our capacities. Here I continue to assume the narrower understanding of capacity skepticism, which focuses on doubt.

in question. Certainly to believe that there *is* one, we would need to take ourselves to possess (right now) the capacity in question; the same holds for believing that there *isn't* one, since to discern the absence of such a reality is just as much to discern a basic truth about it as to discern its presence.[9] But then, without taking ourselves to possess the capacity in question, we will be unable, rationally, to form a belief *either way* about whether there is an ultimate and salvific reality—which is of course to say that we will be categorical skeptics.[10] So capacity skepticism will go together with categorical skepticism in those who possess the former and understand what this involves. (Let us call what we have when these two are combined in this way *complete* skepticism.) In any case, the former is evidently an important type of religious skepticism in its own right.

We have, then, four types of religious skepticism, corresponding to the four objects of doubt we have distinguished. Accordingly, "S is a religious skeptic" might well be taken as equivalent in meaning to the following proposition, which draws these threads together:

S is in doubt with respect to (i) this or that particular religious proposition or limited set of religious propositions (common skepticism), or (ii) the proposition that there is an ultimate and salvific reality (categorical skepticism), or (iii) the proposition—qualified or unqualified—that human beings are capable of discovering at least some basic truths concerning such a reality (capacity skepticism), or (iv) both of the latter two propositions together (complete skepticism).

3. *Passive and Active Skepticism*

Although the attitude of skepticism may be taken as involving simply doubt or uncertainty, there is also another way of understanding it, more

[9] Observe that to discern the absence of a being that, were it to exist, would instantiate such a reality—say, a personal God—is not to discern the absence of such a reality, and thus to discover a basic truth about it, unless there is no *other* way for such a reality to be instantiated.

[10] These two possible objects of skepticism, therefore, while not logically linked, are linked epistemologically—that is, the attitude we take toward the idea that one is true will affect (and should affect) our attitude with regard to likelihood of truth in the other. In objection to this a theist may suggest that it is precisely *because* of our incapacity that God reveals the truth to us, and thus *despite* our incapacity we can come to know the truth about religion. But this reflects misunderstanding: given my definition, if the truth about religion is successfully revealed to us by God, then we must have the capacity in question (even if only because God has given that to us too)—then we must have all that we need to have to be able to form correct beliefs about ultimate things. (For if necessary conditions of correct beliefs on some subject matter are lacking, then *those beliefs* will be lacking too.)

active and voluntary than the first. Doubt, as we have seen, is passive and involuntary. But we might also think here of a *stance* or *cultivated disposition* of skepticism, a kind of "declaration of undecidedness" or "coming out on the side of skepticism," together with ongoing reinforcement through appropriate private and public behavior: seeking to avoid (or else canceling) oral or mental endorsements on either side of the relevant issue; expressing a desire to look further into the issue when asked about it; better acquainting oneself with evidence contrary to the view one finds (intellectually or otherwise) most attractive, and so on—in general, a voluntary and persistent distancing of oneself from acquiescence in opinion.[11]

Now obviously the two notions distinguished here might be realized together (you might find doubt plus distancing, uncertainty plus an ongoing attempt to keep things that way), but what is interesting is that either may also be realized alone. We have already seen this for doubt, which may be unwanted and resisted instead of industriously bolstered. But it is also true of the more active state to which I have referred: though compatible with the first, this second sort of skepticism is capable of operating independently of it. The production and maintenance of such a state might, it seems, be undertaken even by one for whom belief fully or vestigially remains, if he thinks that some good may be achieved thereby.[12] In particular, he may think it would be good to enter into doubt *more completely* and may take up an actively skeptical stance in order to promote that end. Perhaps in one part of himself (or at some times) he is under the spell of a certain belief, but in another part (or at other times) he recognizes uncritical tendencies and sees that the belief is responsive to something other than objectively "good evidence" and so ought not to exist—imagine someone who finds himself believing for no good reason that there is intelligent life on other planets. Or perhaps over time he has lost a great deal of confidence with respect to a certain proposition and so only infrequently is in a state of mind corresponding to the conscious experience of belief but sees that intellectually and perhaps otherwise he would be better off if he altogether lost the belief, though without going all the way over to the other side. Here think of someone who while growing up has always believed that his biological mother is alive and looking for him and is

---

[11] Behaviors of the sort I have described might be undertaken in a less unified and directed manner as well: one might see sporadic acts instead of anything properly called a state or disposition or attitude. In such cases one might be tempted to speak of active skepticism, but I reserve that label for the more entrenched and persistent attitude.

[12] Notice that such statements as "You are being very skeptical" can be made even of a believer if she is actively questioning a proposition she believes.

now confronted with the weakness of the evidence supporting this belief. Faced with a situation like one of these, an individual may decide that he ought to cultivate the attitude that best accommodates the psychological state he sees himself coming to, or needing to come to, which perhaps involves distancing himself from the more definite views on either side—a *skeptical* attitude. Surely all this is possible. But if so, then a more active and voluntary stance of skepticism, capable of operating on its own, is possible and needs to be considered alongside the more passive attitude of doubt.

It is tempting to associate this second sort of skeptical attitude with something traditionally connected with skepticism: namely, the idea of withholding judgment. I think we should yield to the temptation. "Withholding" certainly *sounds* active and voluntary. It apparently refers to something one does and so seems to take us beyond mere doubt. And what is withheld? Well, judgment, naturally. But what does "judgment" mean here? In answer, perhaps most philosophers would refer to *belief*: where the issue concerns *p*, the belief that *p* or the belief that not-*p*. This notion spells trouble for the idea of withholding, however, since belief, being involuntary, cannot be withheld in the fairly strong sense suggested here. Is there anything else that might count as judgment and that can be thus withheld? I think so. I suggest we think in terms of taking sides, identifying oneself with one side or the other of the issue, deciding in favor of the truth of *p* or the truth of not-*p*. There appears to be an *endorsement* here, as in other contexts where the word "judgment" is used (think, for example, of legal contexts). Now something like this may typically accompany the formation of belief, naturally elicited from one by the apparent force of the evidence, but even then it is clearly not the same thing as belief. Unlike belief, such an endorsement is an action done at a time, and, again unlike belief (remember the distinction between "thinking of" and "thinking about" from Chapter 2), it is one that requires thinking *about* the proposition involved. In judging, one is consciously aware of the options and mentally plumps for one or the other. "Judgment" has at least a connotation of finality; the mental judgment that *p* or that not-*p*, I suggest, involves *putting behind one* the issue of *p*'s truth and also the alternative judgment.[13]

---

[13] Judgment, in this sense, may seem similar to what Lehrer and Cohen have dubbed "acceptance." See Keith Lehrer, *Self-Trust: A Study of Reason, Knowledge, and Autonomy* (Oxford: Clarendon Press, 1997), pp. 3–4, where the connection to judgment is made explicit; and L. Jonathan Cohen, *An Essay on Belief and Acceptance* (Oxford: Clarendon Press, 1992), pp. 4, 54, where at any rate an allusion to such a connection is present. But Lehrer thinks of acceptance mainly as a positive second-level (or "metamental") evaluation of a *first-level belief,* and gives short shrift to the idea of accepting a proposition. He

This point of *closure* is precisely what is withheld when one withholds judgment on *p*. In withholding judgment, one enacts a determination to keep the issue of *p*'s truth *open*. This will of course involve not judging (i.e., refraining from mental endorsement) but also, it seems, such other behaviors as are mentioned above, both private and public, which will be needed to *keep* judgment at bay. And withholding judgment, understood in this way, appears to be something I can actualize whether I believe the relevant proposition or not. As in effect we have just seen, even a believer can withhold judgment by purposely keeping the relevant issue open, thus seeking to induce the doubt she sees as appropriate. Indeed, the idea of withholding judgment seems tailor-made for capturing the sort of alternative skeptical attitude one may *take on* even when one's having an attitude of doubt toward the relevant proposition or propositions is itself very much in doubt.[14]

Must we say, then, on this alternative view, that the skeptic takes a position? It would seem that we must. But, it may be objected, is not the skeptic, perched as he squarely is on the fence, supposed to *avoid* position-taking? Isn't skepticism supposed to give one freedom from "positions"?

Two things may be said in response to these questions. First, it may be suggested that by "taking a position" we mean only that the skeptic resolves to *act* in a certain way—to perform the actions involved in withholding judgment on a certain proposition *p*. So far we have no reference to any *belief* with respect to *p* of the sort the objection seems to be referring to, and clearly the "position" that might be represented by a mental *judgment* that *p* is being withheld. But of course there is also a skeptical belief lurking here: namely, the belief that it is good to withhold judgment—call this the belief that *q*. And no doubt there is a mental judgment in favor of *q*. This belief and judgment, however, are unproblematic

---

also suggests that the only purpose for which one might accept a belief or a proposition is to arrive at what is true and avoid what is false. But one might form a judgment of the sort I have in mind here—going along with the truth of a proposition—even when one is in doubt as to whether it really is true, and when one's reasons are prudential or ethical instead of evidential. Cohen's notion of acceptance, though more flexible than Lehrer's in these respects, also has built into it a practical component that is missing from my notion of mental judgment (there is more on related matters in Chapter 6). This makes his notion more complex than the one I am developing here.

[14] Perhaps a difference between believer and nonbeliever here is that one who sees doubt as appropriate while not yet able to entirely rid himself of belief will need to *withdraw* judgment before withholding it in the foregoing sense; as we saw earlier, one who believes will also typically have made the judgment in question. It may also be easier for a believer to *fall into* mental judgment when she is not on her guard. And so for her, perhaps, withholding judgment will sometimes require the mental *canceling* of such lapses.

in this context, since they do not involve believing or judging that p or that not-p, and only the latter beliefs and judgments are precluded in the manner suggested by the objection. Someone who is skeptical about p may have all sorts of beliefs and defend all sorts of positions that do not involve taking sides with respect to p, and q is one of these.

The notion I have been developing seems therefore to be quite coherent and to represent an important alternative way of understanding the skeptical attitude. This means that types of skepticism, and so of religious skepticism, may be distinguished not only on the basis of different objects but on the basis of different qualities in the attitude directed to those objects. In particular, we must now recognize that each of the four types of skepticism we have distinguished may be realized either passively or actively—or both (since the passivity referred to involves not the absence of the actions involved in active skepticism but rather the involuntariness of doubt). Religious skepticism, that is to say, may involve either just doubt, or just withholding of judgment, or both doubt and withholding of judgment. Thus a slightly more complex definition of "S is a religious skeptic" is called for:

S is in doubt and/or withholds judgment with respect to (i) this or that particular religious proposition or limited set of religious propositions (common skepticism), or (ii) the proposition that there is an ultimate and salvific reality (categorical skepticism), or (iii) the proposition— qualified or unqualified—that human beings are capable of discovering at least some basic truths concerning such a reality (capacity skepticism), or (iv) both (ii) and (iii) together (complete skepticism).

On Religious Faith (I)

It might be thought that, having already dealt with matters of belief and of religious belief, this book requires no chapter on religious faith—let alone two! Most philosophers, influenced by common interpretations of such notable figures as Aquinas and Kierkegaard, or else by the theological habits of the often highly doctrinal forms of religion most familiar to them, have held that religious faith *is* (propositional) religious belief or, at the very least, that it entails such belief.[1] Many of these philosophers, notoriously, have criticized religious faith because they have thought religious belief to be somewhat naive and foolish, or stubborn and irresponsible, or in some other way unjustified and unwarranted. Such philosophers are typically not much concerned about the details of religious faith; so long as religious belief is entailed by religious faith, they will say, their criticisms of the latter can be upheld, since religious belief lacks justification. Other philosophers have challenged this view, arguing that there is nothing naive or foolish, stubborn or irresponsible, unjustified or unwarranted about the belief that religious faith entails. But as is evident, they have challenged it on its own terms, assuming, as do the critics, that religious belief and religious faith rise and fall together.

I think this assumption is mistaken. In turning from belief to faith we are indeed switching gears, for contrary to popular opinion, religious faith neither is nor entails religious belief. In fact, in one of its main forms it entails *non*belief and represents a positive response to religious

---

[1] A typical example is Walter Kaufmann, who in *The Faith of a Heretic* (New York: New American Library, 1978) writes: "Faith means intense, usually confident, belief that is not based on evidence sufficient to command assent from every reasonable person" (p. 2).

claims which deserves completely separate billing and is quite compatible with religious skepticism. Thus the extreme responses to religious claims of belief and disbelief, and the various forms of skepticism falling between them, do not take up all the conceptual space available here. Philosophers need more colors in their palette. Between religious belief and religious disbelief there is room for another, and indeed positive, response to religious claims.

To see the plausibility of these perhaps startling assertions we need to engage in a careful investigation of the nature of religious faith, against the backdrop of discussion in previous chapters. This chapter and the next undertake such an investigation. I begin at a fairly general level and with an eye to ordinary language, seeking to view this conceptual terrain from the heights, taking note of its most significant geographical features. Then, still in this chapter, I consider one of the more specific notions turned up by our discussion: namely, the notion of trust, which has received inadequate attention from philosophers but represents an important sort of response to things religious. All of this can be seen as a preface to the presentation and defense in Chapter 6 of my most controversial claims concerning this subject. Let the reader therefore beware! Acquiescence in the claims of this chapter may be expected to make resistance to the claims that follow more difficult.

1. *Finding "Faith"*

"Faith" is a rich, suggestive, and elusive term in our language. As in the case of "religion" and "belief," we are confronted with ambiguity. Indeed, "faith" is multiply ambiguous.[2] Pretty clearly it is religious faith that we want ultimately to understand, though we shouldn't suppose that secular usage will be irrelevant to our quest. And pretty clearly the sort of faith that concerns us is the faith that philosophers of religion seek to understand (though of course it is identified by reference to ordinary contexts of faith-related language and activity)—the sort of faith skeptics usually consider to be out of reach and against which antireligious diatribes are regularly launched.

So what do we find when we venture into this territory? Well, beginning in an appropriately cautious manner, we may say that faith does not appear to entail *everything* that can be found in a religious life (though exactly how much of such a life must be part of faith is left somewhat

---

[2] For an absorbing account of some of this diversity in usage, see William Ladd Sessions, *The Concept of Faith* (Ithaca: Cornell University Press, 1994).

unclear by religious language), but it does seem that faith is *present* in any such life. Perhaps at a minimum it would be agreed that it is what sets the religious person upon a religious way and, so long as her religion lasts, keeps her there.

Here we must already note a distinction commonly made by philosophers of religion, implicit in the relevant language, between two kinds of faith: faith-*that* (or propositional faith), which involves some kind of positive and assenting attitude toward religious propositions, and faith-*in*, which entails such an attitude toward religious propositions but goes beyond it in some sort of positive response to the ultimate reality of which they speak.[3] So, for example, there can be discussion of what it is to have faith *that* God exists and how this differs from having faith *in* God. The two do clearly seem to be different, though just how is not immediately evident. Indeed, both in secular and in religious usage, references to faith-that and faith-in sometimes appear separately, and the notions they denote seem at least sometimes to be independently realized. (Compare such utterances as "I'm just going to have faith that a parking spot will appear" and "She took it on faith that the Torah would guide her aright," with "He had an implicit faith in the power of education" and "Faith in Amida Buddha is needed for enlightenment.")

There is also the (related) fact that although trust of the sort associated with faith-in is apparently not a central feature of certain forms of religion (compare the usual interpretations of Christian and Theravada Buddhist religion in this respect), assenting attitudes toward propositions appear to be common to them all. And such attitudes do seem fundamental to the religious stance, wherever they are found. These considerations suggest that, when analyzing "faith," we ought to regard instances of the two notions mentioned as representing distinct forms of that to which it refers. For the time being, at any rate, I proceed on this assumption. (An objection that will allow us to test it further emerges in the next chapter.)

Now different views about the relations between these two forms of faith are possible. Should we think of faith-in as *entailing* faith-that? (Does faith in God entail faith that God exists?) In other words, is the positive

---

[3] The term "positive" should therefore not be seen as having exactly the same meaning in the two instances of its use here. The positive attitude toward religious propositions involves some sort of affirmation or assent in relation to their content, though to say more at this stage would—despite the commonness of references to belief—be unwise. The positive response to the ultimate reality involves something new; it *adds* something—something like trust, perhaps. (Certainly the latter emotion or action or disposition to action, whatever it is, would be thought by many to fill the bill here.) But precision must await further discussion.

propositional attitude at the bottom of faith-in necessarily to be identified with the propositional attitude we associate with faith-that? Or are the two notions more distinct than this would suggest? I argue, in favor of the latter view, that the item identified by the phrase "positive, assenting propositional attitude" can be realized in more than one way, both by propositional religious belief and by another attitude I shall discuss, and that only the latter is the way of propositional faith. Whereas propositional religious belief is often involved in faith-in, it is never part of faith-that. And faith-in, though commonly grounded in such belief, need not be: it may also be grounded in faith-that. Hence *both* forms of faith may exist without propositional belief. Most of this argument belongs to the next chapter, where faith-that is more fully discussed. (In order not to prejudice that discussion, when I refer to the positive propositional attitude I use the indefinite expression "belief or faith.") Here I want to give more detailed attention to faith-in. But as it happens, the discoveries we make in this chapter will not be at all irrelevant to the defense of the unorthodox claims just outlined.

So what is to be said about faith-in? Many philosophers are inclined to think of it as a matter of trust, a state that does seem obviously relevant: How could it be correct to say that I have faith in God or the Dharma or democracy or the educational system if I am not inclined to place my trust in the items mentioned?[4] But trust, though generally mentioned in this connection, has received little in the way of analysis. Let us therefore consider it more closely. I want to address two issues here. First, what *is* the trust we are talking about? What is its nature? Second, can this notion of trust be applied to all forms of religion? In particular, can it be extended to forms of religion in which the ultimate is not construed in personal terms?

2. *Faith and Action: The Nature of Trust*

So what is religious trust?[5] Several possibilities are suggested by reflection on ordinary language (including religious language) and our behavior in everyday life. For simplicity, let us focus for now on what one is claiming

---

[4] Some might say that a kind of love also belongs to faith-in, but as it turns out, most of what one might want to say about love in this context is better said in connection with the concept of *belief*-in (affective religious belief), discussed in Chapters 2 and 3—this for reasons suggested at the end of Chapter 2 and also later on in this chapter.

[5] I refer to the religious case of trust-in. Analysis here is made a bit more complicated by the fact that religious people may also be heard to speak of trusting *that* so-and-so. This latter form of trust, which is a propositional attitude, is discussed in the next chapter.

to have when one professes trust in a personal God. At first it might seem that if I make such a profession, I am simply referring to a positive propositional attitude of mine, whether of belief or of faith, directed toward the very specific and—as we might say—personalized proposition that God's goodness extends to *me*: that God will be or do for me what I need or want. And perhaps the attitude is held even though the falsity of the proposition in question is not ruled out by one's evidence, and even though there will be bad consequences if the proposition is false. Richard Swinburne claims that some such proposition and some such circumstances are involved when in ordinary life we trust someone, and he seems to be right.[6] Ordinary language links trust to vulnerability: if my interests were not at stake in trusting and if I could not be in at least some degree hurt by doing so, there would be no point in using the language of trust at all.[7]

But it is clear (as Swinburne sees) that there must be more to trust than just a positive attitude toward the proposition in question. There would be no vulnerability, no possible bad consequences (or at least none of the sort we are inclined to associate with broken trust), if I were not disposed to *act* on this attitude of mine. If, for example, I elect to place my trust in my son when he asks me for the keys to the car, I not only hold such an attitude; I give him the keys to the car. (If having trust were simply a matter of possessing the propositional attitude, we could make no sense of my saying when the boy's mother enters the room five minutes later, "I trusted him with the car," a report given in the past tense and clearly referring to an action just taken.) To suppose that he will do what I need or want is only a beginning: it is just to suppose that he is trust*worthy*; it is not yet to trust.[8] And the same goes for religious trust: I may suppose that

---

[6] See Richard Swinburne, *Faith and Reason* (Oxford: Clarendon Press, 1981), p. 111: "To trust a man is to act on the assumption that he will do what he knows that you want or need, when the evidence gives some reason for supposing that he may not and where there will be bad consequences if the assumption is false." This emphasis on a radically personalized propositional content is front and center in the very famous account of religious trust given by Martin Luther—as Swinburne notes (p. 113).

[7] We might add here that all uses of "faith" seem to be connected in some way with the idea of evidence that is not as strong as it conceivably could be. A reference to the latter idea of the sort we have made here, tied into the idea of trust and its vulnerability, accommodates this fact nicely.

[8] Of course, what it is that I need or want may well vary from situation to situation (though quite general needs and wants, relevant to every situation, are possible, and applicable especially where the trusted one is God). Thus when person A believes that B will do what she needs or wants in a certain situation, she may have something very different in mind from what she is thinking when she believes the same about B in another situation. And in the same situation, there may be more than one thing that A needs or wants, of *each* of which she believes that B will do it. She may of course act on either or neither of

God will be and do for me what I need or want, but if I am not disposed to act on this supposition in any way, how can I be said to have placed my trust in God? (It may seem a problem here that those in whom religious trust seems most clearly evident sometimes appear to be doing nothing, simply "waiting on God." But *this* doing nothing involves doing *something*: namely, such mental actions as pulling one's thoughts away from selfish concern and prayerfully centering one's mind on God, as well as refraining from such actions as those involving self-aggrandizement and frenzied pursuit of material security.)

Trust, then, would appear to involve some kind of action disposition, which emerges in *response* to the content of a proposition of the sort in question, affirmed by belief or faith. In the religious case we may say that among the propositions about God affirmed by the one who trusts in God is this sort of particular and personalized proposition (or set of propositions) concerning what we might call God's good will toward the individual in question; in response to it, she, as it were, puts her life into God's hands, deliberately conducting herself in a manner she sees as appropriate to the truth of that proposition.

Some, however, might consider this emphasis on an action disposition to be an overemphasis (or at least to represent less than the whole story about trust). Terence Penelhum, in an important discussion, calls trust of the sort identified by Swinburne *explicit* trust, contrasting it with *implicit* trust, which he suggests is a matter of feeling serene and free from anxiety rather than a matter of action or of an action disposition. And it is the second sort of trust, he says, that represents the ideal of faith.[9] What are we to make of these claims? It seems to me that Penelhum may have confused implicit trust—which seems still to be a disposition to act in a certain way—either with a property that trust sometimes possesses (or a state by which it is sometimes accompanied) or with one of the conditions that may serve to bring it about, or both.

---

the beliefs just mentioned. And so A may trust B in one respect but not in another. Further, the same action may constitute A's trusting B in one respect but failing to do so in another. For example, other things being equal, if I perfunctorily refuse my son the car keys, I fail to trust him in a certain respect: I fail to act on my belief that he will do what I need or want—namely, take care of the car. But I do trust him in another respect, since that very perfunctory refusal is an instance of my acting on the belief that he will do what I need or want: namely, refrain from seriously harming me when I turn down his request!

[9] See Terence Penelhum, *Reason and Religious Faith* (Boulder, CO: Westview Press, 1995), pp. 72–74. A quick answer to Penelhum would involve pointing out that according to our definition of "religion" in Chapter 1, religion and thus (given what I say above) faith do not entail an emotional component. But such a response would be inadequate. Penelhum's view can be seen as a *challenge* to our analyses so far, which, if successful, must lead us to revise them.

As I see it, sometimes—for some persons in some circumstances—the action that trust involves is relatively *easy*, and when it is, it may be appropriate to characterize it as relatively serene and untroubled (or to recognize a corresponding emotional state as typically accompanying it); sometimes, indeed, it may be a kind of serenity that *causes* trust to be easy. But the trust itself is still a disposition to act in a certain way. And although the serenity of which Penelhum speaks may be a religious ideal, I suggest that it is not appropriate to call it an ideal of *faith*. Faith, whether ideal or not, seems incompatible with (at any rate, complete) serenity.[10]

Let us see how these claims can be defended. First, notice that Penelhum himself uses language linking the concept of implicit trust to an action disposition. Implicit trust is said to be characterized by "unreservedness," which is filled out in terms of an absence of reluctance "in dealing with" the trusted one. Clearly, unreservedness is here supposed to be a property of implicit trust, and just about as clearly, what it is said to be a property *of* involves action. Now it may be argued that unreservedness—understood as absence of limitation or qualification—can be a property just as well of an emotional state such as serenity as of an action or action disposition. But Penelhum himself puts paid to this when he says that the one who trusts explicitly acts in ways that "would be wholly and naturally forthcoming" if she had implicit trust instead.[11] Though other words are used, we see here a reference to unreservedness once again, and this time the fact that it is said to characterize a disposition to *act* is evident.

What are we to make of this? It would seem that the emphasis on a form of trust constituted by emotion alone is hard to maintain consistently, and for good reason: Penelhum's linking of implicit trust and action (though it apparently leads to inconsistency in his own account) seems quite clearly correct. Consider once more the case of my son and the car keys. I may—perhaps because of powerfully affecting previous interaction with him—be unqualifiedly serene in the face of my son's request, completely unconcerned about how the car will fare in his hands, but if I betray no disposition to let him drive it, he has an excellent reason to doubt that I nonetheless trust him in this respect. (Of

---

[10] There may be an overlap between the serenity to which Penelhum refers (in ibid.) and certain of the emotions involved in *belief*-in, distinguished from faith in Chapter 2. I say this only to point out a connection, not to offer a reason for construing faith-in as an action disposition. Since I am, among other things, here developing the *support* for an exclusively affective interpretation of belief-in that was promised in Chapter 2, I could hardly take what was said about it in that chapter as significant backing for my interpretation of faith without arguing in a circle.

[11] Ibid.

course, I may have a *belief* here—the belief that he would take care of the car—and this may seem enough, perhaps together with serenity in the holding of it, to constitute a kind of trust. But as we saw above, if I never act on this belief, we never get past the notion that he is trustworthy and to trust itself.) Or again, if my spouse is accused of a crime she insists she did not commit, and I am asked to accept her word on the matter and continue to act toward her as I did before but am not at all disposed to comply, I stand convicted of a lack of trust, regardless of how little I may worry about her future actions toward myself or others. Or (returning to our primary concern) suppose I say that I have placed my trust in God and do indeed feel quite unruffled by the suggestion that God may not exist or is unworthy of trust, yet I take no steps along a religious way, do nothing that might qualify as seeking to draw near to God, and take no risks I would otherwise avoid—in short, I live just as I would if I had never heard of God. What I say is then false; I am a victim of confusion or guilty of lying.

Such examples suggest that the trust Penelhum refers to as implicit is something other than or more than serenity and, in particular, that it involves an action disposition of some kind. Other facts support this view. For example, if Penelhum is right, then certain terms synonymous with "trust" in ordinary language, terms that even more clearly suggest the presence of an action disposition (e.g., "rely upon," "count on"), cannot without loss of meaning be used to replace "trust" in the expressions "trust implicitly" and "implicitly trust." But this seems false. Consider also that if Penelhum's account is correct, then we have "explicit trust" as a label to cover acting on a certain propositional attitude when it is *difficult* to do so; "implicit trust" as a label for a certain feeling state one may find oneself in when one suffers no anxiety in relation to the trusted one; but *no* label to cover acting on the aforementioned propositional attitude when it is *easy* to do so. Is this an oversight? Surely that last phenomenon is common enough and deserves some consideration here; and surely it has something to do with trust. (Can it really be that my action of giving the keys to my son ceases to be a case of trusting simply by virtue of ceasing to be difficult? Or—to take another example—can we not make sense of a woman saying, with reference to her action of allowing her daughter to visit out of town overnight, "It used to be easy to trust her, but not anymore"?) But Penelhum's account appears not to have room for any such thing. It is tempting to suppose that this is because his term "implicit trust" has been misapplied. A third fact to take note of is the connection between trust and vulnerability. As Penelhum himself admits, the one who trusts implicitly makes herself vulnerable in the presence of the trusted one, putting up no defense against the trusted one, looking for no protection from him, dealing with him unreservedly.[12] Notice that we say not only that the individual's trust makes her vulnerable—which might suggest that the vulnerability is caused by some belief or feeling state of hers—but that in trusting she *makes herself* vulnerable. The vulnerability in question is entailed by the trust and tends to be expressed in action (even the omissions I have referred to can be counted here, since omissions are but a subclass of actions).

So is there a better way of carving up the relevant conceptual terrain that accommodates such points while also taking account of the differences that Penelhum has drawn to our attention? I think there is. Part of this approach we have already seen. Let me clarify that part now and then develop the view a bit further.

The first thing to observe is that when trusting someone is difficult, we speak of *choosing* to trust ("I didn't want to trust her, but I had no other choice") and so take notice of the action involved. At other times we have no sense of difficulty, and then it is possible to infer that no disposition to act need be involved, and to focus instead on the positive emotional state that may seem to account for the absence of a sense of difficulty. But this is a mistake. What we need to recognize is that in the latter sort of case the lack of difficulty is due not to the absence of any disposition to act but to the *easiness of the action* (which may of course itself in some way be causally linked to an emotional state). Actions that are easy to do are still actions.

To spell out this idea more clearly, I need to underline the fact that it is indeed an action *disposition* to which I have been referring. Strictly speaking, to trust someone is not to act in the relevant manner—the manner I have been mentioning—but to be disposed to do so. For I may speak the truth when I say of my partner that she trusts me even if she is at present engaged in activities that have nothing to do with me (or asleep), just as I may speak the truth when I attribute to her certain beliefs that are not now activated. What I mean in both cases is that she possesses a certain disposition, which is the sort of thing that may at any given time be either activated or unactivated.

With this distinction between actions and the dispositions they may express more clearly exposed, we can make some headway. Let us look at the various possibilities. Persons often do use expressions of the form "A trusts B" (including such as are in the first person, "*I* trust so-and-so") when it is evident that A is not then acting toward B in the relevant way—so the reference cannot be to an action. But what is meant in such cases is not the very different point that A has certain feelings in relation to B;

[12] Ibid., p. 73.

rather it is that A is *disposed* to perform the relevant actions in the appropriate circumstances. Sometimes the expression used is "A trusts B implicitly"; what is then meant is that A is *naturally* disposed to perform those actions, finding them easy, performing them without worry, hesitation, or questioning whenever the situation is right, without even consciously reflecting on the belief involved. A disposition of this sort we might want to call a *strong* trusting disposition. But notice that it is not the only one: someone who performs the appropriate actions unhesitatingly and without question may be said to have a strong trusting disposition whether what she did was easy, unreflective, and unaccompanied by negative emotion or not. (Thus when it is said that A's trust in B is strong, only the context can help us decide whether A trusts B implicitly or not.)

Now sometimes the expression used is instead the distinctive first-person "I *will* trust so-and-so." Here we see a reference to one's own intention to do an action which, if it is done, *activates* the disposition in question; if I do the action I refer to, I trust (as we might say) occurrently.[13] When one uses the expression "I *will* trust," one is consciously reflecting on what one is doing. It is more likely to be used where, perhaps because of worries of the sort mentioned by Penelhum, trusting is difficult. In cases where both these conditions are satisfied we have what Penelhum calls *explicit* trust (here one has to work to maintain the relevant disposition). Finally, where the difficulty of trusting is accompanied by some hesitation, questioning, and perhaps occasional or fairly frequent failure, we may say of the disposition in question that it is *weak*.

This seems to account for everything that needs accounting for here: the whole gamut of trusting states, from strong to weak, is represented. Moreover, it seems straightforwardly applicable to the religious case of trust in God. One who trusts in God is, in one of these ways, disposed to act upon a belief or faith that God will be or do for her what she needs or wants, even though, given her evidence, there is a chance (not necessarily one she has reflected upon) that the latter proposition is false, and even though there will be bad consequences if it is.[14] That is, she is disposed to perform those actions she sees as appropriate to the truth of the proposition in question, given her purposes and (the rest of) her worldview. This trust may be reflective or unreflective, conscious or unconscious, troubled or relatively untroubled, difficult or easy, implicit or explicit, weak or strong, and distinctions may accordingly be drawn.

---

[13] Similar points apply to the common "You can trust him [or her]."

[14] For simplicity's sake, the chance of falsity and its bad consequences will not be mentioned in all future references to trust, but such a reference should always be understood as tacitly present.

But there is no distinction between trust that involves an action disposition and trust that does not.

Perhaps a defender of Penelhum would insist that my account still leaves room for trust as a certain feeling state (lack of anxiety, or serenity) existing *over and above* the forms of trust I have identified. Maybe Rubin "Hurricane" Carter, the African American boxer wrongfully convicted of murder, who said of the Canadian activists who helped secure his release from prison and befriended him that for the first time in 40 years he *trusted* someone, serves as an example of this sort of trust.[15] It certainly seems that Carter was here referring simply to a more settled emotional state, free of anxiety over what might follow personal contact and interaction. And what about Jesus, who (as Penelhum notes) tells his disciples that their anxieties show they do not trust God adequately?[16] We certainly seem to be told here that a state in which one is *free* from worry is a state in which one trusts God.

I suggest, however, that such examples do not show what they are often taken to show. Trust, on my account, is constituted by a disposition to act on one's belief or faith that a certain proposition reports what is the case. Given the sort of content we have seen the latter proposition to have (especially in the religious case, which has a much broader scope and more thoroughgoing application, in matters of life and of death), it is easy to imagine that worry or anxiety of a certain sort might function as an *obstacle* to the development or maintenance of such a disposition—perhaps an obstacle that needs to be removed or managed before one can truly be said to possess that disposition, or to possess it fully or strongly. (And perhaps, as earlier suggested, to the extent that this obstacle is removed and not just managed, one may be caused to trust more implicitly.) Jesus can—quite naturally, I think—be seen as making just this point. The trust he asks of his disciples, when implemented, involves stepping out, "setting one's face toward Jerusalem," acting in ways that will speed the coming of God's kingdom—yet here they are, sitting around worrying, letting *that* rule their lives. They need to deal with their anxieties so that they will more readily do the actions involved in trust.[17]

---

[15] From a CBC television broadcast, February 4, 2000.

[16] Penelhum, *Reason and Religious Faith*, p. 68. (The relevant New Testament passage is in Matthew 7.)

[17] It may be useful to consider also the famous story in Matthew 14 of Peter walking on the water to meet Jesus and then sinking into it when his trust fails. Peter goes from acting *on* his confident belief that he will be safe, to thinking (and worrying) *about* it. This thinking and worrying—what Jesus in the story calls doubting—causes him to stop acting on his belief and undermines his implicit trust. It does not follow that it was in *not* worrying that he earlier *had* trust.

Notice: on this view one seeks to trade inaction or weak trust not for a purely affective state, serenity, but for a condition in which one's disposition to act on what one supposes to be true of God is *stronger*. One may find a measure of serenity along the way, and this affective state may be causally related to the achievement of one's goal, but it is not itself the goal. Indeed, one may need to get along without it: a *will* firmly set on trusting God may be as important here as serenity, as suggested by Jesus in the same passage when he emphasizes "seeking first the kingdom of God." Jesus seems most concerned about what we might call *religiously debilitating* anxiety, and it is not clear that all anxiety deserves this label. For I may be quite anxious in a situation calling for faith and yet act unhesitatingly in the appropriate manner, thus manifesting a strong trust—it is just *harder* to act under such circumstances than when anxiety is completely absent.[18]

As for the Hurricane: here too we must beware of confusion resulting from an emphasis on the removal and replacement of what may *obstruct or impede* the disposition to act in trusting ways. Where there have been such obstacles, it may be tempting to think of trust as constituted by their removal, together with the setting in place of contrary attitudes. But such thinking is mistaken, for among the various obstacles that may stand in the way of trust, anxiety is but one. In the Hurricane case the relevant obstacle seems to have been more a matter of suspicion than of anxiety as such. Are we to suppose, then, that the Hurricane's trust amounted to freedom from suspicion instead of freedom from anxiety? Surely not. It is a mistake to view either of these states as a form of trust. They simply represent possible stepping-stones along the way to trust. (And the stepping-stones may not be expected to be exactly the same in every case.) The Hurricane really trusted his supporters only when, suspicion erased, he found himself disposed to interact with them in positive ways. Had he not been so disposed, his statement would have been based on either confusion or a lie.

A stronger argument for the claim under consideration—that over and above the forms of trust I have identified there is the form represented by lack of anxiety or serenity as such—is one that reminds us of certain common expressions we may not yet seem to have accounted for. When, for example, a mother says of her teenage daughter, "I can't trust her anymore," or "She betrayed my trust," she seems clearly to be referring to

---

[18] Consider, for example, an individual, temperamentally disposed to be anxious, who worries upon leaving his car whether he really locked it or whether he left the lights on. Such a person may often go back and check, but he needn't do so: he may train himself to walk briskly in the direction of his goal despite the anxiety—that is, he may train himself to *trust* in himself!

some involuntary feeling state that she once had but now has lost. Is this not precisely the state to which Penelhum refers?

We need to remember, however, that one's trust is removed whenever some condition causally necessary for it is removed. And if the mother's trust has been implicit, consisting in a natural and unhesitating disposition to allow her daughter certain privileges, grounded in the largely unconscious and of course involuntary belief that she will be responsible and not upset the life of the household, then her trust will be removed as soon as the belief just mentioned is undermined by her daughter's unexpected use of drugs or stealing or whatever. And then indeed she will say, upset over what has taken place and *referring to the trust she had,* that she cannot trust the girl anymore, or that her trust has been broken. Strictly speaking, it is not true that she *cannot* trust her; rather, she cannot trust her *in the way she did before*; though it might be foolish, it is at any rate possible for the mother consciously and explicitly to adopt a *policy* of trusting her daughter.

Is it then no longer a disposition to act in a certain way that we are seeing here? I do not see why we should say so. It is only the (mistaken) assumption that a *natural* disposition exhausts the relevant possibilities that may lead us to do so. Clearly, the mother's natural disposition, which operated smoothly and spontaneously, is gone, but it does not follow that there can be no disposition here at all. Since the mother, if her policy of trusting her daughter is successfully adopted, will tend to act in all relevant circumstances as she did act when she believed and trusted implicitly, we may surely say of her that she is disposed to act in that way; it is just that now the disposition has a different cause: namely, the adoption of the aforementioned policy and the cultivation of trust as a habit instead of the good track record or parental affection that caused the disposition as originally instantiated. (And of course the disposition and the causal story appropriate to it may be affected over time by the daughter's improved behavior.) I suggest, therefore, that the analysis of trust we have developed is quite capable of handling the apparent anomaly suggested by the present objection.

I have spent some time defending the important notion that trust and a disposition to act in certain ways are necessarily linked. But what about my other claim—that the serenity emphasized by Penelhum does not represent the "ideal of faith"? Now it might seem that if serenity is to be distinguished conceptually from trust, it can hardly be part of faith, let alone its ideal form. But remember that what falls under the category of faith-in is not entirely clear. Although trust is primary, perhaps other elements belong there too. More to the point, perhaps *serenity* belongs there. If so, serenity could perhaps be the ideal of faith without being the ideal of trust.

Reflection, however, suggests otherwise. Why? Well, complete serenity would seem to come only when the goals of religion are achieved. Faith sets one upon a religious way and keeps one there, we have said. One who attains serenity (or at least complete serenity) would seem to have arrived at its destination. Even Jesus of Nazareth, who, as Penelhum shows, seems opposed to anxiety (or at least religiously debilitating anxiety), was not always serene. The ideal of faith, as realized by Jesus of Nazareth, might rather be seen in his submission to crucifixion, despite considerable anxiety ("Let this cup pass from me"). The serene Jesus is the *ascended* Jesus, "seated on the right hand of God." Now this does not mean that serenity is not a proper goal of the religious; Penelhum rightly associates it with complete liberation. But that is just the point. When complete serenity and liberation have arrived, we walk no longer by faith but by sight. Perhaps in moments of intense religious experience—as also suggested by the life of Jesus—one may approach that serenity, but so long as faith is required, it would seem of necessity to some degree elusive.[19] We should say then that serenity is a *goal* of religious faith, though not its ideal *form*.

Such a conclusion ties in with the fact, yet to be more fully defended as such, that faith (whether imperfect or ideal) is voluntary. On this there is a great deal of agreement. We are asked to *put* our faith in God, to *have* faith in God. (The imperative seems typically directed either to those who have not yet undertaken such a commitment or to those who need to take steps to prevent or halt its derogation.) This sounds like something one must *do*, and something pretty much *anyone* can do. But serenity is not like that: it is not something almost anyone can achieve just by trying to. Some are fortunate enough to experience it; others hardly ever do, despite their best efforts. No doubt one can do various things to remove obstacles to serenity, but that is another matter. We are not asked to remove obstacles to faith but to *have* faith. Now if faith in God is a matter of taking certain claims concerning God and God's will toward me as guides for my behavior (and thus becoming disposed to act thereupon in appropriate circumstances), this makes sense, for then faith is up to me. It does not seem to make sense if an emotional component is essential to faith.

Here we might add a related point: if an emotional component consisting in serenity or freedom from anxiety is essential to faith-in, then whether you have faith of this sort or not is at least in part a function of

---

[19] In part, this is so because to trust God must always be radically different from trusting a fellow human being. In the latter case I may have no anxieties at all, since matters of life and death are probably not at issue or in the balance. But trusting God involves being disposed to act on the belief or faith that God will take care of us in life's most difficult moments and also at its end. Here complete serenity is rarely forthcoming, or even psychologically possible.

the type of *personality* you possess (for clearly some personality types are much more given to anxiety than others). But this seems wrong: the idea that faith is in any way dependent on involuntarily acquired tendencies of the sort we use the label "personality" to cover (e.g., a tendency to be introverted instead of extroverted) is highly counterintuitive. In the same connection we might note again that faith is supposed to be something one can acquire just by trying to, in order—among other things—to help one *deal* with the troubling issues of life, including issues with which one is presented by one's personality quirks. This, needless to say, faith could not be if it depended on *not possessing* such quirks.[20]

3. *Is Trust Present in All Forms of Religion?*

We have been talking a lot about God. Let us now consider this question: Can the notion of trust we have been developing properly be extended to all forms of religion, including nontheistic ones? A tempting argument for a negative answer runs like this: religious trust requires a personal object; the object of ultimate concern in some forms of religion is not personal; therefore, religious trust is not to be found in all forms of religion. There are problems with this argument's first premise, and the conclusion does not follow.[21] But let us focus on the problem premise, as it seems simply to declare a prejudice in favor of personal objects of trust. Now perhaps it will be said that the ultimate reality must be thought of as capable of *doing* this or that before trust can be placed in it: when one trusts, one is disposed to act on one's belief or faith that the object of trust will do something for one; and only personal beings are capable of doing something in this sense, of performing actions. But this view is overly narrow—and that is indeed why I earlier spoke in terms of the object of trust being *or* doing what one needs or wants. Clearly, I put my trust in nonpersonal objects incapable of action all the time, as, for example, when I trust a rope to hold me as I swing across a ravine. Why then should the religious person not place her trust in the ultimate even when it is construed nonpersonally? In both cases, what one is doing is

---

[20] This last point suggests that at least some degree of serenity or some lessening of anxiety might be expected to be an *effect* of successfully having faith. But what faith causes and what faith *is* are different matters. (I am grateful to Daniel Howard-Snyder for helping me see more clearly the point about faith's effects.)

[21] The conclusion fails to follow because in certain nontheistic forms of religion the ultimate is thought of as in some sense *mediated* by personal beings, and so there is the possibility of reposing one's trust in one or another of these beings as a *way* of relating to the (nonpersonal) ultimate.

choosing to act on the belief or faith that the object of trust has the character, the nature, required to satisfy one's needs. But, it may be said, trust makes no sense unless the object of trust may decide *not* to be or do what one needs or wants. The rope example is again a counterexample here. What ought to be said is more general: trust makes no sense unless the proposition believed, or with respect to which one has faith, could be false. And this phrasing accommodates both agents not doing the actions anticipated and nonpersonal objects not having the character ascribed to them.

Someone supporting a negative answer to our question may now change tack and argue as follows: "For the ultimate in nontheistic forms of religion to be the object of trust, it must at the very least be thought of as the *cause* of any transformation of life and character that is attendant upon pursuit of the religious way. (After all, in theistic forms of religion salvation is construed as a *gift*, and one relies upon God to give it; we need some analogue for this in nontheistic religion before it makes sense to say that trust is to be found there too.) If this condition is satisfied, then we can say that the religious person trusts in the ultimate, being disposed to act on the belief or faith that the anticipated results of pursuing the religious way will indeed be forthcoming. The trouble is that in nontheistic forms of religion it is typically not the *ultimate* that is thought of as the cause of salvation or liberation but *one's own action* in uncovering the true self (or perhaps the truth that there is no self) beneath the distracting and misleading appearances generated by confusion and egocentricity. Therefore, the aforementioned condition is not satisfied, and so the ultimate in nontheistic religion is not properly construed as an object of trust."[22]

Difficult questions of interpretation lurk here, with regard to both the nature of nontheistic religion and the language of causation. But the argument can be answered without going far into these. First, it is not obvious that there is nothing corresponding to the theistic mystery of freedom and grace in nontheistic religion. Even for those religious persons who do not hold that there is a personal God to rely upon, there is the experience of gift—by which I mean the sudden experience of insight or transforming power that comes in the midst of religious practice, for which the recipient feels profoundly grateful. And one may surely come to *trust* in the source of such religious sustenance, associating it with the ultimate reality to which one's practice is directed—perhaps even if that is a reality about whose detailed nature one would be prepared to say very

---

[22] Such an argument is suggested by a passage in Penelhum, *Reason and Religious Faith,* pp. 127–128 (and the barest hint of the previous argument is to be found on p. 33.)

little. (It should be noted, in this connection, that we must beware of the fallacy of inferring from the fact that the ultimate is not taken to be personal that it is taken to be *non*personal. It is also possible for religious nontheists to rest in ignorance here, holding neither that the ultimate is personal *nor* that it is nonpersonal.)

Another reply begins from the fact that whatever may be said of trust in the transcendent, religious nontheists clearly place their trust in the religious way. Just as one may trust a rope to take one to the far side of a ravine, so the monistic Hindu or nontheistic Buddhist trusts in the religious form of life in which he participates to take him to the luminous awareness that Atman is Brahman or to the realization of his Buddha-nature. So it is misleading to say that one's own action and a sort of self-reliance is the sole focus in nontheistic religion. One must walk, it is true, but first there must be a path to walk upon, and one who walks upon a religious path puts his trust in it; he is disposed to act on the faith or belief that it will be for him what he needs or wants it to be: namely, a way to liberation.

Now, having achieved this recognition, we may move on to the realization that trust in an ultimate reality is hidden in this trust in the religious way. For a religious person cannot suppose that a certain religious path will lead to liberation without supposing the ultimate reality associated with that path to exist and to have a character *conducive* to such liberation, and any action suggested by the former proposition is obviously appropriate only given the truth of the latter. Hence, in acting on the former supposition one necessarily acts on the latter as well. But what is it to act on the second way here if not to place one's trust in the ultimate, to act in the belief or faith that it will be for one what one needs or wants, that it has the relevant character? Trusting the religious way, therefore, necessarily involves trusting the ultimate to have that character.

Consider again the rope. Suppose you are swinging across the ravine because you have heard that on the far side is a magical kingdom in which your pursuers will be changed and become your friends. You are trusting the rope to provide a means of salvation, but you would not do so if you did not suppose there to be a magical kingdom on the other side, with the character you have been led to believe it has. So in acting on the belief or faith that the rope will take you to salvation, you are acting as well on the belief or faith that what you encounter on the other side will be for you what you need it to be. You trust both the rope and the kingdom. Notice: this is so even if you have in your head no thought of a magician or king on the other side who will personally see to it that your needs are met; despite our proclivity for associating magical kingdoms with magicians or kings, there is no reason to suppose that a magical kingdom needs such individuals to be capable of functioning as the source of well-being or as a worthy object of trust.

I conclude, therefore, that trust of the relevant sort must be present in all forms of religion. Whenever the religious person acts in pursuit of a religious way, she necessarily trusts in the ultimate reality she associates with its destination, whether that reality be construed personally or not. For her action manifests a disposition to act on the belief or faith that the ultimate exists and has the character presupposed by success in the religious way. Call any such action in pursuit of a religious way—whether it involves loving concern for the needs of others, prayer, meditation, or whatever—a *religious action*. Then we may say that any religious action manifests or expresses trust in the ultimate.

A couple of distinctions do seem called for here, but they do not undermine the account. First, although all religious actions express trust in the ultimate, sometimes the religious person may express trust in the ultimate more *directly*, by acting more directly on the belief or faith that it will be or do for her what she needs or wants (the story of Abraham leaving his comfortable home in response to what he perceived as God's call comes to mind here).[23] But such actions are religious actions too, so in linking trust to religious action we do not leave them out. We might also wish to distinguish actions that set one on a religious way—one's initial commitment—from other actions taken *along* the way. Although in the former case one often more explicitly decides what the direction of one's life will be by, for example, consciously putting one's life into God's hands (perhaps for the first time), there is no reason, given our analysis, to consider this any more a case of trusting than some case of directly or indirectly acting on the relevant belief or faith in the days that follow. For in both sorts of case one is disposed to act on the belief or faith that God will be or do for one what one needs or wants, when this may (regrettably) not be the case.

4. *Trust and the Nature of Faith*

If such trust as we have analyzed were not just necessary (as we saw earlier) but also sufficient for faith-in, it would follow from my account that any religious action whatever instantiates faith in the ultimate. I want now to suggest that it is sufficient. Ordinary language strongly suggests the

---

[23] The relevant notion of "directness" can perhaps be explicated in terms of how central the proposition in question is to the theoretical or practical inference on which the action is based. Is it a main premise, maybe the only premise consciously considered, or perhaps a distant presupposition that one would list among one's premises only if one were giving a fully detailed and thorough account of the reasoning behind the inference?

appropriateness of saying of anyone who trusts in God, for example, that he has *faith* in God: the two notions seem coextensive. It may be argued, however, that religious love—specifically, emotional attraction and attachment to the ultimate—is entailed by the latter but not by the former. Faith in God may be said to involve not just trust in God but love of God; the one who has faith in God finds in God a beauty far exceeding that of any earthly thing and is emotionally drawn to religion as a result. Yet this seems mistaken, for though the state of mind in question may often be possessed by one who has faith in God, it is not *entailed* by such faith. One might, for example, recognizing at some level the importance of honoring God above all else, place one's faith in God by taking small steps along a religious way, aiming to generate, among other things, precisely this emotional love one knows it is appropriate to have but finds one lacks. I am not saying that this is a common or desirable state for the religious person to be in, even at the beginning of a journey of faith, but it does seem possible—in which case, love of the sort in question is not conceptually linked to faith.[24]

I conclude that trust of the sort we have been discussing *is* both necessary and sufficient for the faith we have been calling faith-in, and that the latter is accordingly to be understood as a disposition to act on the belief or faith that the ultimate will be or do for one what one needs or wants—even when on one's evidence there is some chance (whether consciously recognized or not) that this will not be so and when bad consequences are to be expected if it is not so. More formally, we may say that "S exemplifies religious faith-in" or, in other words, "S has faith in *x* (a putative ultimate and salvific reality)" is equivalent in meaning to the conjunction of the following propositions:

(1) S believes or has faith that *p* (where *p* is the religious proposition that *x*—a putative ultimate and salvific reality—will be or do for S what S needs or wants).

(2) S lacks evidence rendering *p* certain.

(3) If S is disposed to act on her belief or faith that *p*, and *p* is false, S will suffer bad consequences.

(4) S is disposed to act (directly or indirectly) on this belief or faith: that is, to do what seems appropriate to the truth of *p*, given S's other purposes and the rest of S's worldview.

Because of the connection between religious propositions and religious practice (see Chapter 3, section 1) and also what must, given our purposes

---

[24] See also n. 4 of this chapter.

(including those generated by self-interest), seem appropriate to the truth of the religious proposition here mentioned, it follows that what such faith amounts to is a disposition to *act religiously:* one's faith in the ultimate may be said to be defined by the extent of one's religious actions and disposition to perform them. This leads to another interesting result. Though faith-in is not the whole of just any religious life—since its defining features do not include what religion typically does include: namely, emotional dispositions—it does seem to embody precisely what is referred to by the *definition* of "religion." That is, given the two definitions, anyone who has religious faith-in can be called religious, and anyone who is religious has religious faith-in. The *conceptual* connection between religion and religious faith-in is thus a very tight one—indeed, the two notions are logically equivalent.[25]

5. *Faith: Propositional and Operational*

Our discussion has taken many twists and turns. It is now time to draw together its various threads and clarify our conclusions. Faith, as we have seen, can be detected in all religion: when it takes the form of faith-that, it involves some sort of positive attitude toward religious propositions (the nature of which we have not yet discussed), and when faith-in, some sort of positive response to the ultimate reality of which those propositions speak. That response we have found to amount to trust, which consists in a disposition to act (directly or indirectly) on the proposition that the ultimate will be or do for one what one needs or wants when, given one's evidence, there is a chance that this will not be so, and when there will be bad consequences if it is not so—which is to say, a disposition to perform religious actions. Because of the fact that such trust may be indirectly

---

[25] For some, the notion of faith-in I have here developed may still seem unduly barren of positive feelings or emotions directed toward the ultimate. I recognize that such feelings are common among those who possess faith-in, but I have nonetheless excluded them from my definition for reasons similar to those considered in relation to the definition of religion (see Chapter 1, section 5, elucidatory remark (ix)) and in relation to the differences between faith and hope (see Chapter 6, section 2). In brief, what is driving me here is the need to maximize *inclusiveness,* in line with the connection between faith and voluntariness (in particular, accessibility—more on that in the next chapter), and also the need in a definition like this to cover not just how things *are* but all the relevant *possibilities.* In any case, the reader should not forget that given the content of the proposition p mentioned in the definition of "faith-in" (and also the conceptual connection between faith-that and positive evaluation, discussed in the next chapter), someone—anyone—who believes or has faith that p must see what it refers to (and, indirectly, must see x) as good and so cannot fail to evince at least *that* laudatory attitude in exemplifying faith-in.

manifested, propositions other than the one just mentioned may come into play. Indeed, if I am correct, then *whenever* one acts on a religious proposition and one's action is a religious action, one may be said to be expressing religious trust, either directly or indirectly.[26]

Now without prejudicing the discussion of the next chapter, we can say that sometimes the propositional attitude in which such trust is grounded is belief. (Clearly, religious people are often believers.) An example of what I am talking about is provided by the sort of implicit trust one can encounter any Sunday just by walking into a Christian church: a natural disposition to act on the proposition that God exists and cares for us, grounded in unquestioned belief of that proposition. In such cases, what we have is faith only because trust is *added* to belief; belief by itself is not sufficient. But as we will see, the propositional attitude may also be something other than belief, in which case it constitutes a form of faith in its own right, capable of existing independently of the faith that consists in trust and deserving its own name. Here we bump into what philosophers call *propositional* faith, and I suggest that we choose a name for the faith that is trust that can parallel the label "propositional faith" (doing so will permit us to avoid cumbersome or awkward expressions such as "faith-in," or "the faith that is trust"). Because such faith involves acting on religious propositions in pursuit of a religious way, and thus, as it were, "operationalizing" them, I propose "operational faith." So we have propositional faith and operational faith. The latter, I hope, is better understood after this chapter (though, of course, the matter of its compatibility with non-belief has yet to be more fully addressed). The former is the main concern of my next chapter.

---

[26] Notice that not just *any* case of acting on a religious proposition is a religious action, for one's action might (through some weird circumstance of misunderstanding or perversion) not occur in pursuit of a religious way.

On Religious Faith (II)

The central idea of this chapter is that of religious faith without propositional religious belief. Let it be emphasized immediately that in supporting this idea I am not arguing that someone could have religious faith without any beliefs whatever, or that there are no particular beliefs (concerning value, say) that are necessarily possessed by one who has faith, but only that it is possible to have such faith without *religious* belief. Even so, the claim is a strong one and may seem radical. To see why, we need only recall my comments at the beginning of the previous chapter concerning the sort of career that "faith" has had in philosophy. Most philosophers assume that religious faith *is* religious belief—or, at the very least, that it entails such belief. But this assumption, as we are about to see, is mistaken. (Having to some extent prepared the ground for this claim in previous chapters, I am now prepared to plant it firmly in the minds of my readers.) Religious belief is indeed commonly a *part* of religious *operational* faith, as actually exemplified, and where this is so, philosophical assessments of faith which assume that it entails belief are at least relevant. But that this is so is a contingent fact: neither the operational faith you need to get going on a religious way nor even the ideal form of such faith entails belief.

Now it is true that *some* sort of positive propositional attitude is entailed, but when this notion and its relation to faith are more carefully scrutinized, it turns out that belief is not the only thing that can fill the bill. The "something else" that can fill the bill, far from being or entailing belief, is *incompatible* with it and, unlike belief, capable of being voluntarily adopted. When it occurs as part of operational faith, one does not find a complex consisting of propositional belief plus trust. Rather one finds a

voluntary attitude of assent to a religious proposition or religious propositions, undertaken in certain special circumstances (propositional faith),
and a commitment and consequent disposition to act on this assent in
pursuit of a religious way (operational faith). Since the voluntary assent
is—given the proper circumstances—a form of faith in its own right,
those many philosophers across the centuries who have considered there
to be a purely propositional form of faith not necessarily linked to operational faith turn out to be correct. But in the pet saying of a friend of
mine, this is "more by luck than by good management," since they have
almost always confused propositional faith with propositional belief—seeing operational faith as actually exemplified in Christianity, say, and looking just long enough to observe what is of interest to them: namely, the
curiously unquestioned *belief* that is so commonly a part of it. In my view,
indeed, there has been a lot of confusion in philosophical discussions of
faith, and it is time to seek a more adequate account.

But how are these claims and my alternative construal of faith to be
defended? Well, we can identify three plausible criteria against which
interpretations of the nature of faith can be assessed—criteria that are
satisfied by my account, and (so I will show) better satisfied by it than by
any account suggesting that faith is or entails a species of belief. They are
the following: (1) an account of the term "faith" should make sense of, fit
with, or accommodate the broad patterns (and, where possible, the
details) of that term's ordinary usage; (2) an account of "faith" should
preserve in as robust a form as possible the notion that faith is voluntary
and potentially meritorious (this follows from the previous criterion,
given what ordinary usage actually suggests, but as we will see, it is also
independently warranted); (3) an account of "faith" should be religiously
and philosophically illuminating and fruitful—that is, it should cohere
with much else that we are inclined to say in philosophy of religion and
help to clear up puzzling matters in this discipline, and it should also take
our thinking about philosophy of religion further in interesting and
important ways.

Now the third criterion is one that could be fully applied to the
account of faith I am developing only after (inter alia) proper discussion
of the justification of faith and the implications of conclusions drawn with
respect to that—and I am not developing such a discussion in this book
(though some clues as to how it might go appear here and there). The
other two criteria, which were already to some extent influencing my
thinking in the previous chapter, receive more explicit attention in this
one. I begin by fleshing out the view sketched above, drawing on certain
facts concerning the contours of "faith" and of related terms, especially as
they occur in nonreligious contexts, applying as I go some of the results

of our own earlier discussion and comparing what emerges with the views of certain others who have been moving in a similar direction. Then I give more specific attention to how the language of faith is ordinarily used in religious contexts, arguing that religious forms of speech call for my view and that the universal emphasis on the voluntariness of faith is especially confirming. Finally, I consider various objections to my account. In answering them, I am particularly concerned to demonstrate what I call the religious integrity or authenticity of beliefless faith.[1]

1. *Propositional Faith as a Nonbelieving State*

Here I want first to describe in some detail, and with examples, my view of *propositional* faith—faith that *p*. Much of what is new in my account of religious faith hinges on this notion. Since in some respects it is also an elusive notion, it will be good to get as clear about it as we can, right away. To that end let me exhibit, using examples, the typical path from a faith-less state of mind to faith that *p*. By identifying the steps involved, we will permit all the essential elements of the latter state of mind to become visible.

So think of a runner who is considering whether he will do well in the important race that is about to begin. Loosening up and stretching behind the starting line, he broods about how on this day of all days his condition is not exactly favorable to success, because of various physical ailments. Going over the relevant evidence, which at first he is inclined to read very negatively, he notices that it does not *establish* that he must fail;

---

[1] That religious faith can be beliefless (in my sense of "beliefless") has been suggested by others. See F. R. Tennant, *The Nature of Belief* (London: Centenary Press, 1943), p. 78; H. H. Price, *Belief* (New York: Allen & Unwin, 1969), pp. 484–485; James L. Muyskens, *The Sufficiency of Hope* (Philadelphia: Temple University Press, 1979); Richard Swinburne, *Faith and Reason* (Oxford: Clarendon Press, 1981), pp.115–117; Louis P. Pojman, *Religious Belief and the Will* (London: Routledge & Kegan Paul, 1986); Joshua Golding, "Toward a Pragmatist Conception of Religious Faith," *Faith and Philosophy* 7 (1990): 486–503; Robert Audi, "Faith, Belief, and Rationality," in *Philosophical Perspectives*, vol. 5, ed. James E. Tomberlin (Atascadero, CA: Ridgeview, 1991); William Ladd Sessions, *The Concept of Faith* (Ithaca: Cornell University Press, 1994); William Alston, "Belief, Acceptance, and Religious Faith," in *Faith, Freedom, and Rationality*, ed. Jeff Jordan and Daniel Howard-Snyder (Lanham, MD: Rowman & Littlefield, 1996); and Peter Byrne, *The Moral Interpretation of Religion* (Grand Rapids, MI: Wm. B. Eerdmans, 1998), pp. 67–68. Nevertheless, it is hard to find a thorough development of the view. And in what is said there is no clear mention of the idea that propositional faith is incompatible with belief (suggestions in Tennant compatible with the incompatibility view are not developed). Moreover, no one distinguishes the state involving voluntary assent and that involving *action upon* one's voluntary assent as separate forms of beliefless faith.

on at least some occasions in the past he has done well when feeling *un*well, and he knows of a few other runners who have also clocked good times in such adverse conditions. But all in all the evidence on which he reflects still is insufficient to cause in him the *belief* that he will do well; it takes him from disbelief to doubt but no further. At this point he realizes that he will have to do something about his frame of mind if he is to have any chance of beating the odds. Winning the race, or at least placing in the top three, would obviously be a good thing; so he tells himself to contemplate that good thing for a bit. As he focuses his attention on it, the unsettling feelings associated with his doubt recede to the background; there is no longer room for them at the forefront of his consciousness. Keeping that picture before his mind as he positions himself with the other runners, he mentally affirms over and over that it corresponds to the way things are: "Yes, I will do well, yes, I will do well. . . ." This pushes him forward into a new place, mentally speaking, one in which his doubt remains—after all, he has no new evidence and would, if he were asked, give the same assessment of the old—but in which it is overlaid by an attitude of a very different kind toward the proposition that he will do well.

Here is another example. Suppose that my assistant, many miles away, and inaccessible to me for the time being, has assured me by telephone that he will remember to complete a certain important task later that day. He has sometimes forgotten this sort of thing before, so I don't really believe that he will do it, though not quite disbelieving it either. After hours of worry it occurs to me that this is a waste of mental energy, and that I should just go with the idea that he will complete the task as I want him to. So I imagine that he is preparing to do it, and doing it successfully, just as he said he would. Focusing on this picture and affirming to myself as often as needed that he will complete the task, I am, while still nonbelieving, moved to a new mental place where my worries dissipate and I am able to get on with other things.

A third example. My wife's friend is in New York on September 11, 2001, with plans to attend a meeting at the World Trade Center that morning. After the terrorist attacks my wife is naturally very concerned about her friend's safety. One or two mutual acquaintances in New York whom she manages to contact say that her friend had a last-minute change of plans; others are not so sure. Altogether it is far from obvious that she has escaped harm. But realizing that there is nothing she can do but wait for the smoke and the evidence to clear, my wife decides to clear her mind by doing yoga and focusing on the idea that her friend has indeed escaped harm. She knows this may well not be the case but replaces her conscious attention to that fact with a visualization of the brighter possibility and a mental affirmation of what it contains: "So be it, so be it. . . ." And after leaving the yoga mat and moving on to the tasks of the day, she still works at sustaining her new attitude through periodic reminders to herself of the stance she has taken up.

One final example. A young woman abused as a child is in therapy after pressure from friends and family, who find her low self-esteem and rather dark view of human nature oppressive. In discussions with her therapist she is able to produce long lists of what she takes to be facts supporting the position that she is bereft of value and that human nature in general is irredeemably bad. Clearly, these are things she confidently believes. Over a considerable period of time the therapist—with (among other things) his own unwavering kindness and sensible good cheer—is able to make a few dents in the crusty exterior of his client and in her confident pessimism, and at a favorable moment he insinuates the suggestion that the young woman use her imagination to represent the world to herself less pessimistically still so as to open herself to any further evidence there may be for an optimistic position. After all, he continues, there is at least a possibility that the pessimistic view is mistaken, and that would certainly be a good thing! This practice would have to be a serious commitment, he reminds her, and no superficial experiment, but the value that might be achieved thereby is worthy of such a commitment. The young woman, thus persuaded to give a more positive view of the world a chance, with her therapist's support moves from faltering beginnings to a place where, when the still dark view to which she is more naturally disposed comes to mind, she is able to avoid endorsing it, instead presenting herself with the alternative that she is okay and that human nature is basically good. By mentally endorsing *that* view, she becomes more open to evidence supporting it in her environment. And although her therapist never learns of her moving all the way to belief of this proposition, her new disposition in connection with it is fairly well entrenched by the time she leaves his care.

Now what I am inclined to say about these examples is that they are very naturally described as representing cases where someone has propositional *faith*. The runner, in the face of doubt, has chosen to have faith that he will do well; I respond to my worries about my assistant by having faith that he will complete the important task; my wife decides to have faith that her friend has escaped harm in New York; the pessimistic client, after much nurturing and through considerable effort, manages to have faith that she is really okay and that human nature is basically good. Notice that the third and fourth examples show that descriptions of states of affairs with respect to which one might have faith will not always be phrased in the future tense but may also be phrased in the present or even the past tense. We might further notice that faith may represent either a short-term response to exigency or a more ongoing disposition, as in the fourth case. But either way, what we see is not just a single action or a few but rather an action *policy* of a certain kind. And as the fourth case also suggests, not only doubt with respect to a proposition but even disbelief is compatible with having faith that the state of affairs to which it refers obtains (though completely confident disbelief might make such faith psychologically impossible).

There are many other conceivable cases of propositional faith: I might have faith that I put enough money in the parking meter, faith that I will pass a course, faith that I have right now the *ability* to pass the course, faith—after societal collapse—that a new and better government is forming, faith that I will get a job, faith that the individual for whom I am campaigning will win the election, faith that someone will discover and prove the falsity of a murder charge on account of which I lie rotting in jail, faith that poverty will be wiped out or that democracy will spread throughout the world or that my friend is not the criminal that some pretty striking evidence suggests he is, and so on and so on. And, of course, I might also have faith that God exists or that the Buddha told the truth about enlightenment, or that there is an ultimate and salvific reality of some sort or other. I would suggest that in each scenario, insofar as we have reason to speak of faith at all, we will find certain distinctive elements.[2] These appear most clearly in the four examples with which we began. Let us now consider them more closely.

Where *p* is the proposition involved, we find, first, the absence of evidence causally sufficient to produce *belief* that *p*. As reflection on our examples suggests, not only is it possible to adopt propositional faith in the absence of propositional belief, but such faith is positively *incompatible* with belief. More support for this interpretation is provided as the chapter progresses, but already we may note that viewing the world in the relevant way appears to require intentional action in the case of faith, whereas it would not if belief were present. And the phenomenological qualities of this viewing and also of one's response to it are clearly different in the two cases. (These points are developed below, where the third and fourth elements are discussed.) Indeed, faith that *p* may function as a kind of alternative to belief: it is precisely in circumstances where one finds oneself without evidence causally sufficient for belief and yet needing or wanting or feeling obligated to take on a certain view of the world that it is adopted. (It does not follow, notice, that belief must always represent the more worthy condition. Indeed, faith may have its own distinctive advantages which often make it preferable to belief.)

---

[2] In certain superficially similar situations, one might find not faith but some other attitude one could have in the absence of belief, such as acting-as-if or hope (see n. 7). But the point is that we may *also* find just what we saw in the first four examples above, on account of which we must expand our conceptual repertoire, making room for beliefless faith.

Second, we should notice that the person who has faith that *p* will think of what is reported by it and of what its truth would facilitate as in some way *good* or *desirable*. As William Alston writes with respect to the example of faith that democracy will win out, "If *S* were strongly opposed to universal democracy, it would be somewhere between inapt and false to represent *S* as having *faith* that democracy will triumph."[3] But here we need to be careful. Does it follow, as Alston suggests, that *S* must have what philosophers call a *pro-attitude* toward the proposition in question? The answer depends, I think, on how much one builds into that notion of a pro-attitude. Probably it would be viewed by most philosophers as involving not just a favorable opinion but also a strong enough *approval* of the truth of the proposition to entail a *desire* that the proposition be true—which takes us beyond what is essential to propositional faith. Something may intellectually be seen as desirable—as *worthy* of desire— without actually being desired, when relevant psychological obstacles are present. And such may be the case when someone chooses to have faith. Take the political example: perhaps the person running for election is a serious rival of mine who defeated me in the primaries, and—being somewhat undeveloped emotionally—I feel a lot of resentment toward him and really do not want him to win; indeed, I harbor a strong secret desire that he will lose. Nevertheless, whether from party loyalty or obligation (maybe in a weak moment I promised our people that I would support him) or because I want to achieve some benefit for myself, here I am, campaigning for him, and in a situation where—because of a protracted slump in the polls—I have to have faith that he will win if I am to project the needed positivity. Along lines such as these it seems possible to develop examples of cases where one has faith that *p* without a desire that *p* be true. Accordingly, so as not to be misleading, I suggest that we avoid the notion of a pro-attitude and instead deploy the weaker notion of a *favorable evaluation* of the state of affairs reported by *p* (and, by extension, of the truth of *p*). This *is* entailed by faith that *p*, as Alston's example and similar examples clearly reveal.[4]

---

[3] Alston, "Belief, Acceptance, and Religious Faith," p. 12.

[4] The notion of a favorable evaluation must not be confused with that of a positive propositional attitude: one obviously might have *such* an attitude toward a proposition— one might be confident that the world will end tomorrow, say—while looking upon the prospect of its truth with horror. It may further be mentioned that one can affirm or assent to a proposition—have *this* positive propositional attitude, also involved in faith (see below)—*without* favorably evaluating the state of affairs it reports. For example, a scientist may for a shorter or longer period assent to a hypothesis without in any way considering what the hypothesis claims is true to be a "good thing." (I am grateful to William Alston for reminding me of the latter point.)

A third element of propositional faith—which may come to be exemplified by someone who recognizes, in connection with some proposition, the applicability of our first two elements—is what might be described as a disposition to *purposely picture the world accordingly* and focus one's mental attention on this representation. More fully: in taking on an attitude of faith I tenaciously represent the world to myself, through the power of will and imagination, as having a certain character, and I determine to continue (at least for some time) representing it in that way. Here we see one of the clear differences between propositional faith and propositional belief. When I have faith, I consciously and deliberately don a pair of glasses that give everything—or at least the relevant things—a certain hue (and it may be difficult to keep the glasses on). I know that it is the glasses that produce this effect, while not denying that it might match what I would see without glasses if my vision were sufficiently penetrating. The experience of belief, on the other hand, is like wearing the glasses without knowing it (and here, of course, there can be no associated difficulty, for the representation is not voluntarily produced). Describing my experience at the time of activated belief, I would say that the world is showing or presenting *itself* to me.

So the first three elements needed for propositional faith are weak evidence, a favorable evaluation, and a policy of tenaciously representing to oneself the state of affairs thus favorably assessed. The last item in the recipe is what I call a *policy of assenting* to that state of affairs or, perhaps better, to the proposition reporting it. The precise nature of what goes on here is actually quite hard to identify clearly: sometimes, for example, one might want to say *con*sent (hence the "so be it" of one example above), and the word "endorsement" is also inviting. But the main idea is that of some ongoing positive mental response to the picture with which one has presented oneself (in addition to the continuing favorable evaluation). We would not go far wrong if we spoke of continual *affirming* or *judging* (recall Chapter 4's discussion of what it is that the active skeptic withholds, while filling out what we said about that to include repetition over time). But the phrase I most commonly employ—aiming to capture everything relevant—is "voluntary assent."

It is important to remember that it is *voluntary* assent. What I have in mind involves *deliberately going along with* the imagined state of affairs in relevant contexts (as opposed to questioning or criticizing or ignoring the proposition reporting it, or simply keeping the possibility it represents at arm's length).[5] And as this confirms, here too we have to speak

---

[5] I take going along with the content of a proposition in this way to involve and to require going along with any propositions one sees it to entail.

in terms of a deliberate adoption of and subsequent adherence to a certain *policy*—a policy paralleling and intertwined with the one involving the imagination, mentioned above. Such a policy may, as we have seen, be of shorter or longer duration, and the relevant contexts may be many or few. (Sometimes it may be needed to deal with a particular short-lived emergency or crisis; sometimes—as in the case of the assent involved in religious faith—it may penetrate every situation in which one finds oneself and represent a long-term commitment.) By speaking of a "policy," I mainly hope to communicate that we are talking about something intended to continue at least for a time; something more than simply a single action or series of actions that leaves no cognitive residue. Indeed, if these policies are successfully implemented, what we really have is something like a *disposition*, though one intentionally initiated and sustained, to respond with assent to an imagined state of affairs.[6]

Now it might seem natural, when considering what I am calling voluntary assent and describing in terms of deliberately affirming and going along with a proposition, to speak instead of taking for granted or treating as given or, more simply, of *assuming* the truth of a proposition, where this is done in the absence of belief. But although they might serve to underline the dispositional aspect of voluntary assent, these modes of expression also tend to push to the background or leave out altogether what I want to keep front and center in what I have to say about propositional faith: that what such faith requires of us is often done (and renewed) consciously and explicitly, that it is something one could even do for its own sake and not only in the course of doing something else. Beliefless assuming, for example, as normally treated, tends to disappear within the complex state we call *acting on* an assumption. It is not very natural to construe the assumption part of acting-on-an-assumption as a belieflike element to which one might give separate attention—as a separate and cognitive form of commitment or independent bearer of value.[7]

---

[6] An interesting point about this assent—one that enhances my distinction between propositional faith and its believing counterpart—is that at least part of its functional role is to provide *support* or *reinforcement* for the persistent representation to oneself of the relevant state of affairs. (None of this is needed in the case of belief and so is not part of the function of any assent that may accompany *it*.) The runner of our first example is enabled to *keep* the picture of success before his mind by his repeated assent to its content. Such repeated assent helps to prevent the picture from slipping out of focus and thus to prevent the unsettling feelings associated with doubt from reemerging into consciousness.

[7] A related phenomenon, that of acting-as-if, has even less in the way of a belieflike cognitive state attached to it and apparently involves nothing like that assent which is my focus here. Very roughly, although in acting-as-if, one is *behaving* as one would if one believed, one is not necessarily *thinking* as one would in that state. I may (as I was recently) be in the

And other expressions that might be thought useful here, such as "accept-ance," at least as most relevantly employed in the literature, tend similarly to conflate what I am calling assent with *acting on* one's assent. I therefore avoid these expressions. (More on acceptance in a moment.)

But further explication of my own expressions is still needed. In exem-plifying voluntary assent as part of faith that *p*, one is saying yes to that proposition. One is actively preferring *p* over its denial, and not only in the sense of thinking a world in which *p* is true to be *better* than one in which it is false. This yes is in some ways similar to the yes—to the mental endorsement, the judgment—that we saw, when discussing the idea of withholding judgment, may accompany belief. But in the case of belief, such a yes is elicited by one's perception of the evidence, and any ten-dency to continue saying yes may be expected to be involuntary: what is involved here is mostly a matter of *noting* or mentally *recording* (what one takes to be) the truth of *p* in response to what the evidence apparently shows with respect to *p* and its denial. When one has propositional faith, on the other hand, one must *submit* to the intellectual governance of the proposition in question (here again we bump into the idea of consent), and doing so requires action that is deliberate and often difficult. It is the enacting of an explicit decision, which takes us outside the realm of belief and the judgment associated with belief.

Another way of coming at the voluntary assent of propositional faith is to say that, though lacking both confidence and belief, when assenting in this way one is still taking *p* to be *true* (perhaps in the only way that "tak-ing" really makes sense), for one has resolved to think of it as such. If the resolve continues, one will naturally be in the process of developing a *habit* of taking it in this way, and doing so may accordingly come to require less in the way of deliberate effort.[8] Where the resolve really amounts to a long-term commitment, it may also be that *p* becomes one's "position"; in such circumstances one may well put it forward as one's view, be disposed to defend it against claims that it is certainly false, and

---

home of an elderly person I do not know very well and hear sounds that certainly might be the sounds of someone suddenly taken by a heart attack but might also just be the strange sounds this individual normally makes. In such a situation I may (as I did) rush downstairs anyway to make sure all is well (which thankfully it was). Here I clearly do not *believe* that there is a problem, and neither do I *assent* to the view that there is (while running down-stairs I am not mentally endorsing any representation I have made to myself of this stranger gasping on the floor), but I nonetheless behave as I would do if I so believed.

[8] Paul Draper has reminded me of a particularly apt comment made by H. H. Price: referring to the nonbeliever who engages in religious actions, Price says that what he is doing is "something like what an actor does when he throws himself into his part" (*Belief*, pp. 484–485).

so on. (Of course, even someone thus disposed, if he really has a grip on the concept I am explicating here, will not think of himself as *believing* that *p* or as attempting to bring such belief about, and he will respond in the negative to the question "Do you believe that *p*?" and also to the question "Do you think it is true that *p*?," when this latter question is reducible to the former. He will see himself as instantiating an important *alternative* to belief. If asked about his state, he will say, "I am voluntarily assenting to the proposition *p*; having cast in my lot with it and standing behind it, I am viewing and interpreting the world in light of *p*.")[9] Although such a disposition is not entailed by voluntary assent, I suppose one might become in a sense *attached* to one's position (utilizing terminology from an earlier chapter, we might say that the person who voluntarily assents to a proposition may over time come to believe *in* that position), though in a much less psychologically absorbing and more "eyes-open" fashion than is common in the case of propositional belief, for as our examples reveal, one will recognize that one has not resolved any *evidential* problem and will still believe that the evidence is weak (recall the glasses metaphor).

In responding to the proposition that *p* in any of these ways, one brings it about that the proposition exerts a certain intellectual influence—even dominance—in those aspects of one's mental life where the truth or falsity of *p* matters. Certainly this is true in situations where the assent is part of one's response to a crisis or the needs of some other particular situation: one urgently fills one's mind with a picture of the state of affairs in question in the act of endorsing it and concentrates much mental energy on the support of this attitude. But it is also true (though here constant vigilance is needed) where it is part of a long-term commitment: in the latter case, if one has been exercising the necessary intellectual discipline it will be *p* that most readily comes to mind, along with an occurrent moment of mental assent to the truth of *p*, when relevant questions are raised or comments made by others (e.g., "I wonder whether it is *p* or not-*p* that is true"). In every case of voluntarily assenting to the truth of a proposition, other propositions incompatible with it will quite naturally recede to the background of one's attention, even if they are not believed false.

So much for explication of the fourth element of propositional faith: voluntary assent. The four elements I have detailed are all necessary, and jointly they are sufficient, to produce the state of mind I am calling

[9] It is in part because of the possibility alluded to here of having one's state confused with belief, a possibility to which many persons of faith may be expected to be alive, that we should not think of one's voluntary assent to the proposition *p* as *entailing* a tendency (or a stronger tendency) to respond in the affirmative rather than in the negative when one is *asked* whether *p*.

propositional faith. And now I want to emphasize (as briefly mentioned earlier) that faith of this sort may also be directed toward *religious* propositions. Though most of my examples have been secular, they reveal how naturally the language of faith may be applied in circumstances of the sort enumerated. But then if such circumstances arise in connection with a religious proposition, we may surely speak in a parallel fashion of having faith that God exists, or that Samsara is Nirvana, or whatever it might be—*even when belief is absent*. Indeed, when we consider how religious persons sometimes hold on to religious propositions in the face of what appears even to them as weak evidence, it seems apparent that such faith is rather common. (Notice that they will typically call what they experience "faith" while also speaking of "clinging to belief," on the mistaken assumption that their experience is compatible with belief.)

But we also need to notice some distinctive features that must be present before we can move from speaking of faith directed to a religious proposition to speaking of propositional *religious faith*. In the religious case, for one thing, the attitude of assent involved in one's faith will be less arbitrary, less restricted to particular contexts, than it sometimes is in secular contexts. Though not only religious propositional faith is like this, where propositional faith *is* religious, we are, as suggested earlier, really talking about a long-term commitment to view the world a certain way, not simply a temporary assent for the sake of some specific, limited purpose (for example, assent to the proposition that I am capable of swimming across the lake when I need to be able to do so to escape a kidnapper). This feature follows from a constraint that, intuitively, must apply both to religious faith and to religious belief—a constraint I articulated as follows when discussing the latter: such a state ought to be appropriate or conducive to the practice of religion (even if it may be possessed by someone who is not practicing). Clearly, only a *commitment* at the cognitive level is appropriate to what goes on at the conative level in religion, when the cognitive state involved is one of faith.

Another feature of propositional religious faith arises from this shared constraint—that the religious character of her state must be *recognized* by someone possessing such faith. Perhaps it would be harder to have faith with regard to a religious proposition without making the connection to religion than it would be to believe a religious proposition that way, but since it does not appear inconceivable, and since the connection to religion seems, for the reason given, to be required, let us introduce the feature in question into our understanding of propositional religious faith. Bringing all the relevant elements together, then, we can say that "S has faith that p (where p is a religious proposition), and S's faith is religious faith" is synonymous with the conjunction of the following propositions:

(1) *S* lacks evidence causally sufficient for *S* to believe that *p*.

(2) *S* considers the state of affairs reported by *p* to be good or desirable.

(3) *S* tenaciously and persistently represents the world to herself as including that state of affairs.

(4) *S* voluntarily and committedly adopts a policy of assent toward that representation—or, more broadly, toward *p*.

(5) *S* recognizes the religious character of her attitude.[10]

2. *Some Operational Corollaries*

Now as will no doubt be recognized, it is plausible to suppose that when one has faith in the propositional sense I have sought to delineate, one is commonly disposed to act in yet *another* way (though a way embracing what we have already considered)—that is, to act *on* this faith, doing those actions one sees as appropriate to the truth of the proposition to which one has given one's assent. (Indeed, one generally adopts such an attitude of assent at least in part because one intends to provide oneself with a *basis* for theoretical or practical inference, or a *guide* for behavior.) And, by definition, propositional faith involves assenting to a proposition where there is at least some chance, given one's evidence, that it is false and where there will be negative consequences (the non-occurrence of the good state of affairs that generates the favorable evaluation) if it *is* false. If all this be accepted, then we appear to be led to a second form of beliefless faith: acting on propositional faith can count as a manifestation of faith in its own right—specifically (and this will come as no surprise to the attentive reader), as a manifestation of *operational* faith.

Consider again my secular examples. What we see in these cases, I suggest, is not just propositional faith but a nonreligious version of operational faith, a disposition to act on a (nonreligious) proposition in circumstances of vulnerability of the relevant sort, the truth of which is

---

[10] In "Non-doxastic Faith: Audi on Religious Commitment," *International Journal for the Philosophy of Religion* 37 (1995): 75, Dana M. Radcliffe claims that the proposition "I have faith that God loves me but I neither believe nor disbelieve that he exists" is incoherent. As a supporting example, Radcliffe proposes "I have faith that Uncle Ed loves me," arguing that it is "evident" that one who utters this statement is referring to someone believed both to exist and to care. But such a dismissive response to the idea of propositional faith without belief will not do in the face of detailed arguments and examples of the sort I have provided. In any case, it seems clear that someone might be in doubt over whether her uncle loves her and decide, despite this doubt, to assent to the proposition that he does. What would we call this if not faith? (Notice that my believing my uncle to *exist* when I say some such thing may well be evident without its being evident that I believe he *cares*. Radcliffe needs both these things to be evident, but, as I have suggested, this is not the case.)

140 Prolegomena to a Philosophy of Religion

taken on (nonreligious) propositional faith. Sometimes this sort of operational faith involves acting directly on the propositional faith that so-and-so will be or do for one what one needs or wants. At other times this proposition is further to the background, or the filling for "so-and-so" becomes as vague as "the universe." Whatever the case, it is possible to see a kind of trust even in nonreligious or secular operational faith: it is natural to say of me, if I act on my propositional faith, not only that I have faith *that* my assistant will complete the important task but also that I have faith *in* my assistant (trust in him). In the case of the missing friend, acting on propositional faith might be said to amount to faith in the universe (or that chunk of it with which the individual in question is then in contact); in the case of the overcoming of a negative attitude toward self and others, we find faith in oneself and in human nature. In all such cases, one sees a kind of operational faith grounded in beliefless propositional faith. And it is only natural to infer by analogy that I may appropriately be said to have faith in God or in the ultimate (*religious* operational faith) even if all I am doing is acting on a beliefless attitude of voluntary assent to the relevant religious propositions in pursuing a religious way. Religious belief, that is to say, is not required as a basis for operational faith.

Let us briefly consider now how this understanding of faith is related to the discussion of the previous chapter. The trust involved in operational faith, we have seen, amounts to a disposition to act in a certain way. It does not entail an emotional component of the sort that might be said to presuppose belief (complete freedom from anxiety in relation to the providence of God, for example, of a sort that would require beliefs entailing the existence of God). It is even arguable that the most admirable sort of operational faith is that exhibited *in spite of* anxiety—or, more generally, in spite of the absence of emotional reassurance. This kind of faith, as we saw, might make a better candidate for the ideal of trust than Penelhum's serenity. Now if these points are correct, then there should be nothing preventing propositional faith as I have described it from satisfying the "positive propositional attitude" requirement of operational faith. The fact that belief is to be found undergirding many actual examples of operational faith is but a contingent fact. Indeed, propositional faith, where it exists (and it exists more commonly than one might suppose), allows the trusting disposition of operational faith to come into its own. It is not where trust is easy and emotionally supported but where it is grounded in an explicit and difficult commitment that we will see what the religious person is really made of.[11]

---

[11] It may be suggested that another way of understanding faith, one that I have not considered, puts some of my points in a different and perhaps disconcerting perspective. If, as

3. *Related Views*

I now consider how my account of faith as allowing—and in the purely propositional case, demanding—nonbelief is related to certain apparently similar moves in the literature.

Richard Swinburne, whose view on the nature of trust I have already described, speaks of acting on religious assumptions without belief and recognizes that doing so can be seen as a kind of faith (he calls it "pragmatist faith").[12] Indeed, Swinburne is an important pioneer in this area. But he does not develop his view very far, and from what he does say it appears that he lacks any inclination to identify the assumption part of "acting on assumption" as a distinct form of faith; indeed, the distinction between faith-that and faith-in (between what I have called propositional faith and operational faith) is not to be found in his writings.

In an article by Joshua Golding we find a critique and a development of Swinburne's idea. Golding argues, much as Swinburne does, that one's faith might involve, instead of belief, an "assumption for practical purpose." This notion is developed as follows: "Given that person N pursues goal G, N makes an action-guiding assumption that P for the purpose of pursuing G if and only if insofar as N pursues G he tries to do those things which are, if P is true, more (rather than less) likely to result in his attaining G."[13] Golding's discussion is illuminating and rigorously developed, but his definition shows that he too conflates the elements of assumption

---

I argued in the previous chapter, the object of trust need not be a person but can be a path, what is to prevent it from being a proposition? That is, if I act on the idea that a certain proposition will be for me what I need or want—namely, true!—in a situation where it may not be true and where there will be bad consequences if it is not, surely I can be said to be placing my trust in that proposition. And if it is a *religious* proposition, then this may count as religious action and so (indirectly) as trust in the ultimate, as we saw in the previous chapter. A further definitional point is that it must then count as faith-in or operational faith. But—and here's the rub—isn't placing one's trust in a proposition the same thing as trusting *that* the proposition is true? If so, it would seem to be the same as *faith*-that, which is to say that faith-that and faith-in here turn out to coincide. But I would resist this slide at the point where the inference is made from faith in a proposition to faith that it is true. Even if there is such a thing as faith in a proposition, just because it *is* broad enough to accommodate everything I have discussed under the heading of operational faith, this will not be the same thing as faith-that, which, though not identifiable with belief, is similarly cognitive or intellectual. Acting in a manner *appropriate to* the truth of a proposition concerning something's trustworthiness, which is what you see where there is faith in such a "something" (and so also where there is faith in a proposition), must be distinguished from more narrowly *taking it as* true. And it is only this "taking" that you see in faith-that.

[12] See Swinburne, *Faith and Reason*, pp. 115–117.

[13] Golding, "Toward a Pragmatist Conception": 492; see also 487.

and action upon it, construing the former as solely in service of the latter and so clouding the nature and distinctiveness of propositional faith.

The situation is not much improved by James L. Muyskens.[14] Muyskens does speak of *hope* as a positive propositional attitude capable of supporting a kind of trust (and so faith) when belief is absent, but it seems intuitively clear that propositional hope and propositional faith are not the same thing. A closer look at the nature of hope confirms this intuition. Propositional hope is a complex state consisting in belief and desire—if I hope that I will win a million dollars I clearly want this state of affairs to obtain (that is, I am disposed to experience a felt attraction to it in suitable circumstances), and I also believe it to be in some respect good and at any rate possible, given my evidence—and both belief and desire are involuntary. Propositional faith, on the other hand, is voluntary: the one who has it moves past hope and intentionally casts in his lot with the proposition in question through the act and disposition of assent discussed above.

Now perhaps Muyskens would say that the favorable evaluation that is also a part of such faith requires precisely the belief and desire of hope, that while propositional faith is not the same thing as hope, it nonetheless entails it (faith, on this view, does take one past hope but takes hope along). This seems false, however. Although hope that *p* represents a condition *sufficient* for a favorable evaluation in respect of *p* of the sort in question, it is not *necessary*. As we saw earlier, though such an evaluation must involve the *belief* that it would be a good thing for *p* to be true or that its being true is desirable, a *desire* for it to be true (of the narrow sort required for hope) is not entailed.[15]

But what if we focus now on the distinctive properties of *religious* propositions, our central concern here, and speak of future possibilities *filled with good things for oneself and others*, such as complete fulfillment in God? Even here, I think, desire might conceivably be absent. The power of the ego and its concerns is such as to make it possible for someone to think of such things as good yet—given the need to renounce certain attractive goods in the present in order to realize these things later—to think of

---

[14] See Muyskens, *Sufficiency of Hope*. For a similar account, subject to the same criticisms, see Pojman, *Religious Belief and the Will.*

[15] Contra William Ladd Sessions, who in *The Concept of Faith* (p. 115) writes that "G seems good to S if and only if S desires G." (Of course, if we want to use "want" and "desire" in the broader sense applicable in *any* discussion of action and motivation for action—as in "I have to get up early because I want to take the garbage out"—then we have something applicable to a voluntarist understanding of faith, but the explication of propositional hope needs more than this.) Another point to note here is that a favorable evaluation of the sort in question, unlike hope, is compatible with the belief that *p* is certainly false (I may think that it would be a good thing for me to win a million dollars while considering there to be no chance that this will ever occur).

them without desire and thus without hope.[16] It is of course *natural* for hope to arise in such circumstances, and so hope is contingently connected to faith: the person who has faith that *p* may, and typically will, also hope that *p*. Where hope with its desire component exists, we may indeed find extra motivation for the additional step of assent needed for faith. But the connection *is* a contingent one; faith apparently can get along without hope, and might even be taken up in order to acquire it. (I argued in the previous chapter that someone might adopt faith in part to acquire a love of God replete with the relevant emotions. Just so, a person not much given to passion of any kind or else struggling with contrary desires might conceivably adopt faith in part to engender a desire and hope that she sees it would be good to have but finds she lacks.)

A third major approach, and the closest to mine, is that of William Alston.[17] Alston clearly distinguishes between faith-that and faith-in, construing the former as capable of being instantiated in the absence of belief—though not claiming, as I have done, that it entails nonbelief. When it is so instantiated, says Alston, faith-that involves *acceptance* (a notion he takes over from L. Jonathan Cohen, though the details of his development of it are his own).[18] Broadly construed, acceptance requires

---

[16] I mean without any desire at all, and not, as a critic might maintain is more appropriate, without *non-overridden* desire. It is a dogma to say that we must always have *some* desire when we see something as good. We may see that we have an obligation to do something and so think of it as a good thing to do without desiring it in the slightest. In the religious case, someone could decide to have faith because of a perceived obligation or because of a purely rational appreciation of the goodness associated with religion or (as pointed out immediately below) in order to *improve* her emotional state, any desire for religious goods having been prevented from springing up by the power of the ego and attractive associated goods, or by an emotional handicap, or for some similar reason.

[17] See Alston, "Belief, Acceptance, and Religious Faith." A fourth approach that might be thought deserving of mention is that of Robert Audi (see, for example, his "Faith, Belief, and Rationality"). But even though Audi is concerned with faith-that and recognizes a distinction between faith-that and belief, he still considers the former to be compatible with the latter. And though he seems to be talking about something like our assent when discussing what faith-that amounts to when it does *not* involve belief, what exactly he has in mind is unclear. A fifth major approach to (and development of) the view that faith is distinct from belief might be said to be Wilfred Cantwell Smith's; see his *Faith and Belief* (Princeton: Princeton University Press, 1979). But Smith's account is in fact not relevant here, since what he has to say involves a conception of belief quite different from mine: as it turns out, even if faith that *p* does not include what *Smith* calls belief (the *doubtful opinion* that *p*), it may entail what I have called belief. So, the proper clarifications having been made, Smith can no longer be seen as affirming anything like the claim I am developing and defending here.

[18] See L. Jonathan Cohen, *An Essay on Belief and Acceptance* (Oxford: Clarendon Press, 1992), p. 4: "To accept that *p* is to have or adopt a policy of deeming, positing, or postulating that *p*—i.e., of including that proposition or rule among one's premises for deciding what to do or think in a particular context, whether or not one feels it to be true that *p*."

taking a proposition "on board" and keeping it there, including it "in one's repertoire of (supposed) facts on which one will rely in one's theoretical and practical reasoning and one's behavior . . . *and* thereby being disposed to *use* [it] in one's thinking, feeling, and behavior" (so an initial mental act that engenders a continuing disposition, and also a continuing disposition to make use of the proposition thus taken on board). Its components, says Alston, are very like those he takes to be constitutive of propositional belief (mentioned in my Chapter 2): a tendency to affirm the proposition when asked whether it is true, to take on board and make use of what one supposes to follow from it, to use it in theoretical and practical reasoning where applicable, to be surprised if it turns out to be false, and to act in (other) ways that would be appropriate if it were true, given the accepter's purposes and other beliefs.[19] The main differences between acceptance and belief, as Alston understands them, are the absence from the former of the *confidence* that is (as he supposes) a part of the latter, and its replacement by the voluntary mental act and consequent disposition involved in taking a proposition "on board."

Now it may seem that there is little to choose between Alston's account of acceptance and the notion of assent central to my account of propositional faith, since the latter is at any rate functionally very similar to the former, and especially to that part of acceptance involving the "taking (and keeping) on board" of a proposition. But exactly here we see a difference between Alston's account and my own, which results in a considerable and important difference in our overall understandings of faith. For what I include in voluntary assent is only a *part* of acceptance (the part involving the "taking on board" of a proposition) and thus is only a part of what Alston is willing to link with propositional faith. Much like the other writers discussed above, Alston combines what I call propositional faith with, among other things, a "(tendency to) action on the basis of" component, and he considers the *conjunction* of these things to be a possible way of instantiating propositional faith—whereas I would suggest that the latter component is not in any way involved in propositional faith but ought to be reserved instead for operational faith. Why is this my suggestion? Well, given my arguments in the previous chapter, once one takes religious propositions on board *and* acts on them, there is nothing *left over* that we might identify with trust or faith-in: the latter, I have argued, involves precisely (and only) that action disposition which Alston has assimilated to faith-*that*. So if our aim is to distinguish faith-that from faith-in, and if convinced by my earlier arguments concerning the latter,

[19] See Alston, "Belief, Acceptance, and Religious Faith," pp. 8–9.

we will have a reason to distinguish—in something like the way I do—the faith involved in taking a proposition on board from the faith involved in acting on it.[20]

Alston appears to me to take a different approach in part because of his view that a "(tendency to) action on the basis of" component belongs to *belief*. If we are replacing a conception of propositional faith in which a reference to belief is dominant, and think of belief as involving an action disposition of the sort in question, the replacement may indeed seem to require a similar connection to action. But once we see the reasons for distinguishing conceptually between belief and action upon it (discussed in Chapter 2) and recognize that there can be no room for faith-in without this distinction, we will no longer be inclined to endorse such a move. In sum, there is good reason to associate belief and voluntary assent strictly with what philosophers call the *cognitive* element of faith—with the way the world is seen by the person of faith—and leave what they call the *conative* element to bring up the rear, as it does where propositional faith (a way of seeing) is complemented by operational faith (a way of acting in light of how one sees).[21] The notion of acceptance, which combines the two for purposes of practical decision-making and the pursuit of external goals (goals external to the act of "taking on board" itself), whatever its usefulness in other contexts, and despite incorporating in its own way much of what I would want to include under faith labels, does not seem to me to allow drawing the line in an appropriate manner between the types of religious faith.[22]

[20] It may be wondered how I view the relation of the other items on Alston's list to propositional faith. I do take at least assent to propositions that S sees as following from p as part of its nature, and I can do so consistently with rejection of a parallel move in the case of belief because faith is voluntary: when one voluntarily assents to a proposition, one commits oneself to all its discernible entailments—indeed, in the typical case one assents to p at least in part *because* of what one sees it to entail. Belief, on the other hand, being involuntary, carries no such commitments (see Cohen, *Essay on Belief and Acceptance*, pp. 27–33). A tendency to affirm p when asked about it and surprise when it turns out to be false I do not take to be part of the very meaning of "propositional faith": the former for reasons similar to those given in Chapter 2 when discussing Alston on belief; the latter because surprise of the sort referred to here is likely only when one believes (it is the sort of thing you might expect to be caused by belief but not by the more "eyes-open" approach of faith). There might be *disappointment* in the case of faith when a proposition is discovered to be false, but even this is to be expected only where the accompanying favorable evaluation is instantiated by hope.

[21] The distinction is of course not absolute if the way of seeing represented by propositional faith is *voluntarily* adopted, and so involves action—but let that pass.

[22] In other words, though the two sorts of disposition are hard to distinguish in practice, they require this conceptual distinction. To readers with different intuitions I suggest the following. In work like mine and in discussion of it we may be witnessing a stage in the evolution of a concept—certainly not enough attention has yet been given to thinking

Another reason for taking the approach I do is one I have already alluded to; here I want to fill it out a bit. Though other writers who think faith is distinct from belief construe that part of the former which I am calling voluntary assent as purely practical in nature (thus granting a seeming legitimacy to moves like Alston's, which may then seem to represent the logical next step), it ought not to be so construed. Voluntarily adopting a religious view of the world when one lacks belief may be much more than a practical matter—much more than an action taken for the purpose of achieving goals beyond itself—and in the deepest instances of propositional faith, it is. It may, for example, be generated by a love of God, or of the ultimate, quite as profound as the sort of love that sometimes accompanies propositional belief and is sometimes part of affective religious belief. (Earlier, I said that operational faith, which entails some cognitive component, whether of faith or belief, may be taken up in the absence of what would usually be called the love of God; here we see that such love—albeit of a sort that does not involve the belief that God exists—may *precede* both propositional faith and operational faith, and that both forms of faith may be the *result* of such love.) Though it is often ignored by religious writers, there is a sort of love of God which the one who seeks after God *without* finding may possess—a deep longing after God and a world suffused with religious meaning that has mystical, ethical, and aesthetic overtones, in addition to any prudential or self-interested elements it may embody. (There is a clear connection to propositional hope here; I would take the love of which I am speaking to entail such hope while, in its richer qualities, transcending it.) And for such a one the act of giving mental assent to a religious picture of the world, and determining thereafter to view the world in that light, may be an act of love.

Seen thus, the initiation of propositional faith can be construed as a religiously meaningful form of action in itself; it need not derive its significance only from the fact that it facilitates another form of action. One might take on board a religious view of the world in part because one finds that very action (quite apart from the other actions to which it may lead) a way of expressing one's love of God. It might also be seen as a way of expressing one's love of the world—as a way of paying tribute to the

---

about the relations between faith-that and faith-in, and ordinary language, while to some extent supporting this distinction, also fairly often displays insensitivity to it—rather than competing attempts to delineate a concept already fully developed. In that case, my work on faith-that could be seen as suggesting and putting forward for consideration a direction we might take (a direction in at least some important ways connected to tendencies in ordinary language) in order to account clearly and sensitively and fruitfully for everything that needs accounting for here—including such facts as I now go on to mention in the text.

wonder of life and the magic and mystery of the universe, or a way of honoring one's deepest values and relationships. But if so, then we have yet another reason for disentangling the cognitive from the conative in matters of religious faith, and for declining to accept "acceptance."

4. *Religious Language and the Voluntariness of Faith*

In this and previous chapters I have several times made or mentioned the claim that (whatever else we may say of it) faith must be understood as voluntary. Here I want to give this claim more extended attention, in connection with a closer look at typical religious references to faith.

Three important intuitions, I suggest, need to be captured by any understanding of the concept of faith's voluntariness. These might be informally expressed as follows: if you want it, you can have it; if you have it but don't want it, you can drop it; and you shouldn't expect to keep it without doing something about it. In other words, faith is accessible to, and can be produced by, anyone who seeks to have it (call this the *accessibility* clause); it can be got rid of, terminated by those who no longer wish to have it (call this the *terminability* clause); and it is vulnerable and will be lost in the absence of sustaining activity (call this the *vulnerability* clause). One should, I think, stay as close to these intuitions about faith's voluntary nature as one can in developing an understanding of faith. And although there is not as much sensitivity as one might like, in ordinary religious discussions of the voluntariness of faith, to the possibility of different types of faith, what I have said here seems to apply indifferently to whatever types there may be: it seems that anything deserving the label of "faith" is subject to the points I have raised.

Notice the implied references to action in each of these points: faith is intimately bound up with what we *do* (or fail to do), if it is voluntary. The suggestion is also that the link between faith (or its absence) and our actions is direct: it is not just that how we live may over time have some influence on whether we have faith or lack it but rather that, if I try, I can have (or lose) faith right now through an act of will and that without such exertion faith will definitely be lost.[23] Notice, finally, that accepting

---

[23] Does this notion of voluntariness imply that we have incompatibilist free will if faith is voluntary? I would say no. What is most important here—actions, actions one chooses to do, perhaps the expending of effort in doing them—appears to reside within what compatibilist and incompatibilist conceptions of free will have in common rather than within what divides them. This is not to say that in *religious interpretations* of faith these notions do not sometimes appear in incompatibilist dress. But that is because of independent commitments of the religious person, which need not influence us here.

the voluntariness of faith—in particular, its accessibility—does not commit one to the view that just *any* way of being a person of faith can be realized by *anyone* through a conscious choice. Perhaps some way of instantiating faith (implicit trust?) even presupposes beliefs or other dispositions that not just anyone has, so that if someone lacking the relevant dispositions were to seek to access it, they would inevitably fail. We need not infer that, were this the case, faith could not be seen as voluntary, or fully voluntary, after all; so long as *some* way of becoming and being a person of faith is available to the one who seeks it, the relevant requirement of accessibility is met.[24]

I have not plucked this understanding of faith's voluntariness out of thin air. It is well supported both by institutional deliberations and theoretical discussions in philosophy and religion and by the ordinary religious talk of your "person on the street." It is well known, for example, that in the tradition most preoccupied with talk of faith, namely Christianity, theologians and church councils have explicitly declared that faith is voluntary (by which they have meant at least that it is such as can be chosen and given up).[25] It should also be noted that theologians and ecclesiastics have often spoken of faith as *meritorious* and *virtuous*—notions that go well with an understanding like my own: how can I be credited with or praised for something I do not take a hand in myself? Looking further, we can see that religious writers (both inside and outside Christianity) have emphasized the accessibility of faith: not only those specially favored by life in respect of intelligence and other desirable personal qualities, or individuals who hold certain particular beliefs or have achieved certain other attitudes few possess, may have faith but anyone who (appreciating the goals of religion) truly seeks to have it. The religious life is open to all who are *genuinely interested*: those who seek will find; the Way, though easy to miss, is always present and accessible; anyone willing to follow the religious teacher or guru and submit to the rigors of the Path may achieve enlightenment. This accessibility view is of course also implicit in everything that is said and done by the religious to

---

[24] Thus the reference to faith in the accessibility clause is slightly different from the reference in the other two clauses: in the former we are talking about *some* form of faith; in the latter about *any*. And this seems intuitively right. For the former applies to those who do not yet have faith, and at this stage we would need a reason to discriminate between the different possible ways in which faith can be instantiated (as we have seen, it certainly seems that so long as one or other of them is accessible, faith is accessible), whereas the latter, since they apply to those who already do have faith, cannot be discussed *without* reference to specific ways of instantiating faith: namely, those actually instantiated. But even here, at a deeper level, we can see an element of nondiscrimination, because we apply the latter two clauses to *all* the ways in which faith is actually instantiated.

[25] See Swinburne, *Faith and Reason*, p. 200.

spread their faith and in the invitation thus extended: proselytizing and missionary activities of all kinds suggest that anyone who truly seeks to have faith may have it.

If we take seriously this open-door policy of religion, we will, I think, be inclined to say that—whatever else we should say of it—faith is to be understood as the sort of thing that can be intentionally produced and that the class of those who may thus produce it is wide and inclusive. As for terminability and vulnerability: well, there is, in addition to points already made, the known tendency of religious people to *warn* the faithful against the loss of faith—against "backsliding" (the perhaps not wholly deliberate return to old patterns of behavior inconsistent with faith) and also apostasy (the deliberate forsaking of faith). Ever-present vigilance is apparently required to stay on the religious way; much of what is said in religious contexts, indeed, would make little sense if this were not taken into account.

Such voluntarist talk on the part of intellectuals and ecclesiastics and developers of religious tradition would seem to be in harmony with ordinary usage of the term "faith" across a wider range of contexts. As already noted earlier in the book, the nonreligious are frequently told to *put* their faith in God or to *have* faith in God. The religious also commonly tell others (or themselves), when things look grim, to have faith that things will get better—that divine assistance or support will be forthcoming—or to have faith that the Bible or some other scriptural record is true. Such imperatives make faith, whether operational or propositional, sound like something that is responsive to what we *do*, something that anyone can have if they but try. I suggest we look now at some other relevant examples of religious language to confirm this interpretation. (In considering such examples we will also, more generally, be able to gather evidence that the account of "faith" developed in the previous section stacks up well against ordinary religious uses of the term.)

The following sentences may provide a representative sample:

1. "Perhaps this illness is meant as a test of my faith."

2. "When she joined that cult, she was going on blind faith."

3. "You should just take it on faith that what the Koran says is true."

4. "We walk by faith, not by sight."

5. "I listened to the voice of God in my heart and received the gift of faith."

6. "Just step out in faith, and God will provide."

7. "If you have enough faith, you will be healed."

8. "My grandmother had a simple faith, but it carried her through life."

9. "He wasn't sure Zen practice would help but said it was an act of faith."

10. "Reading Kierkegaard inspired him to take a leap of faith."

11. "Because of what she was told at that university, she lost her faith."

12. "Following the narrow way involves hardship and risk; faith takes that risk."

Most of these sentences clearly suggest that faith is a matter of action and is voluntary in the way I have suggested. Consider sentence (1): one's faith can be *tested* in the relevant sense only if it is within one's power both to keep it and to give it up. The reference in (2) to the faith of a new cult devotee suggests voluntariness as well (a trust involving action appears to be referred to). More than a strong suggestion of the same notion appears in the admonition of (3) to "take" the truth of the Koran on faith; (4) identifies faith with "walking," which obviously makes most sense if faith is voluntary; (6), similarly, suggests that faith comes into being (and is sustained) when one "steps out" and so intentionally *does* something. There is more initial ambiguity in (7), the sentence linking faith to healing, but it is not hard to see here a reference to something one can do such that, if one does it, one will be rewarded (and the idea of a *reward* for one's faith makes no sense if faith is involuntary; one is rewarded for what one does). Sentence (9) explicitly identifies the instance of faith to which it refers with an act. The Kierkegaardian "leap" mentioned in (10) equally implies action. And finally, in (12), faith is identified with following a narrow way full of hardship and risk—obviously not something properly construed as involuntary.

The sentences cited, best interpreted on the assumption that faith is voluntary in our sense, provide substantial support for that view. (Because of the religious importance of this emphasis on voluntariness, even if religious people using such sentences typically go on to speak of what they have just referred as requiring belief, and so fall into confusion, it is clear that the way to resolve the confusion is not to say that faith is not voluntary after all but to admit that it does not require belief. There will be more in defense of this view later.) But the attentive reader will have noticed that certain sentences were left out of the foregoing review: sentences (5), (8), and (11) seem to point in another direction, away from the view that faith is voluntary, and may therefore not be used to support the case I am building in this chapter. It would be useful, however, if we could show that they do not count *against* it either, that when interpreted in light of the understanding of faith I have developed, they can be made consistent with the claim that faith is voluntary, as here understood, and that the interpretation in question is not implausible.

I think we can show this. Take sentence (11). People who talk about losing their faith usually sound as though there was nothing they could do about it and often seem to be sad about the state of affairs they are in. Surely if faith were voluntary, a critic may claim, what such persons are saying would not make any sense, for then they could *have* faith again just by trying to (or else they could have refused to give it up in the first place); further, then we wouldn't find the sort of situation referred to here involving a disposition that (though now lost) was around from very early on, produced by such things as parental influence or powerful feeling instead of a deliberate choice to have faith.

That argument fails, however. To answer it we need only recall what was true of the mother (described in Chapter 5) whose trust in her daughter was broken by the latter's unexpected misbehavior, and to remind ourselves of what our understanding of voluntariness in faith actually requires. The faith that people "lose" is the implicit, unreflective faith of their youth. We might even say that their trust in God—and it is usually theistic faith that such expressions refer to—is broken by unhappy experiences or the unexpected force of arguments against religious belief. The belief goes, and then (since there is no belief to respond to anymore) the implicit trust goes, and faith is lost. But just as the mother may explicitly choose to act on the proposition that her daughter is reliable despite the broken *implicit* trust, so the former believer may voluntarily commit herself to the proposition that God exists and is trustworthy and act on it, thus (if I am right) bringing both faith-that and a new incarnation of faith-in into being at once. And so faith may, in a sense, be voluntarily regained. Indeed, anyone aware of this option might have refused to give faith up in the first place, by replacing propositional belief with propositional faith and never ceasing to act on the proposition that God exists and is trustworthy. In such a case, the *details* of faith would change, but faith itself would continue. The upshot, if I am right about the nature of faith, is that the voluntariness of faith is preserved despite cases of the sort in question, since even in such cases, anyone who seeks to do so may have faith in God.

One may, however, wonder why I refer to faith *in* God at all here. Is it not just religious *belief* that is lost? Don't persons who say "I lost my faith" *mean* that they ceased to believe that God exists, that Jesus is the Son of God, and so on (or that they no longer believe some similar set of propositions from another religious tradition)? If so, my argument collapses: faith is shown to be belief and thus involuntary after all in a manner irreconcilable with my claims. But this is too quick. Even if the interpretive suggestion here seemed correct, other examples would need to be weighed against it. And the suggestion is not obviously correct. To see why, consider that if the usual descriptions are to be trusted, the loss of one's faith is experienced as (in one degree or another) *distressing*— sometimes, indeed, quite traumatic. Arguably, the best explanation of this, especially given the information often available concerning the previous experience of those who report such things, is that the faith in question involved not just the mental disposition of belief *but a way of life built upon it*. When someone's faith is lost, her whole life may be thrown into disarray (and particularly where emotions are causally bound up with faith, such an event can have serious psychological effects). This happens, I suggest, because not only faith-that but faith-*in* is lost in such cases. Of course, given the implicit nature of the latter, it must be understood as having been grounded in firm belief. As in the case of the mother and her daughter, the firm belief is a necessary condition of the faith's implicitness, so that when the former goes, the latter follows. It is because of this causal connection that we may sometimes find ourselves focusing on the belief. But I suggest that to explain the effects of the loss we need to refer to *both* elements. I conclude that sentence (11) poses no serious problem for my case.

As for sentence (8), we can develop a similar interpretation: the simple faith of the grandmother that carries her through life is, arguably, simply an implicit faith that is never lost. In cases of this sort we appear to find the childlike trust idealized by Penelhum—a trust that may indeed have originated in childhood and, because of cultural factors familiar to most of us, has never in any serious way bumped into the problems generated by critical reflection. But since (if I am right) this is not the *only* way that faith-in can be realized, the sort of disposition I have associated with the latter can still be seen as voluntary in the sense I have emphasized.

Finally, we have sentence (5), which might seem to refer to a religious experience or apparent encounter with God of the sort that can generate a confident *belief* that God exists and loves one. (We might imagine the individual in question to have recently returned from an evangelical revival meeting.) Such an experience and the belief that comes with it are involuntary, so here, it may be said, faith is clearly being construed as involuntary. But this again is too quick. Even setting aside the element of "openness" that religious people would link with "listening to God" and would trace to a conscious choice (remember the emphasis on "decision" at revival meetings), we can show that something is being missed here. For consider: Would religious people really want to continue to label as *faith* what the individual in question received if it turned out to be a matter of *belief and no more*? In cases where "faith talk" of the sort represented by (5) occurs, we find the beginning of a *new form of life*, a desire to follow the way of God and a disposition to seek to carry out certain associated tasks to the best of one's ability. The "gift," arguably, is the sense of God's activity in one's life which prompts one, almost effortlessly, to do so. So again we have a reference to implicit trust. (Christians may say—citing the related New Testament passage, Ephesians 2:8–9—that it *is* God's activity that is operative here, and if God exists, perhaps they are right. But notice that even if they are right, it is only *implicit* trust that is thus dependent on God's gift and also that one must *go along* with the prompting in appropriate circumstances to be correctly said to have an implicitly trusting disposition.) Now notoriously, such faith may *not* last a lifetime; one may under the corrosive effects of argument or negative experience be left without the joy or spiritual spontaneity that marked the beginning of the religious life. It is then that faith becomes more obviously a matter of action—of a sort represented by the sentences on either side of (5). But the key word here is "more": as I say, appealing to a wider religious context, we can see that what the individual uttering (5) experiences would not generate something that religious people would call faith if she did not undertake to act upon it. And so it must be more than belief.

As we have seen, the tactic of a critic who seeks to make use of such sentences as (11), (8), and (5) must be to identify faith with belief (and so with something involuntary) or else more generally with something experiential that does not involve action. But as we have also seen, it is not at all clear that it is—or that it is only—belief that is referred to by the most plausible interpretations of the sentences considered: action and action dispositions appear also to be involved. Further, if the understanding of faith I have developed is correct, then even if action is sometimes not involved in the genesis of faith though belief and other involuntary dispositions are, faith still is something that *can* be produced and sustained by action and so is voluntary by my definition.

We seem, therefore, to be able to say in a general way that there is considerable support from ordinary religious language for the account of faith I have developed in these two chapters. Instances of usage that seem inconsistent with it can be accommodated when its conceptual resources are applied. We seem also to have plenty of reason to say more specifically that faith is the sort of thing that must be voluntary in the sense indicated. But if so, then we have a very powerful argument to draw upon in support of our central claim. For if faith is voluntary, it cannot either be or entail belief. If faith were simply a matter of religious belief, then clearly it would be not at all a matter of action but an involuntary disposition, and so the conditions specified by our understanding of voluntariness could not be satisfied: because of the passive disposition that belief entails, there is no way of producing or terminating religious belief just by trying. Even if faith merely entailed religious belief, it could not be voluntary; specifically, faith cannot satisfy the *accessibility* clause if it entails religious belief, for then it is not available to just anyone who earnestly seeks to have it.

If, on the other hand, the interpretation of faith I have advanced is accepted, such problems do not arise. For then anyone who seeks to have faith—whether already possessing religious belief or not—may have it. In their very seeking, those without religious belief show the favorable evaluation we have said is needed for propositional faith; to this may be added the imaginative representation and the assent we have discussed, as well as action *on* the assent, which is sufficient to generate both propositional and operational faith. Obviously, on our view, anyone who ceases to hold the religious view before his mind or ceases to give assent to it ceases to have propositional faith; and, of course, the person of faith who is a believer may cease to have faith simply by ceasing to act on his *belief* in the appropriate manner.

Perhaps it will now be suggested that even if I am right in what I have claimed so far, we still have no reason to think of propositional faith as incompatible with religious belief. Perhaps our favorable evaluation plus voluntary assent represents one way of instantiating the former (a way appropriate to those who lack religious belief) and religious belief another. This, it may be asserted, would among other things nicely parallel what I have said about operational faith, where clearly faith *with* belief is one option. The propositional basis of operational faith, whether assent or belief, should count as propositional faith.

But to see that this claim is false, we need only consult more carefully our definition of voluntariness in faith and the use we have made of it. In the case of operational faith, where faith with belief is one option, we still always have voluntariness, not only because the accessibility clause is satisfied by operational faith *without* belief but also because operational faith with belief is *terminable* and *vulnerable*—if a disposition to act on one's belief is forsaken or not sustained, the operational faith constituted by it must cease to exist. But nothing like this can be said where belief alone is concerned. Belief obviously cannot be intentionally produced, but as we have seen, neither can it be intentionally sustained or forsaken. Now given the structure of our discussion, we could still say that propositional faith is *accessible* to all who seek it even if we allowed that belief represented one way of instantiating it (a way not itself accessible), because our accessibility clause requires only that *some* way of instantiating this or that form of faith be accessible. And so if religious belief were terminable and vulnerable in the relevant ways, we might have the parallel insisted upon by the objection. But it is not. Belief cannot satisfy the terminability and vulnerability clauses.[26] Hence it cannot represent so much as one way for propositional faith to be instantiated. (Of course, as we have seen, this inability does not prevent it from providing an acceptable basis for operational faith, but not just any such basis will *itself* deserve to be considered a form of faith.)

A critic of my view may now try to defeat it by developing a more sophisticated understanding of believing propositional faith, which is capable of admitting a difference between belief simpliciter and faith and also remains true to the intuitions about faith I have emphasized. How might this be developed? Well, we might first consider the idea of whether belief *plus the relevant favorable evaluation* could count as faith. This is suggested (though not unequivocally affirmed) by Alston in connection with an example in which person A strongly wants friend B to get a job and also has strong, belief-producing reasons for supposing that he will. Can we not say that A has *faith* that B will get the job?[27] Choosing a religious example, could we not likewise say that someone believing that Christ will return on the clouds of heaven and also deeply anticipating this event has *faith* that Christ will return?

Some might be prepared to endorse this manner of speaking, but there are good reasons for dissent. First, if belief plus a favorable evaluation were sufficient, then any approving belief would count as propositional faith. But then the belief I have that the winter is over, which refers to something of which I approve, must be an instance of faith—and this seems clearly false. But is there a difference between this belief and the beliefs previously mentioned that explains this fact? Well, yes, it seems that there is: the others refer to something that has not yet occurred; they are expressed in the future tense. So is *this* what is needed to produce a

[26] And even though recognizing religious belief as a form of propositional faith would not prevent the latter's accessibility, religious belief is still doing no work of its own; on the proposed account it rides to victory on the coattails of the voluntary assent I have been emphasizing.

[27] See Alston, "Belief, Acceptance, and Religious Faith," p. 12.

sufficient condition of propositional faith? Should we say that approving beliefs *about the future* count as faith? Certainly, as we have seen, a future orientation is not *necessary* for faith—I might have faith that my friend, whom I haven't seen for months, safely got out of Iraq despite the fighting, and this does not refer to the future at all[28]—but is it, together with approving belief, nevertheless sufficient? It seems not, for I have plenty of beliefs about the future, referring to events that I think are very good or that I even deeply anticipate in a manner involving my emotions, to which no one would be inclined to give the label of faith. For example, I believe that I will see my sons in the summer, and that I will teach a new course on the problem of evil in the fall, but these are clearly not instances of faith. I have no doubt that a fuller understanding of the nature of faith than I have arrived at will someday be developed, but my state of mind in thinking so could hardly be characterized as one of faith. Why not? Is it precisely *because* I lack any doubt here? Perhaps to get the desired sufficient condition of faith one also needs a situation of uncertainty or weak evidence.

This possibility meshes nicely with the future orientation of the examples which may tempt some to speak of faith: what is in the future has not yet occurred and naturally may raise concerns as to whether it will occur. Perhaps we are inclined to call those earlier cases cases of faith only because we assume that there *is* such uncertainty in them which at some level is recognized by the individual in question (whether in fact it is or not). But if to get the sufficient condition of propositional faith we have been trying to put together we need to speak of approving beliefs about the future *for which the believer's evidence is weak,* we are coming perilously close to the view involving reference to a lack of evidence sufficient for belief which the objection was seeking to avoid. For if the evidence here is indeed weak and if belief is involuntary, do we really have evidence rationally sufficient for believing that belief is present?

Suppose we do. What is it about the weakly supported approving belief concerning the future that might justify referring to it as a case of faith? We have seen that no such justification can be forthcoming without voluntariness, so what exactly is voluntary about belief of the sort in question? Given our reflections so far, it must be something made possible by weak support—but precisely what is it? Here a common and tempting answer will be that the believer believes *despite* this challenge to her belief. Such believing may be expected to be difficult, and it is meritorious when done in a good cause—or so it will be said. But is it really true that the

---

[28] Notice that although in these circumstances I might also have the future-oriented faith that I will see my friend again, that is not the faith spoken of here.

believing may be expected to be difficult? Since it is involuntary, it is neither difficult nor easy, for it is not something *done*—it is not an action—at all. It appears that the critic may here be confusing doubts (which, we saw in Chapter 4, are capable of creating *psychological* difficulties) with some sort of *difficult action* that the believer takes and that is responsible for the continuation of her belief in the face of such doubts. But perhaps it will be said that there are also actions taken by the believer that are difficult in the proper sense of hard to do, and that these are indeed in some way responsible—at least in the sense of being causally necessary—for the continuation of her belief and suffice to make her condition one of faith. (After all, if they do represent a necessary causal condition here, then it follows that if she did not do these actions, her belief would cease to exist.) In other words, what the critic is really thinking of as representing a sufficient condition of propositional faith is a weakly supported approving belief about the future *that is preserved—at least in part—through difficult effort.* What sorts of effort? Well, we would normally hear of the believer extending her investigation, continuing in the face of doubts to look for satisfying answers and finding enough intellectual nourishment for the belief to keep it going, or reliving past moments of certainty, or focusing on the positive evidence and trying to forget the negative, or associating with believing supporters, or telling herself that the arguments against her belief will someday be answered even if she herself cannot yet locate the answers, and finding that the storm of doubts lifts on its own after a time. Do these actions show that the believer's attitude of belief ought to count as propositional *faith* as well?

To answer this question, we need a more adequate description of the situation. For concreteness and relevance, think of some Christian believer's weakly supported approving belief that she or someone she loves will live after death in the presence of God, a belief that she shores up with such actions as have been mentioned. Call this belief the belief that *p*. I would claim, first, that we have no good reason to say that this belief is vulnerable and terminable, as the use of "necessary causal condition" in this context is meant to suggest. Just because it is a *belief,* it might very well—because, for example, of psychological factors of which we have no awareness—continue to exist even if the believer were not to do the actions in question. Only if her attitude toward *p* is clearly grounded in and dependent on actions she might not do, whose role in her belief she recognizes, can we have any reason to say that it is vulnerable and terminable and thus voluntary, as faith must be (of course, if it were thus grounded, it would be accessible as well). And that is not the case. Second, although the proffered list of actions suggests that the believer has faith, and perhaps even propositional faith, the faith it bespeaks is of a different sort than faith that *p*. In each case, the possible actions of the believer are much more naturally viewed as expressing *either* a disposition to act on the further belief—call it the belief that *q*—that it is morally or religiously correct to be loyal to p^{29} (and so expressing operational faith of a moral or religious variety instead of propositional faith: think here of the actions of reliving certainty or focusing on positive evidence), *or* faith that the belief that *p* will be intellectually vindicated—call the latter proposition *r*—together with actions appropriate to the truth of *this* proposition (think here of the actions of telling oneself that the objections will someday be answered and extending one's investigation).

Notice that *r* is a *new* future-oriented proposition nonidentical with *p* (it neither entails nor is entailed by *p*). In having faith that *r*, the believer is in a different state of mind from the one she is in when she experiences the propositional attitude directed toward *p*, whose status as faith our critic wished to defend. It is also a state different from belief. For does the Christian afterlife believer really *believe* that her belief will be vindicated? She *tells* herself that the objections will be answered, as she would not need to do if she believed it (one can imagine her imagining a future moment of vindication and giving her assent to the idea that this picture corresponds to reality). So, to sum up, what we learn about faith when we consider the critic's latest option, that of weakly supported approving beliefs about the future preserved through difficult effort, is that we lack sufficient justification for thinking that the beliefs in question *are* thus preserved and that *other* attitudes represent faith in the cited circumstances.

But let us try one last defense of the critic's stance, focused on a subtly different alternative to the previous theme: weakly supported approving beliefs about the future *which the believer voluntarily and committedly judges to be correct.*[30] The idea is not that the believer's belief is *preserved* by the judging element but that when the evidence is weak, that element—which may be there even when the evidence is strong, as we noted earlier—comes into its own: it is more explicit and deliberate, more difficult, and needs to be sustained over time. With doubts swirling all around, the

---

[29] Perhaps derived from a higher-level belief about loyalty to God, in which case the believer's operational faith may ultimately be faith in God.

[30] For bringing to mind how the notion of judgment may be redeployed here, I am indebted to some comments of Daniel Howard-Snyder on voluntarily committing oneself to the truth of a proposition. (Those who think the latter idea can relevantly be developed not as an explicit attitude toward a proposition, as here, but in terms of acting *on* such an attitude—specifically, on belief—are referred to earlier discussion in this chapter and in the previous one where it is argued that these things should be distinguished. It is important to remember that we are talking only about *propositional* faith here.)

alternative to the proposition believed will appear much more (epistemically) attractive than it otherwise would, and work will be required to remain focused on what one believes. *Experiences* of belief will be relatively rare, and the confidence that is the normal accompaniment of belief will be intermittent at best. Might not someone in such circumstances deliberately choose to go along with the proposition in question, voluntarily and committedly judging it to be true while also believing it? If so, we have a state that is rather a lot like the voluntary assent I have emphasized as part of propositional faith. As such, it deserves to be explicitly referred to in a definition of the alternative involved here—an alternative that then turns out to be voluntary precisely because the *judging commitment* is voluntary. No longer do we need to worry about the belief element not being voluntary, since we have another element that requires our voluntary control, which is such that if we withhold it—if we retract our commitment and become actively skeptical!—*we will not instantiate this state.* This state is therefore able to satisfy both the vulnerability and the terminability clause: through active skepticism I can terminate the state, and without committed judging it will be lost, and so it is vulnerable. And although this state cannot itself satisfy the accessibility clause, given that it still entails belief, that is no matter because there is *another* sort of propositional faith that is accessible to someone lacking belief (the sort I have been promoting in this chapter), and thus (according to my own earlier concession) propositional faith remains accessible. It appears, then, that I have no reason to deny that a weakly supported approving belief about the future which the believer voluntarily and committedly judges to be correct satisfies a sufficient condition of propositional faith.

As is so often the case, however, appearances are deceiving: even this strategy of the critic is unsuccessful. For though I could, through active skepticism, terminate the state in question (and though because of the results of not committedly judging, it would in the relevant way be vulnerable) *if voluntary and committed judging were part of it in the first place,* it is arguable that voluntary and committed judging *cannot* be part of it so long as it truly includes belief.[31] The critic is trying to exploit the fuzziness of the cutoff line between propositional belief and doubt—and, in particular, the possibility of a *weak* belief disposition—but this line is not so fuzzy as to permit walking it successfully. Apart from the fact that a sturdy

---

[31] Remember that when in Chapter 4 we said that active skepticism was compatible with belief, we were thinking of a believer who *needed* active skepticism to detach her from what seemed *too* clearly true (whose confidence for whatever reason did not weaken with the evidence) and whose tendency to judge in favor of the proposition believed therefore did not come anywhere close to the difficult, committed stance we are supposed to have here.

conception of propositional faith should not need to depend upon such a tactic, we can point out that even a weak belief disposition must still be such that *normally* or *usually* a belief experience is involved when the state of affairs in question comes to mind. By the same token, if one believes at all, judging will *normally* or *usually* be the effortless noting of (what appears as) the truth of the corresponding proposition referred to earlier. Consequently, there is no room, so long as belief is present, for a difficult judging *commitment*, sustained over time. What the critic has here is a commitment for the exceptions. And, interestingly, even its applicability to the exceptions—to the times when the believing disposition fails to be activated—can be questioned. For while it is reasonably clear that a believing experience may fail to be triggered for the believer by the relevant state of affairs crossing her mind when she is focused on those "swirling doubts," it is not at all clear that this can be the case *when she focuses on that state of affairs, as she must do to judge that it obtains*. If, when she brings the alternatives to mind and focuses on the state of affairs allegedly believed to obtain, a belief experience does not result, we should not say of the individual who now goes on to hold that state of affairs tenaciously before her mind and voluntarily judge that it obtains that she may *still be a believer*; we should rather conclude that she is not. There is indeed such a thing as a weak belief disposition, but a "disposition" as weak as that is not a disposition at all.

I suggest, therefore, that the critic's program fails. Such beliefs as we have examined are just beliefs. The sort of propositional attitude they embody, however hedged about with qualifications and would-be additions, does not involve voluntarily seeing the world a certain way (the actual *seeing* in the case of belief is involuntary), which is what propositional faith requires. Accordingly, our claims to the effect that religious faith neither is nor entails religious belief, and that propositional religious faith is in fact incompatible with such belief, can be upheld. Indeed, they should now seem quite believable! But there may still seem to be a different *kind* of reason for rejecting these claims. Specifically, some will be inclined to think of the notion of faith I have defended as lacking in *religious* virtues. I conclude this chapter by citing certain complaints of this sort and giving my answers.

5. *Replies to Religious Objections*

(1) "Intuitively, we can see that your account is inadequate, because it makes faith out to be a dry and dusty affair, bereft of assurance, whereas it is in fact a wonderful experience of the living God, who is as real to

the person of faith as the grass on her lawn, and a constant source of comfort and joy."

To this I reply that faith and the elements of a typical religious life can easily be confused with each other, a problem compounded by the fact that one way of having faith does indeed seem to be accompanied by comfort, joy, and assurance: namely, the sort of implicit trust of which I have spoken. But faith is not the whole of just any religious life or properly identified with religious experience, even though importantly related to them; and it must be construed as the sort of thing that can pull you through even when the desired emotional states are not forthcoming (as preached from pulpits every Sunday). At least a part of what religious people call the *merit* of faith resides precisely in its ability to do so, which should (at least typically) make beliefless faith more meritorious rather than less, if faith is meritorious at all. Furthermore, the person of faith who lacks comfort and joy because she lacks belief may, as we have seen, possess other qualities in relation to her faith that prevent it from being "dry and dusty"—a passionate love of God, for example. Finally, although I have not emphasized the point in this chapter, religious faith should be construed in such a way as to make its presence in nontheistic contexts unsurprising, not restricted to theistic contexts, as in the objection.

(2) "The kind of beliefless faith you describe is unlikely to *motivate* a religious life successfully. Isn't faith supposed to be what *supports* one in the religious life? Without belief, what reason is there to carry on? How can one keep going without belief to sustain one?"

It is tempting to reply: "Ask those who do it." The fact is, religious people are doing it all the time, carrying on through the dark night of the soul, when belief may be absent or, if present, too weak to represent a powerful source of motivation. So it must be possible. The reasons for carrying on we can only allude to here—in terms of a salvific reality and the favorable evaluation and perhaps hope undergirding faith even when belief is absent. It may also be worth noting that an emphasis on religious attitudes as "sustaining" and "supporting" can be taken too far: sometimes it reflects a desire to have God or the ultimate, however conceived, do everything for us, which itself reflects an ultimately immature form of religion. The one who gets past it, recognizing the complexities and responsibilities (including intellectual responsibilities) of life more clearly—perhaps for that very reason lacking belief—would seem to be capable of leading a more mature religious life, which, given the emphasis on development and growth in religion, must surely be seen as desirable. And, of course, moments of joy and grace are available even to someone like this.

(3) "The beliefless faith you describe seems quite individualistic. Doesn't faith rather require inclusion in a community and participation in its life?"

If it *is* a lonely affair, perhaps that is because many who lack belief do not recognize faith as an option, and so there are few like-minded persons for a person of faith to associate with. Or perhaps it is because those who believe think they are the only ones who can have faith and so are reluctant to admit others (or at least, to admit them fully) into the life of their religious community. Or perhaps both these factors are involved. This situation (supposing it obtains) may of course change in time, and it certainly is not the case that the one who has faith without belief must wish it to be so. Indeed, without an insistence on belief as a precondition of full acceptance, the one who has faith without belief would seem able to evince a much *more* inclusive and communitarian attitude.

(4) "Isn't beliefless faith likely to be simply a pretense or, if not that, a matter of self-*deception*? That is, it seems that to be authentic, faith must involve a wholehearted and honest commitment, whereas without belief, the person of 'faith' must either fail to be wholehearted or else fail to be honest."

Well, I have built into my understanding of faith an emphasis on religiously *committed* assent and *committed* action thereupon. The person I have described burns her bridges behind her and takes on a new form of life, lived in light of the propositions she holds before her mind. Indeed, the nonbeliever's faith involves a more difficult and risky commitment than can be made by the one with belief and should presumably be commensurately valued by religious people. There is, further, no basis for speaking of pretense here unless we question-beggingly lay down as an axiom at the start that the only authentic religious life is that of the believer and that every person of faith knows this. As for self-deception, notice that it could occur only if the voluntary assent is indeed over time transformed into belief. And even that is not enough, since one would need to show that the transformation occurs as a result of some intentional fudging of the facts as opposed to new apparent insights or new experiences, which produce belief willy-nilly, and provide the *evidence* which the former skeptic appeals to in justifying her newfound belief. Now it is, first of all, not the case that all who adopt beliefless faith find their attitude of assent turned into belief over time; second, it is not at all clear that where this does occur, the process involved betrays the slightest trace of dishonesty. We have therefore been given no reason to suppose that self-deception is ever an issue here, much less that it must be.

(5) "Doesn't authentic faith require that *questioning* be given up? How can one give up questioning while remaining a beliefless skeptic?"

The person of beliefless faith who may be said to remain a skeptic does so only in the sense that she neither believes nor disbelieves the religious propositions at issue. Of course, a skeptic may well be bogged down in questioning (by which I mean a sympathetic and one-sided focus on objections to the relevant propositions), keeping the propositions of faith at arm's length as a result. But, as noted in Chapter 4, she need not. Doubt, we saw there, is a state that one may be in even if one does not want to be in it (and so even if one is not exactly inclined to defend evidential inconclusiveness), or has long since left the whole issue behind, or else has recognized alternative ways of dealing with it that do not require the formation of belief. The last point is of course underlined by what I have argued in this chapter: that questioning can be given up (though perhaps with difficulty) even by one who fails to believe, if she is willing to assent to the relevant propositions—thus, as it were, putting the issue of their truth behind her. Such a one deems it more important to have faith and to continue her intellectual and other explorations *that* way than to continue to pursue the sort of questioning mentioned above, which is *incompatible* with faith.

(6) "It's all well and good to talk in a perfectly general way about a skeptic acting on faith that religious propositions are true without believing them, but what exactly would such a skeptic *do*? It seems that when we get down to specifics, religious actions are such as require religious belief—think, for example, of prayer and worship, or meditating on the nonexistence of a substantial self, to pick some paradigmatically religious actions at random. Operational faith entails performing such actions, but that cannot be done without religious belief."

We need to use our imaginations here to get a sense of the full range of possible religious action and also to look carefully at the many actual and accepted religious actions a skeptic can perform. Take prayer, for example. A skeptic who assents to the proposition that there is a God may pray to God on that basis. What is perhaps more important, she may open herself to any God there may be in periods of silence and in meditation on the content of her faith. She may engage in wide-ranging and multi-leveled investigations into the nature of God. She may seek to become spiritually transformed, doing such actions (e.g., serving the poor) and cultivating such dispositions (e.g., detachment from desire for material things) as are recommended by religious traditions. She may submit to spiritual disciplines of fasting and study and attach herself to a religious mentor. She may form or join a religious community, making its purposes her own and acting accordingly, both at times of meeting together and at other times, allowing her motivational and emotional dispositions to be shaped by the regular carrying-out of religious commitments in company with these others, over time realizing some of the fruits of such a life in subtle transformations of the sort to which it is said to lead. What is this if not a religious life? What are its actions if not religious actions? In Chapter 5 we saw that what makes an action religious is that it is action in pursuit of religious goals. The individuals I have just described clearly are pursuing religious goals—indeed, they are pursuing them much more assiduously than many a believer whose religiosity the critic would take for granted, and in the face of greater challenges.

(7) "Although what you describe may be psychologically possible—and even religiously meritorious—for a person whose situation is *normally* characterized by belief (or at least was *at one time* characterized by belief), and so in whom the relevant motivational and behavioral dispositions are still in some degree present, it is *not* psychologically possible for a person who has *never* believed. And so the option you describe should not be viewed as one that can be offered indiscriminately to skeptics."

This objection's claim could be falsified by a simple survey of skeptics who have faith, but since I am a philosopher and not a sociologist, I will not seek to offer such counterevidence (the fact that such counterevidence has not been ruled out by the objection is nonetheless already a problem for it). What I can point out is that the claim presupposes that either the value of a state of affairs in which religious propositions are true *cannot be apprehended* by the skeptic who has never believed, or such an apprehension is not likely to be *motivationally efficacious* in the relevant way. And there seems no reason to believe either of those suppositions; indeed, there is reason to believe both false. What is often overlooked is the fact that even the skeptic who has never believed may not lack belief because of any sort of moral apathy or care-lessness; such a skeptic may come to care very much about the truth of religious claims and may indeed, in a very deep way, want them to be true—perhaps even possessing the love of God or of the ultimate of which I have spoken. (Her avenue into such religious concern is just a different one—a death or birth in the family, a mid-life crisis, a deepening understanding of the nature of the universe, or some other such occurrence.) She may therefore apprehend the value in question very clearly. And this hope or love (buttressed by other considerations I will not be going into here) may provide an intellectual and emotional motivation base that is perfectly sufficient to support a religious commitment.

It may also be observed that a further assumption or presupposition of the objection—namely that the motivational basis for faith present in those faith-full skeptics to which it refers is a kind of hanging-on from earlier days of belief—appears to be false. Some skeptics who formerly believed have motivations suitable to faith, all right, but ones quite different from those present when they believed. For example, instead of acting religiously out of fear of God, as they were accustomed to doing in childhood, they may do so out of love and, indeed, a love that has developed or deepened *after* the loss of belief. It seems therefore that the objection is lacking in more ways than one.

(8) "You have presented your view as one that allows us generously to extend faith to the skeptic, but when you really look at it, it is also taking faith *away* from the *believer*! No religious believer can have propositional faith if it is what you describe: no believer can have faith that *anything*, whereas surely religious believers *paradigmatically* exhibit faith-that."[32]

But although religious believers paradigmatically exhibit faith-*in*, I would say it is only on a confused view of things—a view I am trying to correct—that they paradigmatically exhibit faith-*that*. In any case, propositional faith, as I understand it, need not be viewed as the exclusive preserve of those we call nonbelievers, since with regard to *some* religious propositions even those we call believers might have only faith. Someone who firmly believes that there is a God, for example, might nonetheless be in doubt about more specific propositions of her tradition—say, that Jesus of Nazareth was God Incarnate and is coming to judge the quick and the dead—and take on the latter propositions by faith.

(9) "In your definition of "religion" we find a reference to ultimization or totalization. Now your beliefless faith is supposed to represent a possible form of religion, from which it then follows that a person of beliefless faith and commitment ultimizes in the relevant respects. But surely to do so she would have to evince the more 'complete' attitude of *absolutely confident belief*. It is indeed precisely because you are right about ultimization that we should expect such belief in religion. But then you must be wrong about faith."

The answer here is that the relevant aspect of ultimization is to be seen in the religious person's commitment to the religious way, and this, as we have seen, can be total even if she lacks religious belief. Indeed, because religious belief is involuntary, it would involve a category mistake to think of it as involved in the ultimization of commitment, which must be something done voluntarily.

(10) "Faith of the sort you commend seems to contain a healthy dose of pride. Your skeptic is just too 'good' or too 'smart' to join the ranks of humble believers, too arrogant to submit to God. But of course faith requires that such pride be given up."

---

[32] This objection and my second point in reply to it I owe, respectively, to Bruce Hauptli and Paul Draper.

I suppose the misconceptions present in this last objection are transparent, but some important points can be made by taking them up anyway. If "humble" means "intellectually humble," then many believers clearly have yet to join the ranks! Stubbornness, arrogance, and carelessness are to be found in good measure among believers, as elsewhere. Indeed, such attitudes sometimes infect their treatment of religious possibilities, which seem now and then to be viewed as swords or as shields instead of as invitations to open oneself to mystery. Of course, a skeptic, just like anyone else, can fail to be humble, but it seems clear that if she behaves as I have suggested she must behave in order to have faith, then she humbles herself, leaves questioning aside, and submits to God or the ultimate in a wholehearted manner. Indeed, she may submit to the ultimate though not at all sure how it should be conceived, being willing to seek to work this out as she goes along. Using a religious metaphor, we might say that she is called to a far country the outlines of which she but dimly perceives. The vulnerability and submission and humility required to go are evident. And it does seem a religious *virtue* to display such qualities in this way—perhaps one difficult to exhibit any other way—rather than a vice.

On the Aims of Philosophy of Religion

Our investigations in previous chapters of the nature of religion, belief, religious belief and disbelief, religious skepticism, and religious faith were undertaken not just for their own sake but also because of the larger aims that philosophers seek to carry out in connection with such phenomena, the correct development and pursuit of which are facilitated by a proper understanding of them. But what are these aims? And how *are* they correctly developed? These are themselves prolegomena issues inasmuch as it belongs to the area of prolegomena to determine what, really, we should be seeking to do in philosophy of religion, thus also contributing to an understanding of what really distinguishes this field from others.

Now our very concern with prolegomena already gives us one aim for philosophy of religion: namely, careful (and ongoing) attention to prolegomena! This aim, I have argued, is an important though often neglected one, but as the word "prolegomena" itself suggests, it ought not to be construed as the final or most general aim of philosophy of religion. It is a narrower, lower-level aim. Nevertheless, the way we deal with prolegomena must, as we will see, strongly influence our understanding of what other aims should be cultivated in the field.

I begin this chapter by examining the status quo, seeking to fashion, from certain persistently recurring directions of thought, a clear and coherent picture of what most contemporary philosophers think philosophy of religion should be about and dealing with some important conceptual problems along the way. But even as thus filled out and clarified, the received view (as my creation is generously called) tells only part of the story of philosophy of religion's aims. And so I seek to tell the rest of the story, adding the bits that are missing and weaving them together with the received view in a way that I hope will throw extra light on issues associated with the latter and their proper resolution.

1. *The Received View: Meaning and Justification*

One view (or at least a potential or incipient view) of the aims of philosophy of religion appears so regularly in dictionaries and encyclopedias of philosophy, and also in introductions to the field and mainstream work in it, as to invite the label "received." It is a view focusing principally on the resolution of two sorts of issues: issues of *meaning* and issues of *justification*. But the meaning of what? And the justification of what? And what are meaning and justification? There is a fairly clear answer to the first question and to the first part of the third: philosophers of religion will say they are concerned with the meaning of religious *claims* (or purported claims) and are seeking to establish what (if anything) those claims succeed in saying about the world. The word "claim" is sometimes intended to bring to mind someone's declaration in speech or in writing that something is so—an assertion—and sometimes the propositional content of such a declaration or assertion. Normally, the focus of philosophers is on the latter, and so "meaning of religious claims" has, for most relevant purposes, the force of "meaning of religious propositions." The concern with meaning, most philosophers would say, is in service of the concern about justification. In seeking to clarify religious claims, we may discover that they are meaning-*less* or else incoherent, which would yield an immediate (and negative!) answer to justification questions and render a separate discussion of such questions unnecessary. If, on the other hand, we discern clear meaning and coherence, we may move on to discuss what can be said on behalf of these claims, with a much better idea of which considerations are likely to be relevant, and which irrelevant, to such a discussion.

What I have just said may seem to yield a clear answer to the second question as well: philosophers of religion are concerned with the justification of religious *claims*. This appears to be borne out by what one finds in the aforementioned dictionaries and encyclopedias and the like. Richard Swinburne, for example, neatly combines the two concerns I have mentioned in defining philosophy of religion as "an examination of the meaning and justification of religious claims."[1] But unfortunately, the situation is not quite as neat as that (and the second half of the third question

---

[1] Richard Swinburne, "Religion, Problems of the Philosophy of," in *The Oxford Companion to Philosophy*, ed. Ted Honderich (Oxford: Oxford University Press, 1995), p. 763.

above—about what justification is—will give us even more trouble). We get a hint of the problem when Swinburne says of the philosopher's concern with Christian claims, "The initial philosophical task is to see how far a clear meaning can be given to these doctrines; and the next task is to consider if there are any grounds for believing them true."[2] Grounds for *believing*—which introduces a notion not yet explicitly mentioned, with which philosophers of religion are rather obviously concerned! But Swinburne's reference to belief is almost incidental. One would not go far wrong, in this context, if one read "grounds for believing" as nothing more than an indirect way of referring to the doctrinal claims in question being true or probably true. And so we are back to claims or propositions, the justification of which appears to proceed by reference to truth-oriented criteria and rigorous standards of evidence and argumentation applied directly to the propositions themselves. In this sort of discussion, though one may recognize that there can be *implications* for the justification of religious belief, the latter is not one's first or main concern.

The hint in Swinburne of a different emphasis is, however, turned into a full-blown reality elsewhere in contemporary philosophy of religion. Especially of late, matters concerning the justification appropriate to religious belief—that is, the *attitude* or *state* of religious belief—have received a lot of attention in their own right: there are well-known discussions of whether religious belief possesses such justification only if the relevant religious claims can be justified by public arguments like those emphasized by a Swinburne, or whether justification for religious belief may also be nonargumentative, perhaps generated by private experiences.[3] So, apparently, we may speak not only of the justification of religious claims but also, quite independently, of whether religious belief is justified. The crisp clarity of "meaning and justification of religious claims" is becoming blurred.

And that is not all. For it appears that yet another at least potentially distinct object of evaluation is introduced when philosophers of religion speak, as often they do, of whether and how *persons* are justified in *holding* religious beliefs. Now here we need to tread carefully, because the conclusion that the belief that p is justified (unjustified) for a person or persons

---

[2] Ibid., p. 765. It is sometimes said that understanding the *arguments* that have been offered for a claim may help us figure out what it *means,* and so it may seem that the distinction drawn here between aims concerning meaning and aims concerning justification is not as clear-cut as Swinburne suggests. But this would be to confuse *understanding* the arguments that have been offered for a claim with *assessing* them. Individuals who carve up the terrain in a Swinburnian fashion do not need to deny the relevance of the former to a determination of meaning, even if they deny the relevance of the latter.

[3] For the latest on this from the individual most responsible for its currency, see Alvin Plantinga's *Warranted Christian Belief* (New York: Oxford University Press, 2000).

and the conclusion that a person is justified (unjustified) in holding a belief that *p* are very easily conflated, and it is not always possible to tell which sort of case is intended in these discussions; indeed, often it appears that both are.[4] But the important point is that they can be distinguished. To see this, notice that in the former case we at least *may* be assessing the merits of a certain *thought-disposition type*—here it is *the* belief that *p* that we have in mind—and need not presuppose that it is realized in anyone (even if its appropriateness to this or that mental or social context may be discussed), whereas in the latter we of course always accept that a *token* of the type is *held*—what we have in mind here is *his* or *her* belief that *p*—and evaluate the person who holds it by way of assessing his or her relevant dispositions and actions (the dispositions and actions involved in their coming to, or not ceasing to, hold the token belief in question).[5] Clearly, we have different objects of evaluation here.[6]

---

[4] Of course, sometimes the two expressions are intended as synonymous, as different ways of talking about the justification of a person. When this happens, we are referring to the token belief actually held by the person in question when we say that "belief that *p*" is justified or unjustified for a person, and our meaning is that the person is justified or unjustified in that instance of the belief that *p*. Something like this may explain what is going on in Nicholas Wolterstorff, "Can Belief in God Be Rational?" in *Faith and Rationality*, ed. Nicholas Wolterstorff and Alvin Plantinga (Notre Dame, IN: University of Notre Dame Press, 1983), p. 163: "*A person* is rationally justified in believing a certain proposition which he does believe unless he has adequate reason to cease from believing it. *Our beliefs* are rational unless we have reason for refraining" (my emphasis).

[5] The analogy provided by actions being called wrong in abstraction from any talk of an actor when we also may say that it was wrong of so-and-so to do those actions might be of some use here.

[6] No doubt there are or may be important connections among these concepts and activities. But the distinctions are also important. Perhaps, for one thing, we might have a resolution for at least part of the famous internalism/externalism debate in epistemology if we clearly recognized the possibility of distinct objects of evaluation in this context. Philosophers sometimes respond to this debate by saying that there must be different conceptions—perhaps "subjective" and "objective" conceptions—of justified belief. But maybe the so-called objective notion of justification is properly associated with belief types, and the so-called subjective notion should more clearly and exclusively be associated with persons and belief tokens. Perhaps at the most general level we even have one notion of justification applied to different objects instead of different notions applied to the same object (more on this later). Failure to consider these possibilities leads to unnecessary disagreement. Nicholas Wolterstorff, for example, disagrees with externalists over whether the term "justified" might pick out a certain merit or desirable feature in beliefs; of someone whose beliefs lack that merit but who has perhaps done as well, intellectually, as he can he remarks: "Can it really be correctly said of him that he is *not justified* in believing as he does? I suggest that there is no sense of the English word 'justified' such that that can correctly be said of him" ("Can Belief in God Be Rational?" p. 184). But if externalists could be construed as referring to belief types instead of believers, then no claim about believers lacking justification would follow from what they are here regarded as claiming, and the reason for disagreement would evaporate.

Given the nature of the matters associated with these different objects of evaluation, there is no way of subsuming all of them under the discussion of propositional justification emphasized by Swinburne: we see here important *differences* in emphasis which make far more considerations relevant than would arise with that approach alone (considerations, just for example, of reliability in belief-forming practices and of epistemic duty fulfillment). Indeed, where the focus is on belief in its own right, or on believers, one also finds mention here and there of purely *pragmatic* reasons for believing—reasons commending religious beliefs, and, so it is sometimes said, justifying those who hold such beliefs, deriving from the (non-truth-oriented) benefits they are said to afford for the believer or others. And here we are obviously in a sort of discussion *very* different from the one we are having when we consider whether this or that proposition can be shown to be true or probably true. That being said, it must also be said that most philosophers have a hard time mustering much enthusiasm for such "pragmatic" reasons. As philosophers, they would like, naturally enough, to know whether religious claims are true, and they find most fascinating arguments or other grounds purporting to settle this issue. So even when focusing on the belief response, or on the believer, contemporary philosophers tend to restrict themselves to justificational considerations in some way bound up with the pursuit of truth and knowledge—with what is called *epistemic* justification.

The various complicating facts so far reviewed mean that careful treatment indeed is called for when we discuss the received view's emphasis on justification. And there are other complexities, too. We have focused on the fact of different *objects* of evaluation, to each of which justification language may be applied (here we were prompted by the second of the questions with which I began). But there is also an issue about the *nature* of evaluation and, in particular, about what that central evaluative term "justification" *means* (the second part of the third question). From our own discussion the careful reader may have already discerned that the term is used in more than one way. Can any clarity be brought to this situation?

A veritable plethora of uses emerges when one inspects the term "justification" more closely, even when restricting one's attention to philosophical contexts. In a first relevant sense, justification is a certain positive property that may be possessed by various things, including religious beliefs. Call this the *property* sense. When something possesses the property in question, it is *justified*. This is the meaning we had in mind when we spoke of a belief possessing justification and—giving a little more detail as to what might go into that property—of epistemic justification. A second sense is what one sees in titles of books referring to "the justification of religious belief" and intending thereby to indicate a favorable conclusion as to whether religious belief has the property mentioned. Here "justification" means the state of possessing that property. Alternatively, we might say it means the state of *being justified*. Call this the *state* sense of "justification." In a third sense, justification is *a* justification, a supportive reason strong enough to bring it about that claims or beliefs or persons are in the state just mentioned and thus are justified. So in discussing Swinburne we might have said, in this third sense, that according to him philosophers should consider whether a justification of Christian claims can be provided. Call this the *reason* sense of "justification." Such a reason we may speak of as *justifying* or as *having justified* (that is, having caused to *be* justified in the first sense) the item in question.

There are at least two derivative senses here, which I lump under the reason sense: one according to which justification is genuine support but not complete support ("He had some justification for what he said but not enough"), and another according to which it is just a reason, good or otherwise, of some purported degree of strength, whether partial or complete ("What justification was offered for that claim?"). But we also hit upon another distinctive meaning of "justification" when we consider the process or activity of *providing* a reason of the relevant sort (of providing a justification), whether good and complete in the original reason sense (in which case we can use the terms "justifying" and "having justified" again, thinking this time of *persons* bringing it about that a belief or whatever is justified *through* producing a reason of the relevant sort), good but incomplete, or just a reason of some sort or other. Because it won't affect our discussion, I abstract from these differences to say that what we have here is the *activity* sense of "justification."

So we have the property, the state, the reason, and the activity senses of that term "justification." Is there not cause for alarm at this diversity in usage? I myself do not think that the diversity in and of itself is troubling. For the three latter senses of the term are themselves all pretty clearly derived from or parasitic on the first, property, sense—the state involved is the state of possessing the property; the reason is a reason that brings about (or may bring about) the state of possessing the property; the activity is the activity of providing a reason that may bring about the state of possessing the property—and so a kind of unity of concern can be preserved. Obviously, the main concern is with *that property*. So if there were something approaching unanimity in philosophy on what goes into that property, we might be sailing. We could then, with some idea of what we were talking about (and tidying up a little as we go), identify the received view of philosophy of religion's aims as the view that philosophers of religion ought to seek to resolve issues concerning the meanings of religious claims, and concerning the justification (in a clearly defined property sense) of such claims, as well as of the associated religious beliefs and of those who hold (instances of) them. But there is no such unanimity. There is no clearly defined property sense of "justification."

And *this* is where the *real* difficulties begin. Philosophers of religion, embroiled in a problem inherited from epistemology, whose practitioners are obsessed with the nature of justification but notoriously quarrelsome on the subject, disagree among themselves as to what justification is (and from now on, unless otherwise indicated, it may be assumed that I am using that term in the property sense), with some speaking of truth-conduciveness in one form or another, and others of pragmatic desirability or of aptness for duty-fulfillment, or something else again. So although we may say that the received view emphasizes the justification of all the objects we have mentioned, we cannot yet say that there is a received view on what this *means*. Clearly, some extra tidying up—and perhaps also some reconstructive surgery—is required here.

2. The Nature of Justification

It may be that the problem we have found concerning the *nature* of justification can in part be resolved by applying what we learned in discussing the earlier problem about the *objects* that may possess it. Perhaps at least part of our difficulty is that the term "justification" is applied, often without clear recognition, to more than one object, and part of the solution may accordingly come from more clearly and consistently recognizing and applying this insight. If we do so, we may notice a single notion of justification that can be instantiated in different ways—ways whose differences grow out of the differences between these various things that may *possess* justification. Perhaps this can point to a way forward (see also n. 6).

But now a new problem arises, for any shared meaning would have to be such as could, as it were, spread out over all these objects. Will this not tend to leave us with something pretty thin and unhelpful—not to mention misleading when its use *disguises* the diverse objects? And this problem can be made to seem even more severe when, anticipating later discussion, we introduce an important criticism of the status quo. In its fascination with religious belief, philosophy of religion has neglected the fact that it represents but one of *several* responses one might make to a religious claim—responses I have anatomized in earlier chapters.[7]

---

[7] Notice that religious belief does not *constitute* such a response (the same goes for religious disbelief). In some religious beliefs the state of affairs envisaged might be (say) the

Perhaps most important, religious belief plus action upon it is not alone where *positive* responses to religious claims, sufficient to generate religious practice, are concerned. The person of propositional and operational faith also makes a positive and religion-generating response to religious claims, and his reasons for doing so may be expected to be quite different from those appropriate to belief—perhaps, for example, involving more of an emphasis on the goodness of what certain claims refer to than on their truth. Thus, to restrict attention to whether religious claims or religious beliefs or religious believers are justified is inappropriate: instead of speaking about beliefs alone we should speak more generally about *responses to religious claims*; and instead of speaking of believers alone we should speak more generally of *those who make or offer responses* or, I suppose, *respondents*.[8] So why does this realization make the difficulties concerning the nature of justification more severe? Well, because now we have even more for that property to spread out over. Is it really plausible to suppose that we may have some one property in mind if we say of all these many objects—some concerned with truth and others not, some persons or token states of persons and others not—that they are justified?

I am going to bite the bullet and say yes. But to set up my solution to the difficulties encountered—a solution that seeks to fill out the received view and take it where it really ought to go—we should first step back and clarify the deeper purposes to which any talk of justification must ultimately be answerable. Here the central point is simple and should be unsurprising: the one constant in all the various contexts in which justification talk appears is *evaluative activity*. Unsurprising it may be, but if we focus on this point and more explicitly make it our point of reference, if we reflect on our rather obvious purpose of evaluating various religious phenomena by reference to the most fundamental intellectual standards applied to all the information available to us, we may be able to make some progress and develop the richer—the more discriminating and

---

existence of God, not the *truth* of the *proposition* "God exists," as would be required in a believing *response*. Having said that, some awareness of the phenomena of religion, including its claims, can normally be taken for granted where religious belief or disbelief is formed, and commonly in some way provides the occasion for its being formed. That is, religion *invites* our assessment, and religious belief and disbelief typically are initiated in response to the invitation. Moreover, there is the fact that typically more than just intellectual attitudes are involved when a response of this sort is made (e.g., there is usually action on belief as well as belief, and operational as well as propositional faith).

[8] Perhaps there will be a special interest in those who make *religious* responses, but there may also be occasion for considering others, given that they too make responses to religious claims. Why should only the behavior of the religious be subject to evaluation here?

sensitive and clear-eyed—discussion that is needed.[9] Thus we can, for example, ask what it is that we want to evaluate, and a little thought will reveal rather quickly that this is not just one thing: items of the various kinds we have surveyed so far all belong on the list. Think of whatever attitudes or responses of religious belief, disbelief, faith, and skepticism come to mind (e.g., the belief that God exists, faith that the Buddha nature is realizable, categorical religious skepticism) and set alongside these the propositions in one way or another involved in them, as well as the persons who make such responses. Our next question can be this: What are we looking for when evaluating items in those three categories? In other words, what property or properties would make a favorable evaluation appropriate?

For propositions, it seems that the answer must be *certain truth or probability of truth.* But to see why we need first to recognize that, strictly speaking, it is not propositions as such that we should think of ourselves as evaluating when we make room for this first category, separating it from the other two (it would be odd to think of a proposition *as such* as good or bad), but rather their qualifications for a role in a set of intellectual activities centered on truth and argument, alluded to earlier in connection with Swinburne. (Later we will find this point in a larger context that explains it.) We might, for example, find ourselves investigating whether God exists and considering various candidates for premises that advance that conclusion. In this sort of context, where, as I shall say, a proposition is *argumentatively utilized,* nothing other than the appearance of truth, it seems, should ignite our interest in a proposition.[10] Of course, what we want is *certain* truth or at least *probability* (whatever exactly the latter might be), and philosophers have the task of seeking consensus on where these

---

[9] When I say "all the information available to us," I do not mean to suggest that I think there is some one pot of stable information which anyone (or anyone in our period of history) with appropriate effort can uncover and to which we are all responsible. Information is constantly changing, and we do not all have the same information. Perhaps the best that philosophers can hope for is the consensus on the most relevant information revealed by investigation and its import mentioned here and there in the text. This side of such a consensus, *each one* of us (or each collaborating team) has the task of contributing to its realization by offering up for discussion the results of his or her own application of the most fundamental standards *known to him or her* to information that *becomes* available *in the course of the most thorough investigation he or she can muster.* (The thought expressed here is not just more convoluted but also more adequate than its counterpart in the text. I suggest that the latter be taken as a condensed version of the former.)

[10] Notice that even where we seek simply to advance to some extent the probability of a conclusion instead of seeking to render it probable overall, or to show that some conclusion is epistemically possible instead of trying to show that it is true, our arguments will still have premises about probability or possibility that we hold to be true, and we will still hold our conclusion about probability or possibility to be true.

are to be found, debating the matter on the basis of how things appear to them when most carefully investigated. So let us say that if a proposition actually is certainly true or probable, given our information, then it deserves a positive evaluation; otherwise, it deserves a negative one (given what we look for in propositions and why, *im*probability is not required for an appropriately negative judgment).

What about the various responses to religious propositions? What should we be looking for here? I suggest that we should be looking for a kind of *worthiness* that abstract discussion can help us discern: we should consider which of the various possible responses to this or that religious proposition or set of propositions is worthy of being instantiated or (as I put it in order to recognize the active element involved) *worthy of being chosen or pursued.* But when do we have such "worthiness"? Since the responses we make to religious claims are important, and indeed central to our lives, clearly we want to make the best response we can make—which is to say, that response which information turned up by our most careful investigation suggests is best. This alone would be worthy of choice or pursuit; anything else, it seems, would have to be unworthy. Perhaps some choices in life would be worthy even if not the best that could be made—a car or house might be worthy of choice even if not the best we could choose, so long as it served our basic purposes—but it does not seem that central life choices are among them. Philosophers might therefore fittingly take this comparative idea of "the best response that can be made" as their starting point when evaluating responses to religious claims and view it as providing their fundamental criterion of worthiness. (There is a development of all this at the beginning of the next chapter.)

Now we have been speaking quite generally about a response that is worthy of being chosen or pursued. But sometimes our judgment may well be more restricted: we may say that this or that type of response is worthy or unworthy in a certain narrower type of situation, where the circumstances include ones commonly but not universally encountered: for example, those in which a certain kind of religious experience occurs or a certain kind of need is felt. No doubt philosophers should catalogue the most common types of differentiating circumstances within the larger human condition and think about the responses that would be worthy or unworthy of being made in those circumstances. But it is important to distinguish any of this from talk about token individuals, responses, and circumstances and also from talk about times when token responses are made. The discussion at this level must remain *general,* and indeed, the most attractive and useful judgments philosophers could render here would be ones applying to *all* types of circumstances.[11] And so perhaps we may commend to everyone the belief that there are no gods on Mount Olympus, pointing out the overwhelming evidence in favor of the truth of that proposition and various insidious practical effects of taking up any alternative attitude. Again, philosophers have the job of seeking consensus as to which responses are worthy of being made on the basis of the most careful and sensitive investigation.[12] Notice that if it is faith that gets the nod in the case of some religious proposition, then we have something that *can* be chosen; if it is belief or disbelief, then we have something that can at least be pursued. (What I mean by "pursuit" is that a person can initiate a *course* of action, perhaps involving active skepticism, designed to open her to the results of intellectual inquiry, which may cause it to be the case that a belief of a certain type, vindicated by philosophical inquiry, is involuntarily formed in her in time.) If a response really is worthy of choice or pursuit, then it deserves a positive evaluation; otherwise, it deserves a negative one.

What now of persons? What should philosophers of religion have in mind here? In this case, it seems to me, the relevant desideratum is pretty clearly what we might call *responsibility* or, more exactly, the *responsible governance* of whatever responses are made to religious claims—and some response will be made by everyone—in the midst of the less than ideal circumstances in which we actually find ourselves, where a consensus on most important questions has not yet been reached. Generalizing from what was suggested earlier in respect of token beliefs, we might say that in determining whether some individual has responsibly governed his response to religious claims, we assess the dispositions and actions involved in his coming to, or not ceasing to, make the response in question. We think about whether he has done as much as might be expected of him, given his nature and experience and information, now and in the past, to make those dispositions and actions *good* ones—whether he has done as much as might be expected of him in cultivating relevant virtues

---

[11] Because of this I tend hereafter to avoid mention of circumstances and times when referring to the evaluation of responses.

[12] I make no assumption that a consensus as to what response is worthy determines the truth as to what is worthy. Some piece of information turned up by investigation might be misassessed by all finite human investigators involved in the consensus, and, were we later to learn of this and were it to be information suggesting that a different response is better, we would surely say that we had previously been in error as to the nature of the best response that could be made. But consensus, at least if it is reached as a result of the most scrupulous investigation, is the best *indication* of the truth we can have and is worth striving toward, just as it is in science. It is what really is true about what response is worthy that determines what evaluation of responses is deserved, but philosophers can do no more than their best to deliver up the evaluation that is deserved.

such as open-mindedness, fairness, humility, integrity, and diligence, and the fulfilment of relevant duties such as duties associated with proper investigation.

When thinking about the responsibility or irresponsibility of persons, even more than in the other cases, results of evaluation may vary, for individuals in different situations will make many different responses which, one naturally supposes, will represent rather a wide range of merits and demerits. And, as we have seen, when assessing whether an individual has conducted himself properly, we must inevitably find ourselves considering details of the *particular history and context* of his response. This particularity might seem to limit the impact of what philosophers, in their general and abstract way, can do here. Nicholas Wolterstorff, using the term "rational" to refer to persons receiving a positive intellectual evaluation (and also exhibiting the contemporary fixation with belief), writes: "Whether a given person is in fact rational in [theistic] belief cannot be answered in general and in the abstract. . . . It can only be answered by scrutinizing the belief system of the individual believer, and the ways in which that believer has used his noetic capacities."[13] But philosophers can still work to develop correct general *principles* for determining how to proceed and what evaluation to give in individual cases, and certain interesting results of a general nature may well be forthcoming when these are applied. Both these points are borne out by Wolterstorff's own discussion, which spends considerable time and ingenuity on the development of persuasive general principles of rationality in belief formation, and then uses them to call into question the claim that persons who hold religious beliefs are inevitably irrational in doing so.[14] In any case, once more we can say that where the relevant desideratum is present, the item in question—in this case an individual person or persons—deserves a positive evaluation, and that otherwise a negative one is appropriate.

There is an important disconnection and also an important connection between the evaluation of responses and the evaluation of persons. The disconnection is perhaps obvious: a claim to the effect that some response *r* (that is, the response type) is unworthy of choice or pursuit may not—at least not as things are at present, with controversy as the norm—provide adequate support for a negative evaluation for all *tokens* of *r*. Even responsible individuals instantiating those tokens may be

---

[13] Wolterstorff, "Can Belief in God Be Rational?" p. 176.

[14] Alvin Plantinga and many others have also indicated an interest in such general results by seeking to produce them. See, for example, Plantinga, *Warranted Christian Belief*, pp. 99–102.

unaware of, or call into question, its unworthiness. The connection is connected to the disconnection. It is this: philosophers, in developing their abstract evaluations of possible responses to religious claims and debating their merits, are pioneers and scouts looking for a terrain in which to live; they are seeking to provide an aid and a guide for the concrete choices and pursuits of individuals. To alter the metaphor, they are in the business of assessing and ranking candidates so that we can make a more informed vote. We may therefore expect to find a link between results in these two cases because discussions of the first sort, if systematically and effectively carried out, may well restrict the range of responsible choice. It could be, for example, that philosophical investigations provide good support for the idea that a certain (negative) feature is present in a certain type of response to a religious claim, which makes that type of response unworthy of being chosen or pursued, *and that this becomes generally known* or can be expected to be known at some time by all responsible inquirers (just as the status of the Greek gods is now generally known). Thus the range of what can responsibly be chosen or pursued may become contracted as philosophical investigation progresses; evaluations in the third category will to some extent be calibrated to the accepted results of abstract discussion in the second. Or, at least, we can expect this result, together with a corresponding diminishment in complacency at the level of personal evaluation (where talk of "duty-fulfillment" can often be quite vague and permissive), if philosophers do a *good job* at the level of response evaluation—all of which should make the aim of doing so the more attractive!

Having thus briefly clarified to ourselves what ought to be involved in the main evaluative goals discernible in the neighborhood of justification talk, we may now consider whether such talk can appropriately be reintroduced. Is there is any natural way of linking the various activities and properties we have outlined under a single concept—a concept plausibly viewed as a concept of justification?[15] Of course we could just *stipulate* that a proposition is justified when certainly or probably true (and thus qualified to be utilized in argument), and unjustified otherwise; that a response type is justified when worthy of instantiation, and unjustified otherwise; and that persons are justified in the token responses they make when they have been operating responsibly, and unjustified otherwise. And it is interesting to note that there would be nothing particularly odd-sounding in such stipulations, which itself suggests there may be a natural

[15] What we turn up here may not correspond exactly to what is found in this or that discussion in the literature, for we are, among other things, trying to deal with certain problems those discussions have created and thus need to be open to new possibilities.

semantic connection to "justification" here somewhere. I suggest that we can find it, and render stipulation unnecessary, as follows.

First, notice that although in talking about the evaluation of propositions, responses, and persons, we have always started by talking about what property or properties would make a *favorable* evaluation appropriate, we could have started from the oppositional side instead. Because of our limitations and imperfection, what is perhaps most conspicuous and most concerning and certainly most discussed about us and our activities in evaluative contexts is how we go *wrong*: in the normative sphere, the climate is typically one more of criticism than of praise. So even though the properties we have canvassed—certain truth, probability, worthiness, responsibility—are indeed things we might look for when evaluating, if we do look for them, it is likely to be because they are so often *lacking*. Relatedly, to realize them is to *not* realize their undesirable counterparts. To realize certain truth or probability is to *not* realize certain falsehood, improbability, or doubtfulness; to make a worthy response is to *not* make an unworthy one; to achieve responsibility is to *not* be irresponsible. By the same token, to be deserving of a positive or favorable evaluation in any of these areas is to not be deserving of an unfavorable or negative one.

Notice next that a close look at "justified" and "unjustified" apparently reveals, in a similar manner, that it is what is involved in being *un*justified that sets the parameters for justification talk. But how can we arrive at a more specific understanding of the latter notion? Well, clearly it represents some sort of negative appraisal. But there are many things that may deserve a negative appraisal without being unjustified. For example, though I hate the destruction of lives and homes resulting from freak storms at sea that make landfall and think of the fact of such destruction as very bad, it would be rather odd to speak of that fact as *unjustified*. However, this appears to be because that fact is one which no human being has deliberately produced or can erase. Talk of something being unjustified seems most naturally introduced when we are in the presence of something in some way linked to thought and choice—in particular, something *avoidable* by a thinking being. (So if we suppose the world to be governed by a Thinking Being we might find ourselves making sense after all of calling the destruction in question unjustified. And, of course, we will quite naturally speak in those terms of more specific facts concerning it—such as the fact, perhaps, that disaster assistance is slow and haphazard—supposing as we do that they could have been avoided by us.)

This connection to avoidability is required, I suggest, because talk of something being unjustified makes sense only where there can intelligibly be a *challenge* to its existence or the way we deal with it, which, proceeding beyond but on the basis of the assumption that this *could* be avoided, says that it *should* be (or should have been) avoided—that the *proper* exercise of thought and volition would lead (or would have led) to its avoidance, which is to say that the conformity of thought and volition to what reason requires, in the broad sense of what reasons concerning thought and action most strongly support, would have (or would have had) this result.[16] What we mean when we say that something is unjustified is that such a challenge goes through in its case; and what we mean when we say that something is justified is that such a challenge does *not* go through— that the item in question *need not* be avoided or, equivalently, that it is not the case that it should be (or should have been) avoided, which is to say that it is all right as it is. It follows that to say that something is justified is to say that it is not *un*justified—which shows that it is indeed what we say about being unjustified that sets the parameters of justification talk.

So we have arrived at a broad understanding of "justified" and "unjustified" involving the insight that the latter can be taken as fundamental, which—given the first point above—already marks a connection between justification talk and what we have said about the evaluation of propositions, responses, and persons. Can we now fill out that connection by applying the understanding more fully? I think we can. To begin this stage of the discussion, notice that how someone has governed her response to religious claims may intelligibly be challenged: if it is said that the states and actions involved should have been avoided, what is said makes sense. It is important not to forget that when we speak here of what should be avoided, we speak of what should be avoided *by the individual in question*. We mean that the proper exercise of *that individual's* thought and volition, something she was capable of successfully undertaking, would have led to such avoidance—that certain states and actions of hers would have been avoided had her thought and volition been conformed to what reason requires: that is, had her thought and volition been conformed to what is most strongly supported by reasons concerning thought and action that would have been revealed to her by investigation

---

[16] Are the terms "should" and its normative companions, as utilized here, correctly understood as *moral* terms? Some are inclined to use moral language broadly enough to make anything representing what (in the broad sense) reason requires a moral requirement. Others are not, suggesting that though one way a rational requirement may arise is through moral obligation, it is not the only way: perhaps I am not morally obligated to go out and make something of myself instead of lying about the house, but I may nonetheless clearly see that I have more reason to do so than to do any contrary action; thus making something of myself, though perhaps not *morally* required, is *rationally* required. Not much turns on which way we go here, so long as we remember that it is the intuitive idea of what reason requires—which way, as it were, reason *pushes* us—that is connected to uses of such normative terms as "should," "ought," and "proper."

adequate to her situation. (Everything is person-relative here, and so when we think at this level of what "reason requires," we can think only of what it requires in *her* and of *her.*)

Now apparently it is just when the individual's relevant states and actions evince irresponsibility (when she has not done what might be expected of her in the way of governing them) that we will want to say that they should have been avoided by her in this sense, and just when they do not evince irresponsibility—that is, when they are responsible—that we will think it is not the case that they should have been avoided by her. Thus where there is irresponsibility in the response one makes to religious claims and a negative evaluation is deserved, the states and actions it involves are unjustified, and, by extension, one is unjustified in making that response; otherwise—that is, where a positive evaluation is deserved because of responsible behavior, because (in other words) irresponsibility has not been entered into—all these things are justified.

It may seem, however, that this is as far as we can go, that my concept of justification does not apply where the other two evaluative categories are concerned. For propositions and response types are not states or actions of human beings, or alterable products thereof, and it is easy to suppose that they therefore lack the needed connection to avoidability. But such a conclusion would be overhasty. Propositions and response types are still linked to human thought and volition, to what could and perhaps should be avoided. The difference is that when we say "should be avoided" or "unjustified" in connection with one of those two items, we apply what we say in a completely *unqualified* way: we are speaking at another level about something we think should be avoided by *all of us*. We are dropping person-relativity and saying that for *anyone and everyone* the proper exercise of thought and volition would lead to the relevant avoidance—that such avoidance would be the result were our thought and volition conformed to what reason requires, which here must mean conformed to what is most strongly supported by reasons concerning thought and action that would be revealed to *anyone*, insofar as his investigation was *as good as could be.*[17] (Obviously, only professional

---

[17] This statement can be linked to the idea of responsibility. For from the claim that we all should avoid a proposition or response type it follows that anyone should do so who is aware of what the reasons in question support. And this idea, filled out, says that anyone aware of what those reasons support, and thinking and choosing properly (i.e., in conformity with that), will avoid the item in question. But since such persons *are* aware, this is the same as saying "in conformity with what the reasons *available to them and to their own investigation* most strongly support," which, as we have seen, amounts to "responsibly." It follows that no thinking being thus apprised can fail to avoid the item in question without irresponsibility.

investigators will be in a position to use *this* "should.") And further, we have in mind a specific sort of avoidance.

Let us see how these points can be cashed out in the case of propositions. The relevant reasons or relevant information from investigation in the case of a proposition would surely involve information showing that it is neither certainly nor probably true; such a proposition should be avoided by thinking beings and is unjustified in the following way: *it should not be argumentatively utilized by them* (no one who is conformed to what the relevant information supports would utilize it thus). And so a proposition turns out to be unjustified when it deserves a negative evaluation. Clearly, furthermore, it deserves a *positive* evaluation when it is *justified*, for such an evaluation applies when it *is* certainly or probably true and so when it need not be avoided in the specified way.

What about response types? In what way are we saying that one of these should be avoided by thinking beings when we say it is unjustified? Pretty clearly we are saying that it *should not be made or instantiated*. That is how one avoids response types. And it does seem that any information that might make a response such as should not be made or instantiated will also make it *unworthy of being chosen or pursued*, and that a response that is *not* such as should not be made is *worthy*. For reason will require that a response not be made precisely when there is a better response that can be made—remember here the point about the importance of such responses in our lives—and so when it is unworthy. And if no better response can be made, how could reason be against it? Proceeding in this way, we can show that what needs to be said about the nature of justification dovetails rather well with what was said earlier about evaluation in all three categories. In particular, a positive evaluation in all three categories can be expressed in terms of the presence of justification, and a negative one in terms of its absence.

It may be worthwhile to underline here that in saying that something linked to thought and volition ought to be avoided and is not all right as it is (i.e. is unjustified), we often imply that things should be *different* with respect to it; and in saying that it is all right and need not be avoided we often imply that things *need not be* different. More precisely, and discriminating now between the categories, to say that a subject *S* is unjustified in making the token response that she has made or is making is to imply that *S* should be in a different state (i.e., a state incompatible with her making that response); and to say that *S* is justified is to imply that it is not the case that she should be in a different state. Further, to say that a certain response type *r* is unjustified is to imply that a response of a different type (i.e., of a type incompatible with *r*) should be made; and to say that *r* is justified is to imply that it is not the case that a different response should be made. Only in the case of propositions is there no such implication: to say that a certain proposition *p* is unjustified is not to imply that a different proposition should be seized upon. As we have seen, a proposition is unjustified so long as it should not be argumentatively utilized, and this would be the case even if the only justified state were doubt all around, and different propositions should not be utilized either.

It appears, then, that the problems we have run into in seeking to give a clear shape to the received view, which emphasizes meaning and justification, can be solved. The received view of the aims of philosophy of religion, properly filled out, can be expressed by saying that philosophy of religion should seek to resolve the most important issues concerning (1) the meanings of religious propositions and (2) the justification of religious propositions, the justification of the various responses thereto, and the justification of persons who make such responses, where the nature of justification is understood against the background of our evaluative concerns in a manner at once discriminating and unifying, as outlined above.

3. Building on the Received View: Theory and Practices

I suggest now that the received view, thus filled out, still tells only part of the story of the aims of philosophy of religion and, indeed, betrays neglect of what ought to be viewed as its *most general* or *highest-level* aims, the proper recognition of which (and of the neglect of which) will help us understand why, in discussing the received view, we have been pulled in so many directions at once. (Thus my solution to the problems that arose in previous sections gets some extra support here.) When these additional aims are properly accommodated, the aims concerning meaning and justification we have already distinguished can be seen to be *lower-level* and—like the aims involved in the study of prolegomena—*facilitating* aims, no doubt worth pursuing for their own sakes but also, importantly, for the sake of certain other aims.

What are these other, higher-level aims? I suggest that, taking our cue from the link forged in Chapter 1 between what philosophers of religion do and broader philosophical concerns, we should identify one of them as the aim of *investigating the theoretical value of religious claims in relation to problems in other areas of philosophy.*[18] Philosophy has obvious reason to be

---

[18] The discussion of philosophical problems has sometimes involved questioning whether the development of theories is conducive to problem resolution, so I mean "theoretical" to be taken very broadly, in such a way as to be applicable to any activity aimed at achieving knowledge or understanding (and so truth). It might be thought that one could say something like "intellectual" or "rational" here instead, but these terms are *too*

interested in whatever bearing religion may have on the resolution of its problems in metaphysics, ethics, epistemology, and so on; it is therefore natural and appropriate for philosophers concerned with religion to investigate this bearing. (Clearly, *someone* in philosophy should be doing so, and if not philosophers of religion, then who?)[19] And I suggest that we identify another as the aim of *rationally evaluating religious practice.* For is it not also of the utmost importance for philosophers to try to settle the issue of whether religion is or can be a worthy and responsible pursuit of rational beings when it is so commonly practiced by humans, and so frequently touted as a source of great good, but also so often challenged in modern culture? We therefore have some further evaluative aims, which take us beyond the evaluative aims discussed in the previous section even (as we will see) while incorporating them.

But here we must pause for a moment: Are these additional aims I have introduced really separate, as I have suggested? Doesn't the first one simply entail the second, in the sense that anyone who fully carried out the first aim would ipso facto have carried out the second as well? The answer is no. To be sure, there is an obvious connection between the broader theoretical concerns of ethics (and also the questions of metaphysics) and questions about how a religious way of life is to be evaluated.[20] What the first aim mentioned above is concerned with, however, is not whether the ideas of philosophy have some bearing on religion but rather whether the ideas of religion have some bearing on the concerns of philosophy. The first higher-level aim is restricted to claims of religion that have *theoretical potential* and—insofar as responses to religious claims considered in

---

broad, potentially embracing, as they do, purely pragmatic considerations aimed at something more than or other than knowledge.

[19] Contemporary Christian philosophers of religion acknowledge the appropriateness of this aim in their examinations of how broader issues of philosophy might be illuminated by Christian doctrine, examinations that have been given new motivation by the establishment (in 1978) of the Society of Christian Philosophers and the urgings of its founders, and frequently published in its journal, *Faith and Philosophy.* (A volume resulting from these activities is *Christian Theism and the Problems of Philosophy,* ed. Michael Beaty [Notre Dame, IN: University of Notre Dame Press, 1990]). This approach, which really only resumes in a more analytically rigorous manner what was common earlier in the history of philosophy of religion, ought in my view to be continued but in a widened form that more fully takes account of nonorthodox Christian and non-Christian religious ideas as well.

[20] To maintain that there is a connection here to the concerns of ethics is not to reduce religion to ethics in any sense of "reduce" that might lead to objection. It is only to point out the obvious fact that for any form of religion that is positively evaluated, there is some comprehensive *way to live one's life* that is positively evaluated, about which ethics might well have something to say, given its concern with, inter alia, what reason dictates in the realm of behavior.

their own right are relevant to it at all—to the question whether there are any religious *beliefs* that can be *epistemically* justified (only those that are would normally be taken as capable of leading us to claims having theoretical potential). But the rational evaluation of religious practice may involve something quite different from the examination of *specifically religious theories of ethics* or claims conducive thereto (perhaps things we know in ethics quite independently of religion may serve to support religious practice or its avoidance), and also something other than understanding whether belief of religious metaphysical claims is epistemically justified (after all, perhaps *faith* can provide an acceptable basis for religious practice). Thus the assessment of religious practice appears to take us *beyond* what is subsumed by the aim of investigating the theoretical value of religious claims in relation to problems in other areas of philosophy, and we are warranted in treating the aim of carrying out such an assessment as a separate aim.

It may well seem that not much is new in these broader aims I have introduced, that they are already so clearly acknowledged by contemporary philosophers of religion that an interpretation of the so-called received view must *include* them if it is to be deemed correct. Swinburne himself might be cited here, for he says that purported facts about the justification of religious claims may be used to justify "the practice of a way of life."[21] But although philosophers such as Swinburne do indeed appear to think of questions concerning the meaning and justification of religious claims as being discussed at least in part in order to determine the rational status of the associated form(s) of religious practice, the latter concern is very often underemphasized or left implicit. And the *first* aim, of determining the theoretical potential of religious claims, rarely appears other than implicitly and, moreover, in an excessively narrow form focused on theistic religion.

It is true that the relevance to their field of other areas of philosophy is sometimes explicitly noted by philosophers of religion. Keith Yandell, for example, says in his introductory text that philosophy of religion is "metaphysics, epistemology, and ethics applied to religion."[22] But it is evident that for him (as for most writers) the relevant point about these other disciplines within philosophy is that attention to their results is needed to carry out the examinations of meaning and justification given primary emphasis by the received view. Yandell says just that: "Philosophy of religion combines these enterprises in offering philosophically accessible

---

[21] Swinburne, "Religion," p. 763.
[22] Keith E. Yandell, *Philosophy of Religion: A Contemporary Introduction* (London: Routledge, 1999), p. 367.

accounts of religious traditions [by which he means "clear and literal expressions of key doctrines"] and assessing those traditions."[23] So, for example, recent developments in metaphysics might be exploited to yield various interpretations of the timelessness of God and also to determine how one should choose between them, and various techniques from epistemology, broadly construed, might be utilized to rigorously assess claims concerning the existence of the God whose nature has thus been clarified, or even the degree of intellectual responsibility to be found in theistic believers. All of this is of course perfectly appropriate, as far as it goes. But notice that here the relation between other areas of philosophy and philosophy of religion runs only one way; the sort of relation suggested by our first more general aim is not yet explicitly recognized. This relation, I suggest, is not—as in the case of the carrying out of aims concerning meaning and justification—a matter of metaphysics, epistemology, and ethics having application to religion *but of religion having potential application to metaphysics, epistemology, and ethics.* Perhaps, just for example, the insights of Buddhist thinkers will turn out to be helpful in untying the knots in which philosophy can become entangled where issues of selfhood and free will are concerned. Clearly, the relation runs both ways, and only the explicit introduction of our first higher-level aim of philosophy of religion allows us to see this properly.

Once we do see both of the aims that I have introduced here, we are in a position to tighten up our understanding of philosophy of religion's other aims (and also the problems associated with them). There are several observations here. One is that the single-minded concern with epistemic justification one finds in much philosophy of religion makes sense most obviously in relation to the first more general aim we have identified: the aim of investigating the theoretical value of religious claims in relation to problems in other areas of philosophy. (Ironically, the more general aim that contemporary philosophy of religion shows the least sign of explicitly acknowledging is the one to which its standard treatments are best adjusted.) How much use can one expect to make, theoretically, of a claim that is dubious or a claim belief of which is supported only by pragmatic or, more broadly, non-truth-oriented considerations? I suspect that their tendency as philosophers to want to solve theoretical problems of philosophy, however inchoately or narrowly realized in their activities in philosophy of religion, may also explain the resistance of many practitioners of that craft to the idea (championed by Plantinga et al.) of religious belief being justified without arguments. After all, belief claims nicely fleshed out and supported by arguments that hook up with

[23] Ibid., p. 18.

work in other areas of investigation are so much more obviously potentially useful from a theoretical perspective than beliefs associated with the
vagaries of "religious experience."

But there is also the second more general aim, and here the typical
argument- and belief-centered approach is not as clearly apposite.
(Ironically, the more general aim that philosophy of religion *most* shows
signs of acknowledging is the one to which its standard treatments are
least well adjusted.) When our main concern is not with solving theoretical problems but with evaluating religious practice, the ideas of experiential and of non-truth-oriented support for religious belief are at least not
obviously out of place and should be carefully considered. Even the dubi-
ousness of a religious claim may be no hindrance to its having a rationally
appropriate role to play in religious practice if there is, as I have argued,
an *alternative* to propositional belief—namely, propositional faith—where
positive responses to religious claims are concerned, which *requires* that
the evidence favoring a proposition be weak. The second more general
aim also nicely accommodates the concern of contemporary philosophers with the evaluation of *persons*, including individual religious practitioners. For we may think of that aim as embracing religious practice not
just in the abstract but also in its concrete manifestations. In evaluating a
religious practice, that is, we may be building on our answers to either or
both of the questions, already discussed in the previous section, as to
whether responses to religious claims instantiating that practice are worthy of choice or pursuit, and whether those who make such responses,
including the religious, are operating in a responsible manner. And, of
course, as I have noted, we may expect to find clear connections between
the answers to these questions.

Thus the understanding that I am developing of higher-level and lower-
level aims provides a way of organizing and making sense of all the various activities and interests of philosophy of religion we have collected
under "the received view," and also a rationale for identifying its problems and developing their solutions in the way that we have. Of course,
some more *re*organizing and *re*conceiving may be necessary. In particular,
a more explicit acknowledgment of the first more general or higher-level
aim and of its broader ramifications is needed, and also a conscious
restriction of things purely claim- or proposition-oriented and perhaps
also things exclusively epistemic to matters subsumed by that aim. In pursuing the second more general aim, the single-minded focus on belief
and perhaps also on epistemic justification will need to be relaxed, and a
more deliberate and discriminating discussion of *responses* to religious
claims and the principles of their responsible governance in actual practice—a discussion designed, among other things, to turn up any justified

responses capable of instantiating religious practice there may be—will need to be entered into.

To fill this out a little: when concerned with the evaluation of religious practice, philosophers might naturally and appropriately adopt a "justification of responses and respondents" approach and, after acquainting themselves with the claims embedded in religious practices, consider the relative merits of such attitudes toward those claims as ones involving propositional belief plus operational faith, or propositional *faith* plus operational faith, or some form of skepticism but without faith, or disbelief. And they might also consider the requirements of making and maintaining such responses responsibly. Notice that the term "response" is used quite broadly here and is not restricted to propositional or intentional attitudes alone. Because of the concern with religious *practice,* someone taking this approach is naturally going to be interested in what we might call *complete* responses, especially where positive responses favoring religion are concerned. (Why focus just on propositional belief or propositional faith when your main interest is in the way of life it may inform?)[24] When philosophers are instead, for the broader intellectual purposes of their discipline, looking at the bearing of religious claims on the latter's problems, they will naturally and appropriately adopt a "justification of propositions" understanding and focus directly on the claims themselves, while allowing that their results may have *implications* for the assessment of responses to those claims and of those who make them. That is, the two approaches do also to some small extent overlap in that if reason can show the certain truth or likelihood of a religious claim, a positive response involving belief is surely justified, and so are believers who are properly apprised of this fact. But it is most important here to recognize that each approach maps onto *one* higher-level aim of philosophy of religion and raises issues distinct from those raised by the other.[25]

---

[24] Of course, as we'll see in the next chapter, if a propositional belief is justified, then so is acting on it, which might seem to warrant considering the justification simply of propositional religious beliefs in this context. But the same is not obviously true of faith, and, in any case, here we must once more remind ourselves that we ought at least to remain open to *non*epistemic forms of justification for belief, which, as normally understood, may be deeply intertwined with whether and how one intends to *act* on one's belief.

[25] A criticism of our developing view that may now be suggested is that although we have assumed that religious practices are grounded in religious claims, the former in fact have nothing to do with the latter. But it can be seen, I suggest, that religious practices *necessarily involve* religious claims; the former, however complex, ultimately involve *acting on* the latter and thus exercising what I have called operational faith. Even practices (such as may be found in liberal Christianity) that metaphorize or allegorize certain orthodox claims in order—so it is said—to relate more appropriately to a Divine Reality whose essential nature is contradicted when they are taken literally, are grounded in claims of their own. But are these *religious* claims, entailing the existence of an ultimate, salvific reality? Ultimately they

What we have noticed most recently is that the received view's concerns with meaning and justification, even when properly clarified and filled out, are not, as it suggests, properly construed as philosophy of religion's only concerns, and also that a reciprocal relation of influence between philosophy of religion and the other areas of philosophy is discernible when the additional more general or higher-level concerns are correctly identified. Are there any other legitimate criticisms of the received view?

I suggest one more. A serious omission in the received view (or at least in its received interpretation), also brought into focus by my investigations in this book, concerns an openness to forms of ultimism that have not yet have been articulated by anyone, or made the basis of a form of religious life in the actual world, but await our discovery. Contemporary philosophical approaches to religion, be they critical or commendatory, betray the assumption that the religious ideas already before us are ideas than which none greater can be achieved. Such a notion is evident in the work of conservative religious philosophers who hold that centrally important religious truths were revealed long ago, never to be superseded. It can also be detected in their harshest critics, who are led by what seem to them powerful arguments against traditional religious claims to infer that there are no such truths and that religion's day is fast approaching an end. (In between, of course, are many pure skeptics unsure what to make of it all, but even their uncertainty tends to be grounded in what has already transpired and waits to be lifted by some strengthening of the evidence concerning views well-worn and familiar.)

But what if this popular notion is just misguided and false? What if we humans are at such an early and primitive stage of religious development that apparent pinnacles of endeavor and insight in this area are at most stepping-stones, quite incapable of supporting dogmatic or dismissive generalizations? Even though I will not here examine the merits of a positive response to these questions (a response which is in any case not susceptible of demonstration), it is not obviously implausible and cannot be ruled out. Certainly, to proceed on a contrary assumption would be inappropriate. Yet contemporary philosophy of religion, in embracing an interpretation of the received view focused on the results of the past and the present, tends to do precisely that. I suggest, therefore, that a proper understanding of the (lower-level) aims of philosophy of religion to which the received view draws our attention will emphasize the need to

---

must be: that is, although other claims (e.g., about language or history) may also enter the picture, we may expect the inquiry of which they are a part to be rooted in broader theological views—or else our assumptions (justified in Chapter 1) do not permit us to call what we are dealing with here a form of religion at all.

examine *possible and undeveloped* as well as actually made and entrenched religious claims. Doing so will be of importance both for the broader aim of examining possible theoretical links between philosophy and religion and for the broader aim of rationally evaluating religious practice, since such explorations may, for all we know, turn up theoretically useful notions and also ones which, acted upon, generate forms of religion that deserve a positive evaluation from rational inquirers.[26]

4. *The Aims of Philosophy of Religion—A Proposal*

My proposal, based on the foregoing, for an understanding of the aims of philosophy of religion that will be well-suited to guide its endeavors in the future can be put in a single compendious statement as follows:

> The aims of philosophy of religion should be to bring to bear methods and results from the rest of philosophy in (1) a comprehensive study of prolegomenous issues, including the questions of what religion, the various (actual and possible) religious propositions or claims, and the various responses to religious claims, as well as the proper evaluation of the latter and of those who embrace them, most fundamentally amount to; and in (2) an inquiry geared to determining whether any religious claims are justified, and also which responses to religious claims are justified, and to what extent persons who instantiate such responses—in particular, religious responses—are justified in doing so (these I have called the lower-level aims, whose realization is facilitated by work on prolegomena); and all of this not just for its own sake but in order to facilitate (3) an investigation of what bearing religious claims may have on theoretical problems in other areas of philosophy and (4) a rational evaluation of religious practice (these last are the two higher-level aims).

I now offer some brief contextualizing and elucidatory glosses on this statement.

---

[26] Another problem for the received view that might be suggested arises from the fact that it concerns itself only with the meaning and justification of *religious* claims. Won't agnostic and irreligious ones need to be understood and evaluated as well? Yes, indeed. But nonreligious claims are clearly related to the aims highlighted by the received view and are indeed considered as *part of the process* of examining religious claims: philosophers of religion examine nonreligious views the better to assess the justification of religious ones, which may turn out to be unjustified if nonreligious views can be made plausible enough.

(i) It is evident that, structurally, the governing ideas throughout are those of explication and evaluation, and so, though my statement takes us beyond the received view critiqued in previous sections, it remains faithful to the latter's central idea of an emphasis on meaning and justification.

(ii) The reference to "methods" should be taken broadly enough to include any approach that reflects the "lofty ideal" at the heart of true philosophy, mentioned at the beginning of this book: an investigation of the deepest of intellectual problems and possibilities that is critical yet creative, analytically precise yet imaginative, tough-minded yet willing to follow wherever the truth might lead, and actively seeking an ever richer and more adequate overall understanding.

(iii) The exploration of what *religion* "most fundamentally amounts to" may take a philosopher some distance beyond the results of Chapter 1, with attention perhaps being given also to such things as the distinguishing of *types* of religion and to the identification of general *characteristics* of religion not here discussed.

(iv) The reference to religious "claims" should be seen as including not only generic ultimism and the various actual and possible elaborated ultimisms but also any other main religious claims—for example, claims concerning miracles or the veridicality of religious experience.

(v) The process of determining which *response* to this or that religious claim is justified may be very complex and involve consideration of many other claims not referred to here. To carry out this task, principles of rational preferability are needed (these are the concern of the next chapter). Criteria for the application of such terms as "justified response" have not yet been provided, so these terms should at this stage be understood quite generally; in particular, they should not be understood as ruling out the relevance of non-truth-oriented considerations.

(vi) I have spoken somewhat vaguely of "evaluating religious practice," but since we are obviously considering whether such practice deserves a *positive* evaluation, and since, as previous discussion clearly indicates, a positive evaluation will be forthcoming if and only if some religion-generating response to religious claims or—as the case may be—religious respondent is *justified,* we may say by extension that the aim is to determine whether religious practice is justified.

(vii) We might note, finally, that my statement accommodates both reflection on philosophical issues *concerning* religion and reflection on philosophical issues *growing out of* religion. That the former sort of reflection is legitimized by it will perhaps be obvious. The latter is covered by the reference to specific religious claims (including not just generic ultimism but various elaborated ultimisms) and to a concern with their meaning and justification, with the evaluation of responses to them, and with the evaluation of the specific forms of religious practice bound up with them. What makes the issues involved "philosophical" can be derived from the dual focus on core areas of philosophy such as metaphysics, epistemology, and ethics, which put in an appearance both at the beginning of the statement (where their active or contributory role is emphasized) and at the end (where their passive or appropriative role is featured).

So much for glosses. Let us look now at the question whether certain of the various aims we have discussed (or derivatives thereof) have more of a claim to the first attention of philosophers of religion than others. Can any order of priority be established here? I suggest that perhaps one can. Arguably, considering the challenge that *nonreligious responses to religious claims are rationally preferable to religious ones* should be deemed paramount.[27] If this challenge turns out to be correct in its claim, then a large part of our second higher-level aim is immediately realized: religious practice in all its forms is shown to be unjustified, and the principles for responsible governance of responses to religious claims, though they may not rule out religion for some who are unavoidably ignorant, will lead those who follow them assiduously to the rejection of religion. If it is not correct, then it will be good to consider which sort(s) of religious response survives rational scrutiny and what form(s) of life it makes available to us or requires of us.

We can go further as well. If this challenge turns out to be correct in its claim, then it appears that our first higher-level aim is also realized: that is, religion is shown to be philosophically unprofitable. For if no religious response to religious claims is justified, then *religious belief* is unjustified, and so, presumably, no relevant arguments support the truth or likelihood of religious claims. (If they did, why should religious belief be unjustified?) And in such circumstances, religious claims can hardly be expected to hold much interest for philosophers seeking to solve the larger problems of philosophy, at least given the manner in which those problems and acceptable solutions have traditionally been understood (a manner requiring that the latter be epistemically justifiable).

Are there also implications for the first higher-level aim if the challenge we are considering turns out *not* to be correct in its claim? In particular, is it then shown that religion may be philosophically profitable? Here it is important to keep in mind that responses to religious claims involving belief are distinguishable from those involving faith, and both sorts of response are positive. So it does not follow from some religious response

[27] Together, of course, with the pursuit of any lower-level or prolegomenous aims the results of whose pursuit are required for the successful pursuit of this aim.

to religious claims being justified that belief is justified. Perhaps it is faith instead. And although from the rational success of religious belief it might (in certain circumstances[28]) be inferred that religious claims should interest philosophers seeking to solve the larger problems of philosophy, this does not follow from the success of religious faith—unless, perchance, in other areas of philosophy too, and for at least some purposes of intellectual inquiry, faith turns out to be an attitude prescribed by reason.

All things considered, then, there would seem to be good reason for philosophers of religion to view with some urgency the aim of considering the challenge that nonreligious responses to religious claims are rationally preferable to religious ones. The prolegomenous discussion I move on to now is, among other things, designed to prepare us for the effective pursuit of this aim.

---

[28] Circumstances we cannot at present assume must be realized in order for religious belief to be thus successful—in which the rational success of religious belief derives from the probability of *truth* in the proposition that expresses its content.

CHAPTER 8

On Principles of Evaluation in Philosophy of Religion

In this chapter I undertake an investigation of how best to pursue some of the aims discussed in the previous one. My focus is on evaluative aims, and, even more narrowly, on the evaluation of various actual and possible *responses* to religious claims—believing, faith-full, purely skeptical, and disbelieving[1]—which the goal of determining whether religious practice is justified requires philosophers to examine. Several

---

[1] I assume that these alternatives, described in previous chapters, are the main ones (what I have to say about skepticism, it should be noted, will not be directly applicable to capacity skepticism but only to forms of skepticism immediately directed to religious claims). Any variations, or other attitudes thought relevant, may in any case be factored into the discussion in ways that are readily apparent. It should hereafter be assumed that when I speak of a believing or belief response, I mean the complete response involving propositional belief plus operational faith; and when I speak of a faith or faith-full response, I mean the complete response involving propositional and operational faith. Where I speak simply of belief or faith I normally (i.e., unless otherwise indicated) have in mind only the cognitive aspects of such responses. I do not refer explicitly to affective belief and disbelief, on the assumption that their justification is bound up with that of the relevant propositional state, and so derivative. The same goes for intellectual confidence, which, as we saw in Chapter 2, is distinguishable from belief: although belief does not entail confidence, it seems evident that *justification* for belief entails *justification* for confidence, and justification for confidence of course entails justification for belief. There is still the matter of the appropriate *degree* of confidence, about which philosophers might be expected to make pronouncements (though here we are into finer matters where philosophical recommendations may be expected to be less useful for the inquirer), but it is natural to associate the proper degree of confidence with the degree of probability achieved by the proposition involved or—should non-truth-oriented considerations be deemed relevant—the degree of confidence required to achieve the benefit at which the belief is aimed. Discussion of both affective belief/disbelief and intellectual confidence, though (as suggested) unnecessary for specifying the relevant evaluative principles, is likely to reemerge in their application. But that is another matter.

points can be raised in support of this way of proceeding. (1) Most philosophers of religion are already very well acquainted with the procedures of analysis involved in clarifying the meanings of religious claims and the methods of rigorous argumentation applicable where one seeks to evaluate such claims; the same goes for a variety of issues relevant to what I have referred to in terms of the responsible governance of responses to religious claims. But (2) those same philosophers tend to discuss the intellectual status of the responses themselves with much less thoroughness and sophistication—and this when (3) there is, as we saw at the end of the previous chapter, good reason for them to put the carrying out of such evaluations at the top of their list of priorities. To these points may be added the fact that (4) a discussion of how to evaluate responses will be the most directly useful for the next part of my project, in which I begin such an evaluation. Given these four points, it should be evident that (and how) our restricted focus is appropriate.

As suggested in the previous chapter, the separate discussion of responses to religious claims has been neglected in part because of a confusion of response with *respondent*. Another factor contributing to this neglect is that the issue of the justification of religious practice has tended to be unthinkingly conflated with the issue of justified religious *belief*. What philosophers commonly assume is that to be justified, a religious practice must be grounded in propositions belief of which is justified by good public evidence—as might be said, a *believing* response must be *epistemically* justified. Some, more recently, have been arguing that justification for religious belief, and so for religious practice, may also be provided by the private evidence of religious experience. But either way, responses other than those involving belief come in, if at all, derivatively: instead of finding evidence in support of belief, a philosopher investigating some religious claim may seem to find good evidence in support of *disbelief* and conclude that religious practice grounded in that claim is unjustified; or else she may consider there to be strong evidence on both sides and favor *skepticism*, which—given the pervasive assumption mentioned above—normally leads to the same conclusion. Responses involving propositional faith, which fall outside this charmed circle, tend not to be noticed at all.

My approach in this chapter will be different. Here I make room for faith and explicitly emphasize the need for a response to be considered in relation to independent others, which do not get adequate consideration just by implication when one discusses belief. I also emphasize, in light of the discussion of the last chapter and the distinctions there made, the need to see whether non-truth-oriented considerations might not be relevant to the justification of any one of these responses, in particular the response involving religious belief (even if such considerations are not sufficient to warrant the additional move of putting religious claims forward as solutions to theoretical problems in philosophy). But I start with some fundamental and general questions about criteria for determining when a response is justified and when it is not.

1. Some Principles of Response Justification

I have already argued that the justification of a response is linked to its worthiness and also suggested that in seeking a worthy response we might naturally find ourselves looking for the *best* response that we can make. In considering this idea, we can immediately see that the business of evaluating responses, of considering which response is worthy and justified, is going to be at bottom a *comparative* venture. More precisely:

P1. A response to religious claims is justified at a time t if and only if there is at t no better alternative response that can be made.[2]

But is this way of putting our fundamental principle really the proper one? Is the specified condition really sufficient as well as necessary? Should our formulation not instead be "if and only if it is *the best* among alternative responses"? Though previous discussion might suggest as much, it is time to add a refinement, which will allow us to see that the correct answer to these questions is no. Where a certain response is at least as good as any other that can be made and none is better, it is true of that response that *nothing better can be chosen*. And it seems clear that a response could not be such as *should not be made* by individuals looking for the best response *they can make* in light of relevant information, if this is what the relevant information shows. In other words, a response is unworthy and unjustified, such as should not be made, only if there is a better alternative response. Since to be justified is simply to be not unjustified, it follows that if there is *no* better alternative, a response is justified and that the condition in question here is indeed sufficient.

This conclusion suggests, however, that there are *two* ways for a response to religious claims to be justified, one more demanding than the other: a response may be the best among relevant alternatives, without an equal, or it may be at least as good as any other. In the latter case

[2] In what follows I omit the temporal reference and commonly also the qualification "that can be made" when speaking of responses to religious claims, on the assumption that they will be understood to apply in every case. (The reader will recall that it is not token responses and the particular times at which they are justifiedly made that are at issue here, but response types and the times at which they are examined or recommended.)

we may speak of the response as at least *a* best. Thus a justified response may be justified because it is *the* best or because it is at least *a* best: either way, there is no better alternative. When hereafter I speak of a response simply as "justified," what I say must be understood in this disjunctive sense. But it will also be useful to have specific names for the two forms of justification. Recognizing that if a response is at least *a* best, it is not the case that it should not be made, but if a response is *the* best, it *is* the case that it *should* be made (after all, if a response is the best, all others are inferior and so reason will require their avoidance), let us say that a response of the former type is *negatively* justified and that a response of the latter type is *positively* justified. And so we also have a second principle:

P2. A response to religious claims is justified if and only if it is either negatively or positively justified.

Positive justification entails but goes beyond negative, and though both instantiate worthiness, no doubt positive justification will seem more satisfying where it can be ascertained to exist.

It may seem to some that there must be an asymmetry between a response involving belief and other responses in respect of justification in that the former, if worthy at all, must win out over all competitors and be *the* best. For surely without good evidence of truth a response involving belief is unjustified, and with such evidence it is preferable. Thus a response involving belief can only be *positively* justified. At this stage, however, we cannot rule out the possibility of non-truth-oriented considerations bringing a response involving belief that is unjustified given only truth-oriented ones (i.e., *epistemically* unjustified) up to the level of other responses, or bringing some other response up to the level of a response involving belief that is *epistemically* preferable. If such could be countenanced, even a response involving belief might turn out to be only negatively justified.

For similar reasons we cannot say that a response involving skepticism must be positively justified when neither a believing nor a disbelieving response is justified, though it does seem that when such is the case, some form of skepticism is justified (i.e., either negatively or positively justified). I say "some form of skepticism" instead of "a purely skeptical response" because for a purely skeptical response to be justified, it must also not be the case that *faith* is positively justified, and a purely skeptical response is *positively* justified only if a faith response is *un*justified.[3]

---

[3] It may seem that in restricting the comparative discussion to *alternative attitudes to the same proposition(s)*, I am neglecting how the preferable alternative to the belief that *p* may

It is important to bear these qualifications and distinctions in mind, but even so we can already identify some additional comparative principles of justification that may be of some use in investigation:

P3. If a response to religious claims is unjustified, then some alternative response is justified.[4]

P4. If a believing or disbelieving response is epistemically justified, then all alternative responses are epistemically unjustified.

P5. If neither a believing nor a disbelieving response is justified, then some form of skepticism is justified.

P6. If a faith response is positively justified, then a purely skeptical response is unjustified.

P7. If a purely skeptical response is positively justified, then a faith response is unjustified.

Remembering that propositional faith entails skepticism, we may add:

P8. If a faith response is justified, then some form of skepticism is justified.

Now what we have so far is still fairly general, and it may be wondered how in specific cases we are to go about eliminating alternatives and determining whether a response achieves either negative or positive justification. In the next section we consider the standard of goodness applicable here,

---

be *another* belief—the belief that *q*. Might not generic ultimistic belief, for example, be deemed by someone to be preferable to the belief that there is a God? But we are here thinking of belief *as* a response to a religious claim, and so the question whether there might be a *better* response *to that same claim* naturally emerges. That is our question. In any case, the belief that *q* could not be deemed *preferable* to the belief that *p* unless the two beliefs were assumed to be incompatible or, as in the cited example, unless the compatible belief that *q*, viewed as an alternative, were really being conjoined in one's mind with at least skepticism about the belief that *p*. (If ultimistic belief is said to be preferable to belief in God, we must deem what is said as elliptical for "ultimistic belief *plus at least skepticism with respect to belief in God* is preferable to belief in God.") And either way, the preferability of one of our alternative attitudes is entailed. Now it could be, in some case, that it is *because* of the status of the belief that *q* that the belief that *p* is unjustified, but the belief that *p* cannot be unjustified without some other attitude toward *p* being superior, and if some other attitude toward *p* is superior, then the belief that *p* is unjustified—all just as is claimed above.

[4] But notice that turning this proposition into a biconditional yields a principle that is false.

and that will put us in a better position to give an answer, for it will tell us the *range* of factors that may be appealed to. That discussion will be especially critical to what we say about believing and disbelieving responses, since we already know that something more than facts about how much evidence we have for the truth of a proposition is involved in the justification of a *faith* response (and thus, potentially, in what we say about pure skepticism, since the latter may be prevented from being positively justified by the negative justification of faith). But though we therefore know a little about the justification of faith, this other way of instantiating religion, we would benefit from knowing a good deal more. Indeed, this is one of the areas most glaringly neglected—no one, to my knowledge, has undertaken an explicit discussion of criteria pertinent to the justification of faith or of a faith response to religious claims. As a result, important resources for pursuing what in the last chapter I called the second higher-level aim of philosophy of religion (the aim of determining whether religious practice is justified) simply do not exist as yet in that field. On the basis of these points, and because at any rate some headway on the larger matter of "elimination of alternatives" can be made by focusing on the faith response, I propose in the rest of this section to consider how such a response may be determined to be negatively or positively justified. Because such a discussion has not been undertaken before, I need to go into some detail but not so much as to cause us to lose sight of our larger goals.

General principles always need to be able to stand up to particular examples, so let us begin by looking at some diverse situations in which propositional and operational faith might be taken up and by thinking about when faith would be *justified* in such situations. I continue my practice, initiated in Chapters 5 and 6, of looking at nonreligious examples of faith first. So think again of my examples of faith that my assistant will complete a certain important task, that I am a basically decent human being, and that I will be able to swim all the way across the river and so escape a kidnapper. As we have seen, there are many other possible examples. I might have faith that a certain set of stairs will lead out of a building in which I am lost, faith that a parking spot will open up in a seemingly full lot, faith that I will get a job, faith that someone will discover and prove the falsity of a murder charge on account of which I lie rotting in jail, faith that *no one* will discover a murder I *have* committed, faith that my mother will recover from a severe illness, faith that poverty will be wiped out or that democracy will spread throughout the world, faith that my friend is not a criminal, faith that I put enough money in the parking meter, and so on. In each case, finding myself with a favorable view of what a certain proposition reports but lacking evidence sufficient for belief, I nonetheless choose to *assent* to that proposition while in imagination representing the world to myself as including its truth, and thus have faith. Typically, my faith is not just propositional but also operational: that is, I also *act on* my assent and do things appropriate to the truth of the proposition in question, thus *trusting* in myself or my friend or the universe. And so I may fill out my applications, guided by the picture of myself being suitably employed; or read books, and thus better myself in preparation for release from jail; or take the time to run all my errands for the family before returning to the car.

Now the sort of faith here described (combining propositional and operational components) is not always well-advised and justified. Indeed, it may often be foolish or silly, and thus *ill*-advised and *un*justified, and it is instructive to think about when this might be the case. Consider our examples once again and the plausibility of the following points. (A) If I can ask the owner of the building, standing next to me, how to get out of it, or if a parking spot is clearly visible in an adjacent lot, it would be pointless to exercise the faith associated with those examples. (B) If I don't have a clue how to swim, I need to find another way of escaping the kidnapper. (C) Better than having the faith bound up with wanting to get away with murder is to turn myself in to the police. (D) When the nurse tells me that my mother has breathed her last, it would be good to face her death with courage and prepare emotionally for what comes after rather than to refuse to accept it, clinging to faith. And (E) if another meter violation will land me in court and perhaps lead to a costly fine, it is not a good idea to walk briskly on, completing my shopping for the family in faith that the money I put into the meter is sufficient. It seems clear that in each of these cases our analogue to a religious faith response is unjustified, for in every one of them, faith should be avoided. Assuming that faith, in the relevant combined sense, is in all similar cases unjustified, we can derive some general principles (where in stating these principles I use the expression "the proposition involved," I mean the proposition to which the propositional component of faith would be directed). (A) and (B) suggest the following principle:

> P9. If, in certain circumstances C in which one might have faith, some other disposition or action is more appropriate to the aim apparently sanctioning faith, then faith is in C unjustified.

(C) generates

> P10. If, in certain circumstances C in which one might have faith, it would not be good for the proposition involved to be true, then faith is in C unjustified.

Supported by (D) is

> P11. If, in certain circumstances C in which one might have faith, belief in the falsity of the proposition involved is epistemically justified, then faith is in C unjustified.[5]

And, finally, (E) seems to lead us to something like

> P12. If, in certain circumstances C in which one might have faith, some aim (independent of the aim apparently calling for faith) that should all things considered be pursued by anyone in C can only or best be pursued by not having faith, then faith is in C unjustified.

Call the conditions specified by these four principles (which are of course perfectly general) the More Appropriate Action, the Unwarranted Evaluation, the Probable Falsehood, and the Greater Good conditions, respectively. I suggest that they also apply, mutatis mutandis, to the case of a religious faith response in competition with other responses. Consider a situation in which following the path of argument would clearly lead to a definite answer as to whether the religious claim involved is true (this is like the situation where one can ask the owner of the building how to get out of it), or in which the demands of faith seem likely to be overwhelming and so one settles for hope (plunging into the water to escape the kidnapper may seem too risky). Then something very like the More Appropriate Action principle can be applied to eliminate the faith response from contention. Or suppose that what would have to be taken as a great good if one were to make a faith response turns out not to be, because the entity that some religious proposition hails as worthy of worship is also furnished with some decidedly unattractive properties (trying to get away with murder?). Then the Unwarranted Evaluation principle can be brought to bear. (Of course, here there is a deeper problem than just the unwarranted evaluation, since the religious proposition in question, to identify something as ultimate whose ascribed properties entail that it is not, must fall into

---

[5] In expressing the condition involved in this principle, I might have referred not to epistemic justification for the belief that the proposition involved is false (which comes in degrees of probability—more on this later) but to the *certain falsity* of that proposition. But this would, perhaps rightly, strike many as reflecting an attitude rather too generous to faith, since our principle would then suggest (though not imply) that no evidence for not-p short of completely conclusive evidence can prevent faith that p from being justified. In any case, in order to achieve the clearly plausible sufficient condition for the *justification* of faith I will be seeking to set out on the basis of these principles, I go along with the less generous idea represented here.

contradiction.) The Probable Falsehood principle can be applied where there is powerful evidence against the truth of a religious claim (if God really is dead . . .). And the Greater Good principle is relevant where a response of religious faith, though it might achieve some good, would apparently stand in the way of other important commodities that one should realize and that can only or best be realized if it is not entered into—perhaps commodities in some way bound up with the life of reason (one could play here with the metaphor of avoiding a meter violation, but let that pass). In every case someone aware of the relevant information should avoid making a faith response. In each case a faith response is unjustified. Thus we have:

P13. If one of principles 9–12 applies to it, then a faith response is unjustified.

It is evident that our criterion of "making the best response one can" has implicitly been at work in this discussion—which provides further support for that criterion. But it is important to recognize that it is not only when a religious faith response falls foul of the More Appropriate Action condition that we can see this criterion as corroborating and corroborated by the conclusions we have drawn. If *any one* of these conditions is in place, there is a better alternative response, and the faith response fails to be so much as negatively justified. If the relevant evaluation is unwarranted, some alternative to a faith response must be superior (perhaps a skeptical response, if belief and disbelief are also unjustified), and similarly when reason shows that the proposition involved is probably false (in which case a disbelieving response is likely to trump the others), or that there is a greater good requiring or benefiting from the absence of faith (here the identity of the superior alternative will depend on the nature of the good, but it is clear that there must be one).

Can we now change direction and argue that it is not just sufficient but also necessary that at least one of these conditions obtain for a faith response to be unjustified? Alternatively, if none of these conditions obtains, is a faith response at least as good as any other and so (at any rate) negatively justified? It seems to me that the answer is yes. In other words:

P14. If a faith response is unjustified, then one of principles 9–12 applies to it.

P15. If none of principles 9–12 applies to it, then a faith response is negatively justified.

What we have here are clear criteria of the *presence* of justification, not just its absence. For consider: How could there be in a faith response something that ought to be avoided by anyone with access to relevant information, in deference to a superior alternative, if according to that information there is no other action or disposition more suited to the situation; if the relevant evaluation is warranted and the proposition toward which it would be directed not probably false; and if there is no good more important than the good that might come from having faith which is advanced by the latter's absence? Certainly in the nonreligious cases of faith this seems obvious. If, for example, there is no other means to someone's goal of reaching the exit that is more likely to be successful than having faith that a certain set of stairs will take him there, and if finding the exit by means of those stairs would clearly be good (say because our subject wishes to get home in time to tuck his children into bed), and if there is no reason to think it probably false that those stairs are the right ones, and nothing to suggest something that needs to be avoided or that should be done right now, which our subject can avoid or do only (or best) by *not* taking the stairs—if all of this is true, how could there be anything unworthy, anything that needs to be recommended against, in his having faith that those stairs will lead to the exit and in acting upon that faith? It seems clear that in such circumstances faith is justified. And again, the religious situation seems to follow suit. As one can see by running through various examples, where a faith response is at issue and none of the cited conditions obtains, we have a *new* condition—the nonobtaining of *those* conditions—which entails that there is no better alternative and so provides good reason to declare such a response to be at any rate negatively justified.

So much for criteria of negative justification in the case of a faith response. How about positive justification? Can we say anything illuminating about what might provide it? I suggest the following:

P16. A faith response is positively justified if (1) it is negatively justified and (2) some aim that should all things considered be pursued by us can only or best be pursued by making such a response.

There are echoes of our discussion of negative justification here: instead of a clause referring to there being no greater good that can only or best be achieved when the faith response is *absent*, we have one speaking of an important good—one we are obligated to pursue—to which faith is uniquely *conducive*. I submit that if this condition, together with the condition of negative justification, is fulfilled in the case of a faith response, that response represents *the best* that can be done and so is positively justified.

To see the plausibility of these claims, and the difference between negative and positive justification, consider our nonreligious examples one
last time. Having faith in connection with a parking spot or money in the
meter might not be *dictated* by the relevant information and positively justified (the benefit resulting from finding a spot to park or avoiding a
ticket might be obtainable in other ways as good as faith, or not particularly important), but there might for all that be nothing ill-advised about
it, which is to say that it might be negatively justified. On the other hand,
I might very well be unable to apprehend my assistant's situation while
not having faith in him without flouting important obligations (this
would be the case if, lacking belief of the relevant propositions, the only
way of pursuing his well-being and being loyal to him were one involving
faith). Or it might be the case that although both believing and disbelieving responses to the idea of poverty's eradication are unjustified, a faith
response to such a proposition would help us all contribute to making it
true, and more fully than we could otherwise. For another example, it
might be that faith in myself as a decent human being is needed if I am to
rise above my current malaise, which includes my (epistemically unjustified) sense that I am *not* a decent human being. In such cases the extra
condition of positive justification that I have specified is fulfilled, and
clearly we want to say that a faith response should be made by those
involved. And even such apparently trivial instances of faith as those
attaching to the parking meter or the parking spot *may* represent positively justified courses of action if enough is riding on them. Imagine,
with regard to the latter case, that I am late for an important lecture, and
a large audience is waiting for me, and the only way I can meet my obligations to these people is by exercising faith.

The criterion of positive justification we have developed and the resulting understanding of how the two forms of justification differ appear
therefore to be both plausible and usable when applied to nonreligious
contexts. And there seems no reason why they should not be appropriate
in religious contexts as well. Is a faith response to religious claims negatively justified? Is it moreover the best way of carrying out certain tasks
that are requirements on us? If so, surely we should have faith and leave
alternatives behind.

Returning to the larger flow of discussion in this section, can anything
similar to what I have done for the faith response be done for the other
responses? Now that a faith response has been brought into the mix, it is
easy to see that any other response, to attain even negative justification,
must be *at least as good* as a faith response. Since this point is important,
let us add it to our set of principles:

P17. For any response *r*, other than the faith response, if *r* is negatively justified, then *r* is at least as good as the faith response.

But under what circumstances might some other response achieve (or surpass) that status? Clearly, in such cases, facts about the amount and kinds and quality of *evidence* available for the *truth* of religious claims will represent at least a part of the story. To see whether it is the whole story, we need to face head-on the question of non-truth-oriented considerations.

2. Truth or Consequences?

How wide a standard should we apply when undertaking the rational evaluation of believing, disbelieving, and skeptical responses to religious claims? Many philosophers, as I have suggested more than once, would be inclined to reply immediately that for such responses, if a *truth* standard has been applied (through an examination of relevant evidence), there is no need to introduce other considerations, and if it is not applied, no others will do—that is, no others will suffice to produce justification. Call this view *justificational monism.*

How can justificational monism be defended? A monist might begin very generally by arguing that in a great number of cases we make it a condition of the appropriateness of taking on an intentional attitude that there be good reason to think it corresponds to the facts; what we want are attitudes that are in the relevant way (which varies from state to state) discerning of or sensitive to or attuned to the nature of reality, as represented by good evidence. Take, for example, intentional attitudes such as fear and hope and desire. If we say, as in many circumstances we might, that there is no *reason* for fear, we imply that what is feared is not likely to *be actually forthcoming,* or that it likely will not *in fact* be harmful. And here the language of justification is also often used. Fear that *p* is *justified* in certain circumstances, we will say, only if *p* is at least probably true and its truth may be expected to create a harmful state of affairs for someone in those circumstances; otherwise it is taken as unjustified. (Think of fear that one will have to go to court, for example.) If we think fear to be justified, we will think it justified *by the facts*; and if we think it unjustified, we will think it *not* justified *by the facts.* Similarly for hope: if we know that some good thing is very unlikely to occur, we will say it is not worth hoping for. We will think hope that *p*, where *p* is certainly or almost certainly false, to be not properly attuned to the way things are; we will say that it "gets reality wrong." (Think of hope that a former lover will return.) And to accept *desire* that *p* as justified, do we not have to agree that the truth of *p* would create a *good* state of affairs, as one would be supposing in having the desire? (Imagine the desire that all Catholics be killed: wouldn't we say this desire is unjustified precisely because it is inappropriate to what reason tells us is the truth about value?)

Turning now to matters more specifically related to our discussion, the justificational monist may ask us to notice how these points can be applied. Start with faith. Here too the standard of appropriateness to the facts is implicitly being applied when we speak of justification, even though we are not looking specifically for evidence of the truth of the proposition with respect to which one might have faith. As we saw earlier, if there is good reason to suppose that the problem which faith is introduced to solve is *in fact* no problem, or that what one would favorably evaluate in having faith is not *in fact* good but bad, or that the proposition a faith-full one would have to consider uncertain is *in fact* probably false, then faith is unjustified, for we have reason to think that it does not properly take the measure of reality. Then, as we saw earlier, there is a *better* attitude—to find where the weight of reason lies, we have to look elsewhere. And consider skepticism. Skepticism is a matter of doubt or withholding of judgment, and surely it is only when the relevant evidence is in some way weak that this attitude is justified—which is to say, precisely when there is reason to view it as appropriate to the facts.

Coming, finally, to the central case of belief, we find nothing different. Here the propositional content of the attitude is itself at issue.[6] And in thinking about whether a belief is justified, we will wonder whether that propositional content is true. Innumerable examples could be cited. If we know that a certain man in our neighborhood has threatened a woman repeatedly and has a violent past, the belief that he may harm her is certainly justified; it is justified by what our evidence tells us about the facts. A teenage boy may be thinking "She loves me, she loves me not," but if the circumstances provide reason to think that she *doesn't* love him, we will say that belief of the proposition that she loves him is unjustified. Precisely *because* of what there is reason to think false here, there is no good reason for belief; it is not worth having (regardless of whether *he* has access to the relevant reason: we may notice that he doesn't, perhaps even allowing that he escapes irresponsibility and that his token belief is justified, but we will nonetheless hold that the belief *type* is unjustified). Thus,

---

[6] In the other cases, what is at issue is the peculiar way in which the attitude *relates* someone holding that attitude to its propositional content (desire, for example, relates one very differently to the proposition "There is a God" than does fear), and the often quite *distinct* propositions whose truth would render that relation appropriate (for example, in the case of desire, the proposition that the truth of the propositional content would be in some way *good*).

the justificational monist will say, the language of belief in particular and of intentional attitudes in general provides abundant reason to conclude that when we think about what is needed for religious belief or disbelief to be justified, and thus for any response to religious propositions to be justified whose justification is in some way bound up with that of such attitudes (including skepticism, whose justificational status we saw to be derivable from theirs), we need to focus on whether there is good evidence that the proposition involved is true or probably true.

But to others it will seem less than obvious that non-truth-centered considerations are just inapplicable here. It may be that this is how we commonly use the language of justification in certain contexts, but we can still ask whether we *should* use the language that way in *religious* contexts—and also whether we are permitted to do so by the very general ideas concerning justification developed in the previous chapter. A *variety* of forms of goodness, so it will be said, may contribute to the worthiness of a response (or detract from it) and thus to our reasons for accepting it as justified. The critic of monism may concede that epistemic justification of the propositional belief element of a belief response is *sufficient* for the justification of such a response and so also for the justification of the religious practice it represents, since it is transmitted to the other elements (if a belief is epistemically justified, it is surely rationally permissible to act on it). And a similar concession may be made for disbelieving and skeptical responses. But the critic will claim that only an intellectualist bias—appropriate enough where our ultimate concerns are theoretical but inapplicable outside that narrow domain—would make us say that an epistemic sort of justification is *necessary* in these cases. If there were significant enough non-truth-oriented goods associated with, say, a believing response—perhaps deriving from the *practice* it involves instead of the belief per se—then that response would surely remain justified even if it did not satisfy a truth standard; reason would have to side with it, and criticism would be quelled. Call this view *justificational pluralism*.[7]

The justificational pluralist can perhaps best defend her view by pointing out that the monist's case, though purportedly starting out from very

---

[7] Justificational pluralism will no doubt sound a lot like certain similar and well-known views in the literature, associated with Pascal or William James, variously labeled as pragmatic or prudential or nonevidential. But it is important to notice that the view we are dealing with here, though I sometimes associate it with such notions (and though early on I note a way of linking it with one of the historically important views), is designed as a nonepistemic answer to the questions of how *response types* should be evaluated and what recommendations philosophers should make concerning their worthiness—questions importantly different from those commonly discussed in connection with a pragmatic approach in the literature, which are focused on *token beliefs*.

general considerations, is restricted to the sorts of reasons for belief or skepticism or faith or fear (or whatever) that may *cause* such attitudes to be expressed and that are normally internally related to their maintenance. (Fear, for example, will be caused by, among other things, a sense of danger and will last only so long as that sense is in place.) It is of course natural for us to be influenced in our everyday justificational judgments by whether these are *good* reasons, in the standard sense. (One may appropriately ask, for example, whether there is reason to think something fearful is lurking in the real world.) When we are thus influenced, we are applying what might be called *internal criteria of worth.* The problem is that if we go no further, we completely ignore *external* criteria of worth. Normally, perhaps, and when we spread our net as widely as the monist has done, we will find that attitudes justified by internal criteria are best overall: they are usually the ones we need in order to get where we humans are well-advised to seek to go. Important *purposes,* in other words, are often best served by connecting in the relevant manner with the truth. But, or so the pluralist will say, there are exceptions, and in the case of religion these are much more likely, since here we have to do with beliefs and other attitudes of the widest scope: *framework* attitudes, which provide a way of looking at the *whole* of things. These may have their value and, indeed, may make their best contribution to goods and purposes pursued "lower down," even when they are not narrowly "appropriate to the facts" in the manner emphasized by the monist—an emphasis principally applicable to attitudes more directly and particularly related to those goods. (Believing that there is a God, for example, may—even when that proposition is objectively false or dubious—help us retain our zest for life and *all* its many purposes and so do more good than harm, even if a disregard for truths specifically related to those purposes—truths about where food and shelter and stimulating interaction and so on are to be had— would be harmful and is to be discouraged.)

Philosophers suppose themselves to be looking most generally and deeply at the truth about justification in this area of religion, but, ironically, the pluralist will say, they often ignore the real truth about what there is most reason to do through a misplaced loyalty to a narrower set of "facts." If we look for what is appropriate to *all* the facts, the widest set of facts relevant to the evaluation of a response to religious claims, we may sometimes find ourselves coming out on the side of, say, a belief response that is *not* supported by truth or the probability of truth in its propositional element.

But then what sorts of considerations should we be ready to bring into play? What does the wider set of facts—the set of external criteria—contain? Here is a sample of non-truth-oriented properties that are prima facie good-making, which the defender of a pluralist approach will say might possibly be found in one of the responses we have mentioned and contribute to its justification: being conducive to the fulfillment of moral obligation or the development or expression of moral virtue, being conducive to psychologically healthy functioning, to an interesting life, to understanding, to wisdom, to consciousness (as opposed to ignorance and gullibility, especially about oneself), to creativity, to the general happiness, to communal or cultural enrichment or growth of one sort or another. Philosophical evaluations of responses to religious claims, according to pluralism, should be sensitive to all such considerations, in addition to truth-conduciveness and related criteria, not just in evaluating the faith response but also when considering responses that involve or reject an attitude of belief. Consider, for example, the possible situation in which some religious belief and a disposition to act thereupon are found to be psychologically necessary for us to be properly functioning moral agents, with a sense of moral order and purpose, or where it is determined that a significant deepening of self-awareness is correlated with participation in some religious practice presupposing belief. Surely, the pluralist will say, there are at least conceivable circumstances in which responses to religious claims involving religious belief are justified on account of non-truth-oriented factors such as these and should be sanctioned by philosophers. For these factors have *weight,* and *rational* weight, that no philosophical investigation can afford to ignore. Thus even where the evidence of truth is weak and only skepticism is justified on epistemic grounds, it might still be the case that we should be believers, or at least that a skeptical response is not *better* than a believing one.

So what should we say about justificational pluralism? I am inclined to think that though easy to underestimate, it is ultimately unsuccessful, and that justificational monism is correct. Although the faith response, by its very nature, permits considerations concerning a variety of forms of goodness to be introduced, we should not say the same where the other responses are concerned. (And even the faith response is subject to a requirement of appropriateness to the facts more narrow than a pluralist can tolerate.) Let me now spell out the reasoning supporting this judgment.

Notice first that if we take the pluralist's strongest defense, outlined above, with due seriousness, we appear required to say that she is committed to the view that *any* response could conceivably be justified or unjustified, quite regardless of what its *epistemic* credentials may be. If we are going to admit non-truth-oriented considerations at all, it seems an artificial restriction to say that they can never *outweigh* truth-oriented ones in matters of religion. What could justifiy such a view apart, perhaps, from its usefulness in warding off the present objection? Even if, for example, the proposition "God exists" turned out to be *probably false*, it seems the pluralist would be committed by her intuitions about value to recommend belief of that proposition, were significant enough non-truth-oriented goods to be bound up with it. And so, given this approach, it is conceivable that non-truth-oriented considerations match or outweigh truth-oriented ones with distressing regularity, not only showing responses that are epistemically unjustified to be justified, all things considered, but also showing responses that are epistemically justified to be overall *un*justified.

What this suggests is that the pluralist must take back the concession optimistically made at the beginning of this discussion—the suggestion that epistemic justification of a propositional belief is *sufficient*, even if not necessary, for the overall justification of a response involving that belief. It cannot be so much as sufficient if non-truth-oriented factors can always outweigh it. But this flies in the face of what most of us would take ourselves to know: namely, that if evidence conclusively supports a belief, it cannot be inappropriate for someone aware of this support to hold that belief and to act on it. Thus we appear to have a reductio ad absurdum of the pluralist position. Notice that all of this applies to the faith response as much as to the others, since the pluralist position makes it conceivable that the *less* appropriate disposition and the *unwarranted* evaluation turn out to be justified and their alternatives unjustified. If, as seems plausible, none of this should be viewed as conceivable, then, again, we have the makings of a reductio against justificational pluralism.

Now I hasten to acknowledge that the position I have argued against here does not well represent certain related approaches in the literature. Pragmatist philosophers of religion influenced by William James, for example, as is well-known, say that non-truth-oriented considerations should be seen as justifying a belief, whether religious or nonreligious, only when truth-oriented considerations lead to no clear verdict one way or the other. The idea is that where non-truth-oriented considerations suggest themselves, they should be allowed to have weight and to contribute to justification, provided that our judgments to that effect never override judgments of justification that can be made by epistemic means. But what I have suggested is that, given the larger context in which pluralist intuitions arise, this reminder of pragmatic modesty generates at best an ad hoc reply to my argument: if the nourishing center of pluralism is the notion that there are many different forms of goodness, all of which have weight, and that this is especially so in the case of framework ideas where an emphasis on truth is not obviously relevant to our purposes, then the hierarchy with truth at the top, which a Jamesian pragmatist assumes, *breaks down*, leading naturally to the result that the reductio above attacks.

The critic may object that I am ignoring how an *alternative* version of justificational pluralism can simply put forward the intuition that when (but only when) epistemic, truth-oriented considerations do not suffice to decide the issue, others may legitimately be brought in. But this view strikes me as odd. Non-truth-oriented considerations deciding the issue? Which issue? Surely it is the question "What is true here anyway?" and it is in the nature of the case impossible for non-truth-oriented considerations to decide such an issue. Perhaps it will be said that the question is instead, more generally, "What should we believe?" But this suggests that there is a certain inevitability in believing: *something* must be believed; the only question is what it will be. Such a view ignores the option of skepticism, and also—in connection with it—faith. We appear to be driven back to the idea that certain special *purposes* and *good things worth achieving* are uniquely supported by belief, and that these things should have weight in our thinking about the justification of belief. But then why should we shrink from saying that these can operate, and potentially dominate, even when truth-oriented grounds point us in one direction or another?

In this way, I think, it can be shown that the reductio I have developed will not be as easy to resist as might have been thought. But suppose we accept the restriction that is needed to remove its teeth. There is an important difficulty for a pluralist approach which is unaffected by such a restriction. To see this, we need to make some distinctions—thus avoiding certain confusions that can make pluralist arguments seem more attractive than they ought to.

Notice first that it is one thing to say, where an individual S's questionable religious belief—this *token* belief—is seen to be bound up with a significant non-truth-oriented good such as psychological health, that S's belief ought not to be interfered with (through, for example, damaging objections that we could easily bring to bear) or is not irresponsibly held or even is overall a good thing; it is quite another to suggest that a belief *type* is justified by such reasons—to say, where such non-truth-oriented reasons seem more widely applicable, that human beings *in general,* or in certain commonly realized circumstances, *ought to pursue* (or are under no requirement not to pursue) a religious belief for those reasons. And the latter is what we must take pluralism to be claiming in order to make that view relevant to our concerns.

Two further distinctions are involved here: a distinction between what I call the *factual backgrounds* of these claims and another between what I call their *normative components*. What the justificational monist can say is that whereas the first set of factual circumstances (in which an individual's questionable belief is bound up with a significant good) may not be uncommon, the second (in which a significant good for all hangs on or is best served by the belief of all) is much less to be expected, since there are ever so many ways in which the significant goods on the pluralist's list may be experienced, and it strains credulity to suppose that human beings are so uncomplicated and lacking in diversity as to all be capable—whether religious believers, disbelievers, or skeptics—of fully experiencing psychologically healthy functioning, an interesting life, understanding, wisdom, consciousness, creativity, or whatever it may be, in only *one* of those ways. Perhaps it is conceivable that things should be otherwise. Perhaps there is a possible world in which they are. But in the actual world *this* is how it is. Thus the factual circumstances that the pluralist needs to be able to say are live possibilities in the actual world, in order to make her claim relevant to the work of philosophers offering *general* evaluations and recommendations about response types, seem not to be live possibilities at all. For an even more important point we turn to the different normative components of the claims in question: what the monist can say is that whereas the judgment of the first (that an individual's belief ought not to be interfered with or even is good to have in factual circumstances of the sort in question) may sometimes be plausible, the judgment of the second (that it would be all right for all of us, if the circumstances it presupposes were to arise, to *seek to realize in ourselves a belief we know to be less than probable*) is not plausible. The first judgment, in particular, does not require us to countenance widespread self-deception and a flagrant disregard for integrity (in more than one sense) as does the second. (There may be no self-deception in the first case at all.) If it did, we might be inclined to make a different judgment in *both* cases.

Let us examine the issue involved here a bit more closely. Suppose that in a situation where, say, epistemic considerations show nothing either way, a philosopher nonetheless recommends a response involving belief on non-truth-oriented grounds. Given the involuntariness of belief, no one aware of the epistemic situation can act on the recommendation without fooling himself about what the evidence shows, without coming to believe the evidence on one side stronger than the evidence on the other side, contrary to what is in fact the case and what, at least initially, he believes to be the case. The religious inquirer must inculcate in himself a false belief about the evidence—indeed (given that the evidential support he takes himself to have found will naturally be taken to justify numerous other beliefs indirectly, because of the relevant entailment or probability relations), *many* false beliefs. He must develop a religious or irreligious belief and act on it and thus must come to think certain evidential propositions at least probably true, *when he knows full well that they are not probably true.* Perhaps he becomes religious, singing songs in church and praising God, thinking that there is a God worthy of praise, feeling secure about the support for his belief and various other beliefs formed on its basis but having got himself into this position for reasons quite unrelated to truth. Perhaps he was told it would enhance his creativity, or add to the interest of his life, or be psychologically uplifting. Like other believers, he will think the truth of his belief enormously important and see himself as staking his life upon it, realizing that the appropriateness of many of his emotions, for example, depends upon it. Like others, he may comment that he would be prepared to give it all up if skeptical arguments could be made out, but his commitment to the truth keeps him hanging on!

This is only an example, but it helps us to see that not only do we have self-deception in such a case and the lack of integrity (in the sense of dishonesty) that goes with that (lying to yourself is still lying, and this even if you are upfront with your present self about the fact that you will be lying to your future self!), but because of a deep lack of moral integration this individual also lacks a *morally unified self* (lacks integrity in *that* sense), being, for example, quite unable to issue a positive, higher-order evaluation of his moral commitments.[8] There is a part of himself that must be kept hidden from what has become very important to him and indeed central: a deep, dark secret that cannot be revealed without undermining the central things in his life. Such self-deception and obvious lack of integrity seem not to be qualities that could possibly be countenanced by someone appropriately sensitive to what reason requires. Accordingly, it appears that we could never be in circumstances where a response involving them need not be avoided and thus is justified. Such a response, it appears, *should* be avoided and is *un*justified.

Let me also develop a less obvious point here, which shows, among other things, that self-deception of the sort in question is to be discouraged by philosophers not just because of its intrinsic properties but also because of its *instrumental* disvalue. There is a central set of philosophical values that would be contravened by following the pluralist's recommendation. This set of values is bound up with the pursuit of *wisdom*—a good, by the way, that appears in the pluralist's list. Anyone who thinks, as philosophers are required by their very identity to do, that wisdom is a great (perhaps the greatest) good, and who realizes that wisdom entails continually seeking a deeper understanding *of how things really are*, will

---

[8] On this understanding of integrity, and on integrity as a virtue, see Linda Trinkaus Zagzebski, *Virtues of the Mind: An Inquiry into the Nature of Virtue and the Ethical Foundations of Knowledge* (Cambridge: Cambridge University Press, 1996), e.g., p. 19.

shrink from the sort of self-deception that is at issue here. And the fact that it would concern religious matters, which, as we saw earlier, the pluralist takes as a mitigating factor, will for those who aspire to wisdom only make things *worse*. Why? Because religion concerns the *deepest* things, which matter most of all to the wise. If we form a belief concerning religious matters on non-truth-oriented grounds when the evidence yields no clear answer, we will, given the nature of belief (recall Chapters 2 and 3), tend to close ourselves off from further possibilities of discovery in just the circumstances where the wise will think the nurturing of an open and investigative spirit to be best. (Here, of course, we have not only the general nature of belief to take account of but also the effect of such motives as are involved in such a case: a belief that will do the job that someone influenced by non-truth-oriented considerations needs it to do will be a strong belief, unobstructed by an eye kept open to the evidence, and the stronger and less obstructed it is, the better it will do that job; hence it is just such a belief that the individual in question will seek to have.) To close ourselves off in this way will negatively affect not only ourselves but also those who come after us, who might have benefited from our deeper searching. For reasons such as this, I suggest that no philosopher can legitimately recommend to anyone the self-deception whose encouragement is sponsored by the pluralist's position.

It may be tempting for the pluralist to reply that I am simply ignoring the value to which non-truth-oriented considerations point, value that might well outweigh both the intrinsic and the instrumental badness of self-deception in such a context as this and thus commend itself to reason. Proscriptions of such things as self-deception, she may seek to remind us, are in ethics taken to have no more than prima facie force and are always capable of being overridden by more important considerations. It is not unreasonable to do what is best overall.

The pluralist may also suggest that the formation of a belief can militate against understanding or wisdom in one area or in one respect *while facilitating it in another*, and that there are possible circumstances in which the latter result is the more important. Perhaps, for example, even if Buddhist doctrines are not clearly true or probable, we could all, as a result of Buddhist belief, be coming to see something about the futility of ego pursuits with unusual depth and in a manner that has wide ramifications for the world as a whole. What is interesting is that the pluralist can claim that the beliefs in question may still be truth-conducive *in a wider sense*. Here is a plausible description of the relevant property: being laudable from the perspective of the goal of contact with the truth and avoidance of what is false. Perhaps a response—even a response involving belief—can possess this property while not immediately or directly putting someone in touch with the truth. Perhaps we humans must hold this or that belief if we are to arrive at the truth *elsewhere*, as already suggested, or *in the long run*, even if our belief doesn't get us there right away, either because this response is needed to keep going and make any headway intellectually at all in a certain area, or because false beliefs early in a process of investigation are causally linked to (perhaps by clearing the way for) true beliefs later on. Many examples from various areas of human life and endeavor, such as science and medicine and art, might be adduced in support of this point.[9] Thus the pluralist's case for her position can involve the claim that even the *monist's* concern, properly construed, would require looking beyond the ideal of evidence that shows the propositions involved in a believing or disbelieving response to be true.

I am inclined to think that there is a serious disanalogy between the situation thought to be possible by the pluralist—namely, one in which philosophers have reason on their side in recommending a response to religious claims that they, and those who become apprised of the relevant information, realize at least initially to be less than likely—and what has turned out to be the case in some contexts: namely, that false or less than likely beliefs have been truth-conducive in the long run. This disanalogy is that in the latter case the relevant beliefs are ones that were *thought* at the time to be well-evidenced and were *corrected* by those who held them, individuals seeking *true* beliefs, when new evidence pointed them elsewhere. In the former case, on the other hand, there is at the start an awareness of epistemic *deficiency* and a recommendation to *cover it up*, which, if followed successfully, could serve only to *prevent* a change of mind and indeed to militate against the habits of thought required for such a thing.

In further response to the pluralist we may point out that much can be learned from religion without holding its beliefs. One might, for example, be provoked by contact with Buddhist teaching to consider matters of the ego more carefully and thus arrive at the very same beliefs concerning the futility of ego pursuits on the basis of careful psychological and other empirical inquiry instead of by embracing that teaching, a teaching which in the pluralist's "possible case" is less than likely to be true. If this were to occur, we might be holding the relevant beliefs on a

---

[9] See ibid., pp. 181–183. Of course, one would not typically be in a position, when assessing the value of a less than probable belief, to *see* that it is truth-conducive in the second of the ways just mentioned. But—so the pluralist could argue—because of analogies between the content of a given belief and false beliefs we know to have been truth-conducive in this way, we might be in a position to consider this a live possibility, and that, together with other factors, might prevent a less than probable belief from being unjustified.

basis that epistemically *secures* them, and would this state of affairs not be viewed as preferable by someone who values truth at all?

As for the overriding of prima facie proscriptions of self-deception and attitudes contrary to integrity, there is, I think, a confusion between the notion of *individual bad acts,* which may sometimes be required by a commitment to the good (as when persons hiding Jews lied to would-be Nazi killers), and *negative character traits,* which are much worse and whose badness is interwoven with so much else that opposes the good as to be out of the question. In following the pluralist idea, we would be cultivating the latter instead of simply doing the former, which makes that idea much more difficult to uphold than is here supposed—certainly in conditions like ours, where so little in the way of "overriding goodness" that cannot otherwise be achieved suggests itself.

That concludes my case against justificational pluralism. But having presented it, I still find that the deepest pluralist idea—that we should be sensitive to goodness in all its forms when delivering a philosophical judgment as to the worth of this or that response to religious claims—has a lingering appeal. Human limitation might well lead us to overlook something here, and in this area of human life, where it is rather important that we get things right, that would be most unfortunate. An attempt to determine what response to religious claims is the best we can make might not unreasonably take *this* fact into account along with all the others I have discussed. I therefore suggest a sort of compromise, one that will do no harm to epistemic ideals yet take the central pluralist idea with appropriate seriousness. Philosophers, I suggest, should *start,* in any particular case of response evaluation, by applying a truth-oriented-criterion; they should then go on at least to *entertain* the idea that whatever conclusion as to justification considerations concerning truth support—whether a conclusion in some way affirming a believing response or a disbelieving one or else some form of skepticism—ought to be altered in light of non-truth-oriented considerations pointing to a better or equally good alternative response. If, as I suspect will invariably be the case, none of the latter considerations turn out to have any countervailing or overriding force, the epistemic conclusion must of course prevail. But the presence in my principles (below) of a condition referring to non-truth-oriented considerations signals my respect for the deepest pluralist idea.

What, now, should we say is *involved* in applying a truth-oriented criterion, in reaching for an epistemic conclusion, as I have said philosophers ought to start by doing? The details will no doubt vary from case to case, but we can touch on some of the most general conceptual issues. Should the philosopher look to see whether there is in the available information evidence overall supporting (making at least probable) the truth of the religious proposition in question or the truth of its denial, or whether there is not—inclining toward belief, disbelief, or skepticism according to the results?[10] This approach might seem right, but there may not be an answer to the question of whether there is evidence providing the relevant support for a religious or irreligious proposition—whether, as I shall say, we are or are not left by our information with overall *good* evidence of the truth of such a proposition. This matter may be left *uncertain* by our information—that it is so may itself be part of our information! In such a situation the philosopher may well judge that it is not the believing or disbelieving response but rather a skeptical response that ought to be recommended. But notice that it is not a situation in which she can judge that it is not the case that there is evidence overall supporting the truth of one proposition or the other: she does not know what to say about that, precisely because the available evidence resists assessment.

Another important point is that even focusing on what the available evidence supports or does not support or is unclear about is too restrictive. We need to leave room as well for the information that the *available* evidence is *not enough* evidence—skepticism may in this or that case emerge as the best or a best among alternative responses precisely because *insufficient evidence is available* to make a reliable judgment about the truth of the proposition(s) concerned, and this even when the available evidence is overall good evidence. Here what we are inclined to say at the level of individual responsibility provides a useful analogy. Just as we may say that someone is unjustified in her belief because she has before her an inadequate supply of relevant evidence, even when *that* evidence overall supports her belief (perhaps someone believing a new theory of cosmology irremediably flawed after initial tests of a first formulation of the theory are all disconfirmatory would provide an example), so the philosopher seeking to guide our choices aright might conceivably say, regarding a certain belief type—even after considering all available evidence, and even after finding that *this* evidence supports a verdict one way or the other—that for one reason or another there is simply not yet enough evidence to render a reliable judgment as to the truth or falsity of the proposition involved.

Drawing these points together, we may provide a better idea of what the philosopher applying a truth-oriented criterion should do: she should consider whether there is *sufficient* evidence that is overall *good* evidence of the truth of the proposition that would be believed in a belief response, or of the truth of the proposition that would be believed in a

---

[10] I construe evidence broadly—as anything supporting the truth or falsity of a proposition or blocking such support.

disbelieving response, or whether instead—as I put it—the available information does not permit such a judgment (because it includes no evidence of truth at all or not enough evidence or no good evidence or no good evidence whose supportive force has not been blocked or because the unblocked good evidence is evenly balanced or because the evidential information resists assessment). Application of the truth-oriented criterion will yield one or other of these results and so will support the justification of either a believing, a disbelieving, or a skeptical response. But given our concession to the justificational pluralist, we cannot, using this information alone, generate principles stating sufficient conditions for the negative or positive justification of these responses. Again, from respect for the deepest pluralist idea, I will not consider a sufficient condition of justification to have been satisfied in this or that particular case of response evaluation unless pluralist arguments seeking to revise the conclusion suggested by application of a truth-oriented criterion have been examined and found wanting. This concession, in conjunction with the preceding points, leads us to the following additional principles of evaluation:

P18. A believing or disbelieving response is *negatively* justified if (1) there is sufficient and overall good evidence for the truth of the proposition involved and (2) there are no non-truth-oriented considerations with sufficient force to show some alternative response to be better and thus preferable in the circumstances.

P19. A believing or disbelieving response is *positively* justified if (1) it is negatively justified and (2) there are no non-truth-oriented considerations with sufficient force to show some alternative response to be as good and thus equally worthy of being made in the circumstances.

P20. A skeptical response is *negatively* justified if (1) available information does not permit a judgment of sufficient and overall good evidence for either the proposition that would be believed in a believing response or the proposition that would be believed in a disbelieving response and (2) there are no non-truth-oriented considerations with sufficient force to show some alternative response to be better and thus preferable in the circumstances.

P21. A skeptical response is *positively* justified if (1) it is negatively justified and (2) there are no non-truth-oriented considerations with sufficient force to show some alternative response to be as good and thus equally worthy of being made in the circumstances.

Comparably filled out principles for a *purely* skeptical response, which build on these results and also on P6 and P7, might look like this:

P22. A purely skeptical response is *negatively* justified if (1) available information does not permit a judgment of sufficient and overall good evidence for either the proposition that would be believed in a believing response or the proposition that would be believed in a disbelieving response, (2) a faith response is no more than negatively justified, and (3) there are no non-truth-oriented considerations with sufficient force to show some nonskeptical alternative response to be better and thus preferable in the circumstances.

P23. A purely skeptical response is *positively* justified if (1) it is negatively justified, (2) a faith response is unjustified, and (3) there are no non-truth-oriented considerations with sufficient force to show some alternative response to be as good and thus equally worthy of being made in the circumstances.

3. *Evaluating Responses to Ultimism: Priority and Strategy*

So far we have been proceeding as though any religious proposition(s) at all could be the one(s) involved when we evaluate responses to religious claims. But we should also think more discriminatingly about how the efforts of philosophers in this regard might unfold. In the previous chapter we saw that a priority could reasonably be placed on investigating whether religious responses must always be outclassed by nonreligious ones. In closing the book I want to reintroduce this point and examine it a bit more closely. What it says, when filled out, is that we should investigate whether, for every religious claim, either a *disbelieving or a purely skeptical* response must be rationally preferable to both *believing and faith* responses, and thus positively justified. But how, it may be asked, can every possible religious claim be investigated? Is this not a recipe for investigation even more grindingly interminable than philosophers have already got used to hearing that their profession entails? I suggest that to carry out such an investigation most effectively and with anything approaching alacrity, we are well advised to move to a very general level indeed, where the religious proposition involved is ultimism, the generic religious proposition which, as we saw in Chapter 1, is entailed by every more particular one. If disbelief or pure skepticism turns out to be positively justified at *that* level, then of course it is positively justified everywhere, and no religious response to any religious claim is either negatively or positively justified.

Among various possible approaches to the implementation of this proposal, one might look at arguments for specific religious beliefs or for a generalized disbelief, applying the relevant principles from our discussion above. One might also examine the worth of categorical skepticism. The approach I favor and plan to follow is a variation on the latter. It will involve examining arguments for the conclusion that there is no epistemic justification for belief of either ultimism or its denial. If it turns out that such arguments are successful, then, barring any nonepistemic surprises, some form of categorical religious skepticism is justified and, indeed, positively justified. But, I emphasize, *some form*. Such a conclusion could deliver only a limited result emphasizing the need to instantiate or pursue passive categorical religious skepticism, not *pure* skepticism. It follows that such a conclusion would not yet show whether a nonreligious response to religious claims must be preferable to religious ones. An additional step would be called for to work out the remaining matters: a separate inquiry to determine whether pure skepticism or skeptical *faith* is justified and, if the latter turns out to be justified, to discern what its proper object(s) and associated practice might be and whether the faith response, whatever form it may take, is positively or only negatively justified. If by chance a faith response were shown to be *positively* justified, a victory for religious practice would be snatched from the jaws of defeat, and a surprising reconciliation of reason and religion would turn out to have been negotiated.

But all of that is for other books to explore. What I have provided here is only a map, a view from above of the landscape they must boldly enter.

Index